Gendering the Nation

Studies in Modern Scottish Literature

Edited by

CHRISTOPHER WHYTE

EDINBURGH UNIVERSITY PRESS

© Individual contributors, 1995
Introduction Christopher Whyte; *Chapter 1*
Caroline Gonda: *Chapter 2* Alison Smith;
Chapter 3 Christopher Whyte; *Chapter 4*
Jenni Calder; *Chapter 5* Berthold Schoene;
Chapter 6 Margaret Elphinstone; *Chapter 7*
R. D. S. Jack; *Chapter 8* Adrienne Scullion;
Chapter 9 Edwin Morgan

Edinburgh University Press Ltd
22 George Square, Edinburgh

Typeset in Linotronic Galliard
by Speedspools, Edinburgh, and
printed and bound in Great Britain

A CIP record for this book is available from
the British Library

ISBN 0 7486 0619 X

The Publisher wishes to acknowledge subsidy
from the Scottish Arts Council towards the
publication of this volume.

Dedicated to
Alasdair Ferguson Cameron
2 March 1953 – 17 June 1994

Contents

Introduction

'Nationalism is always bad news for women.' When one of the participants at an academic day seminar I attended just over a year ago came out with this statement, I stopped to think. I wasn't just asking myself if it was true. The tactical implications of the statement interested me. Something of a tension had been developing between English-identified and Scottish-identified participants. (I use these clumsy and long-winded terms to avoid giving anybody the impression that I think 'being Scottish' or 'being English' is a question of language, parentage or place of birth or residence.) The person making the statement was English-identified and if she could get us to accept it she would win several points. It would mean that cultures where nationalism was an acknowledged issue were by that very fact less tolerant of women (and therefore of other marginal groups, be they black, lesbian or gay). One could call them small cultures, minority cultures, nations without a state. My own preference would be to speak of national groupings which have extremely limited political control over the internal organisation and external relations of the territory they inhabit. It is a constantly shifting category. Twenty years ago Catalonia, Slovenia and Latvia belonged to it. They no longer do. Scotland still does. Did I agree that it was harder to be a straight woman, or a lesbian, or a gay man, in Scotland or in Sardinia than in Italy or Greece?

I stopped to think because the statement was part of a larger polemic against nationalism, which it aimed to discredit by appearing to champion women. It is at the places where affiliations overlap that one can most successfully tease out the tangled threads of political, class and gender allegiance. From being something of a cranks' pursuit, nationalism (and it would be better to use the plural form, nationalisms) have become, in the space of half a decade, thanks to the collapse of the Soviet Union, the crucial issue in Europe as a whole (the Europe which extends to the Urals, as opposed to the 'pretend Europe' which stopped at the Iron Curtain). The more savage manifestations of national sentiment on the European continent have supplied plentiful ammunition for supporters of the British Union, be they feminists or Tories, which they have not hesitated to use.

Anyone casting an eye over the canonic texts of twentieth-century Scottish literature would find much to support the statement I quoted at the outset. Scottish literature has succeeded, against all the odds, in emerging from under the shadow of English literature and establishing its own tentative canon. The texts in question are almost exclusively by male authors. Alexander Moffat's group portrait of seven Scottish poets, men to a man, is emblematic. It is disarmingly easy to trip up the writers involved, as in these lines by MacDiarmid:

> And nae Scot wi' a wumman lies,
> But I am he and ken, as 'twere
> A stage I've passed as he maun pass't,
> Gin he grows up, his way wi' her! . . .[1]

If the Drunk Man succeeds in standing for his nation, his representation is limited to its male members, and to the heterosexual ones at that. MacDiarmid's approach is openly and provocatively sexist. More insidious is the lyricism of Gunn's prose, which glosses over and idealises an ideology of heterosexual relations that is very grim indeed:

> Roddie was like a pillar that she herself could lean against. More than once she had had an almost overpowering desire to let Roddie take her and so find peace for herself inside the circle of his strength. She could have wished him to break through the barrier between them . . . She was weak. She was terribly weak. She feared. She did not know what she wanted . . . She knew she could no more have stopped him than have stopped fate. Would she have desired it? Yes, often, madly . . . yes . . . she didn't know.[2]

This is a fantasy of female disempowerment and male empowerment which masquerades as a way for the woman to get what she wants, while insisting that she is incapable of deciding what that is. It is on a par with the fantasy mothers who crop up again and again in the pages of Gunn's fiction, never the intellectual equals of their sons, always ready to provide food or attend a sick bed, never tiring of their offspring or demanding to be left alone for a few hours to read the paper or do an Open University course or just sit and look out of the window and think. If Gunn indulges in a kind of gender kailyard, he has a contemporary successor in William McIlvanney's nostalgic paeans to a heroic masculinity for which post-industrial Scotland no longer (thankfully) has a place:

> He listened. Every breath drawn in this house made him bigger, both told him who he was and put demands on him. He heard Conn sigh in his sleep and wanted to see him grow up overnight . . . He listened to Jenny's breathing, steady, peaceful – the pulse of his family . . . He felt an enormous upsurge of identity, and grew aggressive on it. He almost wished he could fight somebody now on their behalf.[3]

The thought of Docherty's sleeping, unconscious wife causes a sexual arousal (what else is the 'upsurge of identity' as he is 'made . . . bigger'?) which issues in undirected, unthinking aggression. Yet the man is a totem McIlvanney treats with an almost religious reverence.

So if one wants to take potshots at Scottish writers, targets are not far to seek. The problem is that such an approach risks resembling the crudest distortion of feminist criticism. I mean the kind of reading that treats the characters in realist fiction as if they lived next door to us and debates how far we approve or disapprove of the way the women are treated by their men. This book did not emerge as a response to the statement about nationalism and feminism. The chapters it contains were already commissioned at that stage and well on their way to being completed. So it does not set out to defend Scottish literature from hostile, external attack or to prove, once again, in the gender field, that it can match the English formation. Instead, the collection is symptomatic, even exemplary of changes taking place in the overall theoretical debate and in contemporary Scottish culture. It acknowledges and furthers a process of transformation which has implications for 'new' 'nationalist' cultures much farther afield. (I place both words in inverted commas to avoid subscribing to the claims of competing, hitherto dominant cultures to continuity, tradition and agnosticism where national bias is concerned.)

Perhaps the best way to illustrate the connection between the two kinds of change is to quote a passage from Judith Butler's *Gender Trouble* in emended form. The deleted words are reproduced in square brackets immediately after the words which have replaced them:

> The postulation of the 'before' within Scottish [feminist] theory becomes politically problematic when it constrains the future to materialize an idealized notion of the past or when it supports, even inadvertently, the reification of a pre-Union [precultural] sphere of the authentic Scottish [feminine]. This recourse to an original or genuine Scottishness [femininity] is a nostalgic and parochial idea that refuses the contemporary demand to formulate an account of nationality [gender] as a complex cultural construction. This ideal tends not only to serve culturally conservative aims, but to constitute an exclusionary practice within Scottish theory [feminism], precipitating precisely the kind of fragmentation that the ideal purports to overcome.[4]

In its original form, the passage can be seen as warning against the dangers of imagining an Edenic state of society before patriarchy (before history) in which women were empowered and which could in some way be reproduced in a contemporary context. In its modified form, it describes fairly accurately a dominant trend in Scottish cultural nationalism between the wars, a trend which is not dead yet. Scottish culture, we are told, was mutilated by the twin disasters of the Union of the Crowns and the Union of the Parliaments, landmarks in a process of assimilation to England which increasingly diluted a pre-existing core of genuine Scottishness. Often enough this dilution is envisioned in gender terms as an emasculation (the trope of fluids almost invariably prompts male critics to invest national questions with their own sexual energies). The dangers of such a stance are that it is committed to the restoration, not only of Scotland as it was, but of relations between genders, classes, racial groups and differing sexual orientations that would be unacceptably oppressive in a modern context. If we want to bring back a Scotland that once was, what place will there be in it for blacks or lesbians or the children of Pakistani immigrants?

Outdated as it is, it would be a mistake to undervalue the importance of such an approach at a precise historical time. Here the novelist Fionn MacColla gives it moving expression and links it to another, crucial trope of fluids, the Scottish (male) passion for drink:

mental capacity irrespective, job irrespective, position in our society irrespective, the aged, the middle-aged, the child in or out of school, our urban bourgeoisie, our urban and rural labourers, down to what some would have called the lowest levels of society, we all carried about a sense, often an exciting, often a heartbreaking sense, which I can only describe by saying it was a sense that *there had once been a Glory* . . . For some odd reason I remember particularly at this moment from nearly sixty years ago, a little whiskery old man, seeming some distance gone in drink, leaning against the door of the Black Horse public house, looking at the ground, and how he seemed to me to carry round his liart locks a sort of nimbus, not of sanctity but of knowledge that *there had been a Glory*.[5]

It is significant that, before he can speak of the glory lost, McColla feels impelled to elide a whole range of internal differences within the national grouping he discusses.

The passage by Judith Butler is important because it shows how much those working in the related fields of gender, sexual orientation and nationalities have to learn from each other. Eve Kosofsky Sedgwick comments in an illuminating fashion on the parallels between the politics of nation and the politics of gender:

To suggest that everyone might 'have' a nationality as everyone 'has' a gender presupposes, what may well be true, and may well always have been true, that everyone does 'have' a gender. But it needn't presuppose that everyone 'has' a gender in the same way, or that 'having' a gender is the same kind of act, process, or possession for every person or for every gender.

She proceeds to spell out the implications in a North American context:

Does this mean that Canada does not have 'nation-ness'? Or instead that its nation-ness, having a different history from that of the United States, may well therefore have a structure different enough to put into question any single definition of the quality 'nation-ness'?[6]

Just as 'to be a woman' may be a very different kind of activity or experience from 'to be a man', so '(choosing) to be Scottish' is not necessarily the same kind of process as '(choosing) to be English'. Scottishness may be structured quite differently from Englishness.

There may even be a range of possible ways of 'being Scottish'. The way associated with Scottish nationalism in the inter-war period had a concern for linguistic and racial purity which emerges in the *Scottish National Dictionary*'s by now notorious banning of Glasgow speech from its pages as a corrupt and urban dialect,[7] or in those peculiar lines of William Soutar's allegorical manifesto poem 'The Auld Tree' where the tree is liberated from the venomous snake of English and Irish immigration and cultural influence:

> Nae mair nor thrice the Wallace straik;
> And first he sklent the heided snake:
> He sklent it strauchtly into twa
> And kelterin' they skail'd awa;
> The ane haud'n southard to his hame,
> The ither wast owre Irish faem.[8]

We are not cheering on opposing teams on a football field. Indeed, many of us no longer remember (if we ever knew) how a football match works. Perhaps that kind of nationalism, that way of being Scottish, which strikes us as so oppressive now, had its uses at a time when Scottish identity was defined primarily against an over-arching Britishness or Englishness. There can be no doubt that very different strategies are in operation today. One of the most poignant and powerful pieces of writing about national identity in Scotland comes from a black, lesbian, Scottish-identified poet, Jackie Kay. The title is 'In my country':

> walking by the waters
> down where an honest river
> shakes hands with the sea,
> a woman passed round me
> in a slow watchful circle,
> as if I were a superstition;
>
> or the worst dregs of her imagination,
> so when she finally spoke
> her words spliced into bars
> of an old wheel. A segment of air.
> *Where do you come from?*
> 'Here,' I said, 'Here. These parts.'[9]

Critics and university lecturers have begun to challenge the tentative canon of the Scottish Renaissance Movement by asking what kind of texts women were producing at the time and what sort of redefinitions of Scottishness a reading of these texts might prompt. This displacement, or realignment, finds delicious creative expression in Elizabeth Burns's 'Valda's poem/Sleevenotes', where MacDiarmid's second wife, from being on the margins of a recording session, moves to the centre of the text and the scene, becoming our means of access to it. Burns even induces a sense of pity at what the two self-absorbed grand old men are missing:

> I hear their talk and laughter, his and Norman's
> I hear the rise and fall of Chris's voice
> the rhythms of his favourite poems, over and over
>
> In the afternoon I sit against the apple tree
> feeling the dent of bark on my bare shoulders
> I close my eyes and the murmur of their voices
> blurs with the birdsong . . .[10]

It would be foolish to be too optimistic. Older conformations persist alongside the new. While the men in Irvine Welsh's *Trainspotting* are far from idealised, the book does not exactly apologise for the contempt they show their women. And, in a faithfulness to older paradigms that verges on the touching, Welsh's only acknowledged gay character is a double outsider, an Italian immigrant encountered in London. (Given the lack of promising nookie, the narrator contemplates making do with Antonio: 'ah might end up whappin it up the wee cunt's choc-box yit'.[11] The assimilation to the feminine is more than merely linguistic.) To be gay and to be Scottish, it would seem, are still mutually exclusive conditions.

Kosofsky Sedgwick is sensitive to the greater visibility of a situation perceived as anomalous:

> Practically, the existence of habitation/nation systems, and their great variety worldwide, tend to become visible most easily as 'exceptional' stresses on a system (thereby) taken as normal: through personal and political crises concerning exile and expatriation, sanctuary, guest-workers whose status is for some reason deroutinized, changes in the laws of aliyah, emerging or resurgent nationalisms within previously established states . . .[12]

Scottishness is visible, anomalous, problematic in a way Englishness has not yet, and may never become. Indeed, the task of making Englishness visible cannot be the responsibility of Scottish theorists (just as gay and lesbian theorists can hardly make it their business to render visible the eternally elusive, eternally displaced, unrepresentable heterosexual 'norm' of marriage and parenthood). If this anomalous quality of Scottishness is not 'intrinsic', but an effect of existing power relations, it may nevertheless offer a valuable perspective for the study of how nationality, gender and sexual orientation interact. The process is analogous to the one by which Butler uses a lesbian perspective to question the exclusionary narratives of the genesis of the psyche put about by Kristeva and Lacan.[13] Precisely because in small, minority, emergent cultures, national identity can never be taken as given, these are privileged sites for the study of gender and its interaction with other factors in the formation of identity.

This collection, then, serves notice that Scottish texts are being read in new, disruptive and not infrequently discordant ways and the wider world had better sit up and pay attention! Rather than weighing Scottish literature in the scales of sexism to find it wanting, it celebrates the enormous richness of material the tradition offers our interpretive tools. It is perfectly feasible, for example, to read *A Drunk Man Looks at the Thistle* as a cry of exasperation at the constrictions of male identity, a plea to be released from these and from the Christian ideologies that govern them. The national hero also speaks as Christ nailed to a cross which is both the thistle and his phallus:

> *Syne liberate me frae this tree,*
> *As wha had there imprisoned me,*
> *The end achieved – or show me at the least*
> *Mair meanin' in't, and hope o' bein' released.*[14]

The idealised family worlds of Gunn and McIlvanney are alien to the tradition of Glasgow fiction. It has tended to concentrate on gender alienation, on male figures rich in pathos who fail to obtain nurturing from cold and distant wives. The syndrome is not attractive but it does foreground the dissonances and failures in heterosexual relationships, emphasising that female characters cannot be comprehended or embraced (verbally, structurally) by the male author. It is this generic background that gives the carnival scene in Edward Gaitens's *Dance of the Apprentices*, where men and women exchange clothes, its impact of liberation and celebration.[15] Alasdair Gray, too, gains by being read in this tradition. His finest novel to date, *1982 Janine*, has so far received only meagre critical attention. After all, what (heterosexual) critic wants to risk putting his (her) own fantasies on the line? The novel ends with an alarmingly daring gambit when the male narrator claims that, of all the figures in his text, he has most affinity with Janine herself, the trapped, abused and disempowered object of his masturbations. I am, he implies, more like this woman than like any of the men in my mind or in my life.

The chapters in the collection move along two discernible axes. On the one hand, they focus on non-canonical texts, on texts that undermine or enter into competition with a predominantly male canon associated with the older type of cultural nationalism. On the other, they offer unprecedented readings of texts from within that canon, and in doing so demonstrate the limitations of the mainstream critical tradition. So the book not only broadens the range of texts to be considered in any survey of gender, sexuality and nationhood. It aims to reroute, or at least to contest and diversify, our approaches to familiar texts.

Two chapters written, respectively, from a specifically lesbian and a specifically gay stance frame the collection, to avoid any risk of ghettoisation. Caroline Gonda interrogates the terms 'Scottish', 'lesbian', 'writer' and looks at the places where they overlap, or fail to do so. Labels can be a source of both empowerment and restriction. Gonda draws on interviews conducted specially for this piece to highlight the complex self-definition of different authors. Edwin Morgan's coming-out in 1990 was something of a first in Scottish literature, a thoroughly destabilising manœuvre because he had already gained a place at the very centre of his culture from which it would be extremely difficult to dislodge him.[16] His piece is based on an informal talk given at the First Day Conference on Gay and Lesbian Studies in Scotland, held at Glasgow University on 30 October 1993. It is the fruit of many years of meandering through the highways and byways of Scottish writing of the last three centuries, very much in the fashion of a gay man cruising the streets in search of prospective partners or companions.

The main body of chapters is concerned with Scottish fiction since the First World War. Alison Smith argues against the accepted valuation of Catherine Carswell's novels, rating *The Camomile* higher than *Open the Door!* and reading the latter not only against the grain of contemporary expectations but also of what she perceives as the author's desired resolution. Her view of Nan Shepherd's protagonists foregrounds the process by which women become makers of themselves. She does not fight shy of the lesbian implications at the close of

Willa Muir's *Imagined Corners* or underplay the contradictions between Muir's polemical and strictly fictional work. My own chapter takes issue with the uniformly eulogistic stance of Gunn criticism. I suggest that, rather than being a side issue, gender is the principal issue in some of Gunn's most crucial texts and that his gender ideology can help us assess the brand of cultural nationalism he continues to represent on the Scottish scene. Jenni Calder investigates the different bonds, emotional and sexual, within and across genders, in Naomi Mitchison's work of the inter-war period. The experimental nature of her writing, and its possible connection with the author's own biography, are highlighted. Berthold Schoene finds in the 1985 reprinting of Alan Sharp's best-known novel as an unquestioned Scottish classic a pretext for denouncing its undisguised hostility to both women and homosexuals. With sobering hindsight, he argues that the liberated hero figures of the heady 1960s looked on those who were not male or heterosexual merely as obstacles to be ruthlessly destroyed in the search for self-realisation. Lastly, Margaret Elphinstone uncovers the common thread in the apparently very different work of two women novelists, one lesbian, one heterosexual. She maintains that the object of the quest which structures their fiction is gender itself and that, given the inherent instability of gender differentiations, it is destined to remain illusory and mysterious.

Two chapters are devoted to Scottish drama. Kosofsky Sedgwick includes a discussion of Barrie's fiction in her essay 'The Beast in the Closet: James and the Writing of Homosexual Panic', finding *Tommy and Grizel* a limited success not because of 'the acuteness with which it treats male desire' but 'the mawkish opportunism with which it figures the desire of women'.[17] R. D. S. Jack concentrates on the plays and on the range of extreme heroines they offered to an unresponsive, uncomprehending public. He makes extensive use of the Barrie archives held in the United States to show how the dramatist attempted, through rewriting and even self-parody, to conciliate his audience at the expense of his own radicalism. Adrienne Scullion deals with live theatre, television drama and film and looks at how gender configurations emerge in the major locations of contemporary dramatic writing, the home and the workplace. It is her belief that the schizophrenia attributed to Scottish culture is implicitly gendered. She calls for a new critical agenda to provide a way out of the impasse orthodox approaches have reached.

The two drama chapters are slightly longer than the others in the collection. This is because a third chapter, provisionally entitled 'Intimations of Immorality', a study of Glasgow Unity Theatre (1941–51) and of their present heirs Clyde Unity Theatre, commissioned from Alasdair Cameron, had not been completed in publishable form before he died, after a short illness, in June 1994. The uninhibited grief given public expression at his memorial service was testimony to his work as an inspired, unstinting and much loved teacher and colleague. His expertise in his chosen field was unmatched. His fascination with Scottish theatre was neither inferiorist nor jingoistic but coloured by a humour and tolerance to which his unrivalled collection of theatrical memorabilia and kitsch bore witness. How many objects can be made to resemble a thistle? A noted wit and a cook of unforgettable talent, he has left a gap in our lives which will not be filled. By common agreement of the contributors this book is dedicated to his memory.

NOTES

1. Michael Grieve and W. R. Aitken eds *The Complete Poems of Hugh MacDiarmid* (London, Martin Brian & O'Keeffe 1978) Vol. 1, p. 114.
2. Neil Gunn *The Silver Darlings* (originally 1941) (London, Souvenir Press 1969) p. 230.
3. William McIlvanney *Docherty* (originally 1975) (London, Sceptre 1987) p. 54.
4. Judith Butler *Gender Trouble* (London and New York, Routledge 1990) p. 36.
5. Fionn MacColla *Too Long in this Condition* (Thurso, J. Humphries 1975) p. 20.
6. Eve Kosofsky Sedgwick *Tendencies* (London, Routledge 1994) pp. 148-9.
7. Compare Tom Leonard's comment in *Intimate Voices: Selected Work 1965–1983* (Newcastle upon Tyne, Galloping Dog Press 1984), p. 120.
8. William Soutar *Poems: A New Selection* ed. W. R. Aitken (Edinburgh, Scottish Academic Press 1988) p. 203.
9. Jackie Kay *Other Lovers* (Newcastle upon Tyne, Bloodaxe Books 1993) p. 24.
10. Elizabeth Burns *Ophelia and Other Poems* (Edinburgh, Polygon 1991) p. 19, reprinted in Daniel O'Rourke *Dream State: The New Scottish Poets* (Edinburgh, Polygon 1993) pp. 45–6.
11. Irvine Welsh *Trainspotting* (London, Secker and Warburg 1993) p. 239.

Tendencies p. 148.

13. See 'Subversive Bodily Acts' in Butler op. cit.

14. *Complete Poems* Vol. 1, p. 146.

15. See Christopher Whyte 'Imagining the City: The Glasgow Novel' in Joachim Schwend and Horst W. Drescher eds *Studies in Scottish Fiction: Twentieth Century* (Frankfurt am Main, Peter Lang 1990) pp. 317–33 and Edward Gaitens *Dance of the Apprentices* (originally 1948) (Edinburgh, Canongate 1990).

16. See 'Power from things not declared' in Edwin Morgan *Nothing Not Giving Messages* ed. Hamish Whyte (Edinburgh, Polygon 1990) pp. 144-87.

17. Eve Kosofsky Sedgwick *Epistemology of the Closet* (New York and London, Harvester Wheatsheaf 1991) p. 198.

1

An Other Country?

Mapping Scottish / Lesbian / Writing

CAROLINE GONDA

Setting the boundaries for this piece was never going to be easy. Like so many other terms of identity these days, both 'Scottish' and 'lesbian' have increasingly become contested territory, 'debateable ground'.[1] There are the questions of 'new Scots' and 'incomers', of the 'Scottish diaspora', and of what it means to be Black within a predominantly white Scottish culture. There are the questions of what, or who, defines 'lesbian writing' (is it something only lesbians can do?) and of who, or what, defines 'lesbian'.[2] In the end, rather than trying to present a portmanteau creature called 'Scottish lesbian writing', the most important task seemed to be that of beginning to map out three main areas of identity – Scottish, Lesbian, Writer – and the ways in which they do or don't overlap. These spatial metaphors – boundaries, 'debateable ground', definitions, mapping areas, overlapping – are not the only ones available, but they are the kind of images which the writers I focus on here use time and again when exploring the area of identity.

My main texts for most of this chapter will be my transcriptions and notes of the interviews which I conducted with five writers: the novelists, Christine Crow, Ellen Galford and Iona McGregor; the poet, Paula Jennings; and the poet, playwright and prose fiction writer, Alison Smith. Rather than offering an overview of these women's works, I will examine their statements about identity and writing, quoting from their work where relevant. (All of the comments by these writers that I quote are taken from my interviews with them unless otherwise indicated.) In the course of the chapter

I will also draw on published material by two other writers, Maud Sulter and Jackie Kay, who have commented interestingly elsewhere on the subject. Finally, I will consider the work of Carol Ann Duffy, a poet not given to making public pronouncements of any kind about herself or her writing, and who expresses the hope that her poetry 'speaks for itself'. At the opposite end of the scale from those writers I have interviewed, Duffy presents a useful test case: what can, or can't, a reader infer about a writer simply on the basis of her published work, and how does 'knowing' or 'not knowing' a writer's sense of her own sexual identity in particular shape a reader's response to her work?

I begin, however, with an essay by two lesbian poets who are neither Scottish in origin nor resident in Scotland. One, Gillian Hanscombe, is a white Australian resident in England since 1969; the other, Suniti Namjoshi, is an Indian who lived and worked in Canada for many years before coming to England in the mid-1980s. Their essay, '"Who Wrongs You, Sappho?" Developing Lesbian Sensibility in the Writing of Lyric Poetry', is important not only for its reflections on poetic form and lesbian poetic practice, but also for the writers' insights into the tensions between margin and centre, assimilation and difference, visibility and invisibility – insights deepened by their experiences as outsiders in a foreign country and an alien culture.[3]

Most, if not all, of the writers I focus on in this chapter could point to more than one parallel cause of displacement, disorientation, alienation: whether as native Scots who have settled in England; as long-term Scottish residents who are still treated as incomers, or feel themselves to be so; as Black women raised in a predominantly white culture; or as lesbians living in a heterosexual society. The dilemma for these writers seems a stark one: to stake out a place on the margins, boldly asserting one's difference(s) in the face of a hostile society which alternately trivialises and demonises; or to sink one's differences in the hope that the dominant culture will kindly overlook them. (As Gillian Hanscombe's poetic sequence, *Sybil: The Glide of Her Tongue*, puts it: 'We've discussed the choice: to be brave and flayed or be coiled and craven, spat upon, patient among apples'.[4])

As young poets aspiring to write within the lyric tradition, both Hanscombe and Namjoshi had found themselves trapped by the gender assumptions of that form, unable as lesbians to adopt either the persona of the 'I', the speaking, male lover, or that of the 'you', the silent, female beloved. The problem with the lyric tradition was that it had been shaped by white, Western, liberal humanism, and its assumptions: the unspoken equation of 'human' with Man; and the loudly asserted 'doctrine of ultimate realities or the universality of human nature and of the human experience', a tenet which 'completely ignored the facts of imperialism and was therefore unconscious of its assumption of power' (p. 157). Humanism claimed that all human experience was central, not marginal, but the poetic structures and oppositions told a different story: in a tradition where 'imagery itself was gender role stereotyped', how was the lesbian poet to find her place (p. 157)? For Hanscombe and Namjoshi it was 'not possible intellectually to accept that the experience of sexual love and passion was the "same" for all individuals (i.e. Man) and at the same time to accept a displacement to an ill-differentiated margin' (p. 159).

Hanscombe and Namjoshi concluded that a lesbian poet could not find her place within liberal humanism, because liberal humanism did not exist: the first phase of their development concluded with the unmasking and abandonment of 'patriarchal humanism', and the adoption of a new, 'centralist' stance made possible by the context of feminism. Here, a lesbian consciousness and the awareness of speaking to and for a lesbian audience became central in their writing. In the second half of the 1980s, however, this 'centralist' stage came to seem untenable as the political climate of feminism and lesbianism changed:

> The very proliferation of difference within the lesbian sense of identity tended to reduce the word 'lesbian' to merely a matter of sexual orientation. To speak of *the* lesbian perspective became impossible, and of *a* lesbian perspective problematic, since there were 'lesbians' who were making it clear that just about any perspective could be lesbian. (p. 163)

These changes within the more general 'lesbian sense of identity' inevitably affect the individual lesbian writer's sense of her own place on the map: her self-definition and how she positions herself in relation to her desired or probable audience. Working as a playwright for women's theatre groups in the late 1980s, Alison Smith found that audiences 'were less likely to come if you labelled yourself in a particular way, if you set out to designate your audience.' Funding bodies, too, were less likely to respond favourably: 'eventually . . . we had to take the word "feminism" out of what we were doing, because we got more money when we didn't use it! . . . Which is the end. The *end*.' While the glossy magazines write of lifestyle feminism and lesbian chic, eliding freedom of choice and the freedom to shop, patriarchal humanism reasserts its 'universal' values – if, indeed, they ever went away. The American novelist Sarah Schulman notes wryly that 'Reviews that I now get say things like "This isn't a gay book, this is a universal book." That's called a good review; because if it was a gay book, there'd be something wrong with it.'[5] As Iona McGregor puts it, 'we're not allowed to have the full human ticket'. Heterosexual culture, beset by the Platonic image of twinned selves endlessly seeking to fuse, cannot both admire difference and tolerate its own exclusion from it: the options are Colonise or Destroy. (The classic example of the former, in terms of national culture, has been the historical invisibility of Scottish writers' Scottishness in traditional university courses on 'English Literature': great writers are 'adopted' as English, thus becoming central, while the rest are marginalised as 'regional'.)

Not surprisingly, most of the writers I interviewed were preoccupied with questions of categorisation. As I've been suggesting, it's not just the 'full human ticket' which the dominant culture refuses to accord to its 'others', but also the 'full *writer's* ticket': the cultural pressures on writers not to define or label themselves are powerful, and often severely practical. Categorisation affects audience levels, funding, where and how a writer gets reviewed – and indeed where and how her readers can find her books. Here is the Jewish, American-born novelist, Ellen Galford, now in her forties and a long-term resident in Scotland:

> When I went into Waterstone's a while ago I thought 'Bloody hell! . . . I don't see any of my books out', and then I realized there were a whole lot of them in the Scottish Literature section and I thought *AH*! . . . So I'm quite happy to be in Scottish Literature . . . but if there are going to be sort of ghetto strands I want to be in all the ghettos . . . I don't just want to be in Lesbian or just in Scottish or just in mainstream, I want to be on all those shelves.

Galford's desire 'to be on all those shelves', circumventing the problems of category by having as many labels as possible, finds its obverse in Alison Smith's discomfort with any label other than that of 'writer':

I don't find labels at all helpful. Where do you start and where do you stop? Scottish, lesbian, right-handed, Catholic, Invernesian . . . everything is relevant and none of them is more relevant than the other, not really.

Her scepticism about the use of labels goes beyond merely personal dislike:

As soon as you start talking about a group or a separate thing or category or something that you might even call 'gay writing', you're ending up with . . . the limitations and strengths of categorization . . . I really do feel very strongly that categorization or grouping yourself separately is a help to a certain point . . . [but] how do you get beyond that point, how do you push past it?

Smith, who is white and in her early thirties, left her academic post at Strathclyde University because of ill health two years ago and has settled in Cambridge, where she studied as a postgraduate. She sees the issues of categorisation and difference as more problematic in Scotland, where

people are particularly keen to categorize themselves as different . . . from English . . . To be Scottish is to be separate; that's why . . . Scottish women's writing has only really been given a place . . . in the last ten years . . . The idea that there are other forms of difference apart from this one.

The suppression of 'other forms of difference' is a pattern which exists within gay groups, too, as Iona McGregor notes, recalling the pressures 'in the embattled '60s and '70s' to present a united front and conceal the irreconcilable differences which, she argues, are now an important weapon in the fight against stereotyping by the media:

The dominant culture, whatever it is, never sees itself as a whole. It always sees itself as a cluster of individuals . . . . The dominant class never sees its own boundaries.

McGregor, a white Scotswoman now in her sixties and living in Edinburgh, has had two writing careers, the first as an author of historical fiction for children and teenagers, and the second – a comparatively recent development – as a writer of adult detective fiction, something she did not feel able to do until after her early retirement from schoolteaching: 'I felt very strongly that I wanted to write gay fiction, and I've been trying to do that ever since.'[6] She says that she was drawn to historical fiction in the first place because

> [I wanted to write] about people very much in their social setting, in their interaction with their own social class, social background, rather than within one tight little family group, and I think this has quite a lot of relevance to being gay, because one is very much conscious of being differentiated from the rest of society, particularly in the era that I grew up in, in which there was not any gay community of any kind outside perhaps one or two rather obscure clubs in London.

A founder member of the Scottish Minorities Group, McGregor argues that 'minority cultures label themselves when forced to band into a tribe for protection',[7] and says that for those gay writers who do not take sexuality as their subject matter, the importance of a gay perspective must be 'a crusading one – that one is asserting the gay identity and our need to assert the right of that identity to exist, rather than the effect it has on the material'. She sees the gay community as 'very supportive of its writers', but does not feel part of a lesbian writing (as opposed to social) network: 'I think our bond is really more that we are lesbians than that we are writers.'

Of the four writers I interviewed who identify as lesbian, three – McGregor herself, Smith and Galford – did not see themselves as part of a Scottish lesbian writers' network. (The fourth, Paula Jennings, who is a member of Pomegranate women's writing group, has a stronger sense of a collective identity, but that identity is not an exclusively lesbian one.) Asked if she was aware of any such network, Alison Smith was both emphatic and sceptical:

> Absolutely not – never have been . . . I have never in my life in Scotland come across anything that seemed like a collective force [of 'gay writing'] that wasn't artificially put together . . . But in a way I don't know what good a collective force would be . . . I don't have any sense of something to belong to, but I don't know that belonging to something would be a particularly good thing for someone who's writing anyway.

Galford, who also expressed scepticism about whether writers can or should form a community ('I think once you're at the point where you're really seriously writing you've got to be home alone doing it'), has some sense of a social network of lesbian writers, but one which is international rather than confined to Scotland.

An awareness of international connections informs and complicates Ellen Galford's sense of her own identity, making self-definition an increasingly problematic task: 'Certainly the older I get the more I feel lots of different strands of where I come from, and where the people I come from come from, all sort of clashing together.' Her contribution as a member of the Scottish panel at the 1993 Modern Language Association conference addressed these issues directly:

> It was very much about 'What *can* I call myself?' . . . coming in as a sort of inward immigrant, having been here [in Scotland] most of my adult life and yet still having the accent from there, and then of course the Jewish thing and where does that stand inside the Scottish thing, and the lesbian thing inside the rest . . . all these different clashing Venn diagrams – how many edges can you walk on at once?

The idea of 'the lesbian thing inside the rest' indicates what remains constant within Galford's fiction: an unproblematic acceptance of lesbian experience, lesbian identity and lesbian character, whether the character in question is an Elizabethan apothecary, a mediaeval nun, a Hebridean clan chieftain and GP, a Pictish High Priestess, a Jewish taxi-driver, or an eighteenth-century Lithuanian dybbuk with some unexpectedly Scottish turns of phrase ('I hadn't even thought of [them] as Scottish, they were just part of my speech,' Galford says, belatedly alerted to the phenomenon by her Virago editor's puzzled requests for definition). She has never been drawn to the introspective forms of the lesbian *Bildungsroman* (the novel of education and development, or portrait of the artist as a young dyke) or the 'Autobiographical Coming Out Novel', a genre to which she refers with more than the hint of a groan; but she is very clear about the impact on her own writing of coming out:

> I found I had great trouble while I was living what was essentially a heterosexual married life for a short period – I *couldn't write* . . . It was only when I said, OK, I'm a lesbian, I should not be living with a man, I should not be living in a marriage, and came out in my own head and then left that life, that the cork popped . . . I wrote the first short story I had written in probably several years and then started a novel, first novel.

Coming out not only '[took] the gag off' but also brought access to 'parts of me that were blocked off, like a closed-off coal mine': it put an end to her feelings of being 'out on the edges of the world'. In the marriage, she said, 'I was living someone else's life': now, beginning to live her own, 'I felt – curiously enough in the *marginal* sexual category – I felt, OK, where I am now is the centre of the world.' Galford's equivalent of the 'centralist stage' defined by Hanscombe and Namjoshi has been maintained partly in a personal and social sense (her other image of coming out as an end to isolation was 'I'm no longer not invited to the party'), but also in the different sense which she as a comic novelist has of what it means to assume a lesbian perspective and a lesbian audience:

> Even though it's very important to me that I can use lesbian characters, that I can look at the world from a kind of 'lesbocentricity' rather than a kind of heterosexual stance in the way the world is structured . . . I wouldn't feel that I'd write only lesbian novels for lesbians . . . It's lesbian fiction but it's also *fiction* that has lesbians as central characters, and I don't know if every novel I write will always have that . . . I really value the fact that I *do* have a lesbian audience, but . . . I don't feel that I'm writing from a sort of separatist stance where these are my only imagined readers.

Galford's latest project, a screenplay based on her second novel, *The Fires of Bride* (1986), has thrown up different questions of separatism and restriction, marginality and centrality. The novel is set on the imaginary island of Cailleach, 'the outermost island of the Utter Utter Hebrides', and focuses on Cailleach's effects on an artist and 'incomer' (actually the daughter of an expatriate Cailleach woman, as it turns out) and that incomer's effects in turn on the island and its community: it's a lively mix of comedy, fantasy, myth and satire, hardly likely to be taken for social realism.[8] At the Scottish Film Council's 'Movie Makars' conference in Inverness, however, one member of the Gaelic contingent asked: 'Oh, *couldn't* you set it somewhere else? I just feel so uneasy about people from outside writing about the Outer Hebrides!' The question sparked off a passionate debate about the boundaries of Scottishness and the nature of Scottish culture:

> I said, 'Well, this is actually one of the things it's *about* – it's about who's an incomer and who's not and about all sorts of

myths about Celticness and Scottishness . . . I'm very, very acutely aware of this, particularly as someone from a much stereotyped ethnic group myself and who did come to Scotland as an incomer' . . . And then the Central Belt, all the Glasgow and Edinburgh film-makers . . . said 'This is *outrageous* . . . Who is to say who has the right to write about a place? . . . There are people like Ellen and there are people from Pakistan and people from China, Scotland is a very complicated cultural mix these days, there are new Scots from everywhere and their perspective is just as fair as anyone else's!'

. . . But it is a complicated issue, it's one of the things I'm very conscious of, the insider–outsider contradiction.

Being born in Scotland is not necessarily sufficient to gain one insider status, as two Black Scottish writers, Maud Sulter and Jackie Kay, make clear. Maud Sulter, noting British publishers' enthusiasm for Black American women writers, remarks:

This whole dynamic of 'it's okay as long as it's from somewhere else' is endemic in British society . . . And the fact that Black people have been in Scotland for over four hundred years has also to be taken on board . . . It's another disheartening thing, that in a country that claims to have such a radical, rebellious nature as Scotland, there is such a hesitation to take on board other people's voices. The issue is there. It's not somewhere else.[9]

Sulter's comment parallels Alison Smith's sense of Scotland's reluctance to recognise 'other forms of difference': she also shares Smith's critical attitude to labels, describing them as 'only constructive within set situations . . . I wouldn't label my work, because in different situations, in different places and times, the definition would be different'.[10] She emphasises, however, 'the need to name oneself, for oneself, rather than accept easy categorization by other people', and in her poem addressed to James Baldwin, 'Delete and Enter', writes 'we/call ourselves Black and I undoubtedly name myself Zami'.[11] The name 'Zami' has become a term of identity for many Black lesbians since its appearance in Audre Lorde's 'biomythography', *Zami: A New Spelling Of My Name* (1982).

Lorde, in common with other Black American lesbians, found herself under attack from the Black community because of her sexuality, another unacceptably 'other' form of difference within an embattled cultural group. It is not clear to me whether Scottish Black lesbian writers experience the same sense of pressure to keep quiet about their sexuality, or whether in any case such a pressure would not register as significant in comparison to the inescapable fact of being 'other' as Black in Scotland. Sulter and her contemporary, Jackie Kay, now in their early thirties, are no longer resident in Scotland: Sulter lives in Yorkshire and Kay in London. In an interview from the late 1980s, Kay said she couldn't imagine being able to read openly lesbian poetry in Scotland (a position which has clearly changed since then), but the statement seems more a general reflection about Scotland's intolerance than a specific one about potential disapproval from other Scottish Blacks.[12]

Jackie Kay, the daughter of a Nigerian father and a Scottish mother, was brought up in Glasgow by her white adoptive parents, who were Communists. She has a powerfully angry sense of some white Scots' attempts to deny Black people full Scottishness, an anger which fuelled her raw, early poem, 'So you think I'm a mule?', and returns, banked down, in the more recent (and more economical) 'In my country'.[13] Interviewed about her latest play, *Twilight Shift* (1993), which focuses on a gay male relationship, Kay says: 'I can easily translate my own experiences of being outside, of being insulted, into a gay man's experience of the society we live in'; from its context in the interview, her remark seems to cast those experiences as the fruits of racism rather than of homophobia.[14]

Kay's attitude to the relationship between personal identity and writing seems to have undergone some changes since the publication of her first collection, *The Adoption Papers* (1991), the first half of which is a poetic sequence in three voices: the adoptive mother, the birth mother, and the daughter. The same interview from 1993 describes her as 'stunned' that people will come up after readings from the book and ask her 'deeply personal questions' about her own birth mother and whether they have met. She seems warier now of that close identification between writer and work which she asserted in *Sleeping with Monsters*, when she argued that labels and self-definitions were not important because 'it's through your writing that people should get a sense of who you are. Because I write directly from my own experience, people do get a sense of the multiplicity of what I am.'[15]

The sharpest possible contrast to that autobiographical, experiential notion of writing voiced by Jackie Kay appears towards the end of

Christine Crow's *Miss X, or the Wolf Woman* (1990) when the
book's narrator, Mary Wolfe, herself the author of a novel entitled
Miss X, recounts her own death in an exploding aeroplane:

> ... **killed on the spot**. [...]
> Unlike similarity ... total identity is no relationship at all.
> **Total identity is death!**
> *Now* **do you understand that the Writer is always separate
> from the work?**[16]

A white, married Englishwoman who has lived in St Andrews since
1965, Crow is Honorary Reader in French at the University there:
she gave up her academic post in 1986 in order to write full-time.
Miss X, her first novel, exploits not only her 'immersion' in the
predominantly male canon of French literature, but also her interest
in French feminist theory. In the novel's title, both names, 'Miss X'
and 'the Wolf Woman' alert the reader to questions of identity: X,
as Crow puts it, is 'both a censoring device and a mark of the
unknown', while 'Wolf Woman' recalls Freud's coded designation
of one patient as the Wolf Man. There is ambiguity, too, about
whether these are alternative titles for the novel or two names for
the same person. Within the novel itself, Crow unsettles notions of
identity, character and self-formation, as Mary Wolfe reconstructs
both her relationship with the Headmistress she names 'Miss X' and
her own development as a 'HomoseXual'. *Miss X* becomes, among
other things, a conscious parody and dismantling of the Coming
Out Novel:

> I think I had to parody the coming-out story because it is
> going towards a fixed or known goal ... I suppose I almost
> consciously used the coming-out story to ... pull the reader
> along ... but I realise that it's got to be parodied or disrupted.
> Not parodied necessarily in the purely playful, humorous, ludic
> sense, although that obviously is very important to me, but
> parodied in a 'structural' sense, in that it's the congealments
> and closures of the coming-out story itself which I feel I've got
> to unpick in some way. And so although there is a coming-out
> story there, it's got to be much more problematic – because
> coming out from what and to what?

Crow's characterisation of the coming-out story as 'going towards a
fixed or known goal' reflects her more general reservations about
'confessional narrative'. She has a strong sense that 'any investigation

of self that the writer does is a retrospective one', with all the distortions retrospection can bring. Moreover, the very project of tracing the self's development inevitably imposes a fictitious order and coherence on randomness and flux, falsely identifying (in fact creating) events and stages on the way to one's present, culminating selfhood. If the 'fixed or known goal' of that process is a named or labelled identity, the results are yet more problematic:

> When I wrote *Miss X* I was very conscious of wanting to take up a sort of double position towards the notion of the name and the label and so I had started to use the space of the fiction, the different narrative levels and so on, to try to give the reader a feeling of entering into that space where the label or the name was perceived as both necessary to give a shape to an identity, but also very harming the other way round, because it objectifies subjective consciousness, which is what it's all about as far as I'm concerned . . . And in the book one of the big labels is, of course, 'lesbian'.

In *Miss X*, Mary Wolfe first constructs and then comes to reject her self-definition as a 'HomoseXual', realising belatedly that 'There is no such thing as *A HomoseXual*', nor yet '*A HeteroseXual*' or '*A BiseXual*'. She also renounces her previous notion of 'HomoseXuals' as outlaws, rebels and scapegoats, who must go in fear of 'a Pack of Men and Women . . . waiting to eXclude us from the fold'.[17] Crow is well aware of the reality of homophobic oppression and the political potential for the oppressed of naming themselves, but she remains wary of 'the very notion of identity, whether it's labelled as lesbian, heterosexual, feminist, whatever', saying that 'since we are objects to ourselves as well as subjects, we're going to be affected by how we see ourselves as well as how others see us'. Once the term 'lesbian' crosses 'a boundary from political to subjective, private experience', she feels, the women who use it 'are actually oppressing their own open-endedness, their own growth, paradoxically or ironically using a term which is probably a male term anyway'.

In Crow's novel, 'lesbian' becomes a metaphor, a way into ideas about the self and its relation to others, and about the objectification of subjective experience in oneself or in others. 'I think I very much used the lesbian image and plot to set going those things for a reader of either sex or whatever position, because I suppose I feel that ultimately they are universal processes of identity even if we come through very different routes towards them.' Of *Miss X*, she says that 'now it is like a mirror that I can look into to remind myself of that problem'. Despite that mirror image, she maintains that *Miss X* is not autobiographical 'on the level of the plot', but says that the work does reflect her own powerful sense of 'negative images . . . *false* ways that people see literature or that people read or people see lesbians or selves or women' and of the need to find ways to 'prevent those false, simplifying views of things from working'. Mary Wolfe then becomes 'not exactly a scapegoat but . . . a sort of *tabula rasa*' for presenting and challenging those negative views: 'That would explain more why I can't see her as a character . . . because the things that are important to me as a person are done to her ironically.'

Not all reviewers have been equally alive to the irony: *Miss X* has been variously described as 'a crypto-gothic fairytale . . . and a semi-autobiographical account', as 'a detective thriller/who dunnit . . . and a coming out story' (all genres which have been popular with lesbian writers in recent years).[18] Of the two serious critical accounts of *Miss X* to date, the first, by Mary Orr, half-jokingly suggests filing the novel 'in the pending tray marked "Feminist anti-*Bildungs-roman*"'; the second, Nicki Hastie's 'Lesbian BiblioMythography', sees it as a 'touchstone novel' for the 'desirous reader' examining her own shifting and changing identity – a reading which also pleases Christine Crow herself.[19] She remains preoccupied with the operations of selfhood and with ideas of the self as 'both autonomous and bonding'. Despite her determination to challenge categories and boundaries, she says: 'I think that the re-affirming of boundaries is just as important to me as the breaking down of boundaries . . . In my [current] writing, on cultural paranoia, it's more like going towards an edge in order to come back from it.'

Many of Crow's preoccupations with boundary, category, identity and difference are shared by Alison Smith, who is a great admirer of *Miss X*. Smith describes herself as working to 'talk about and explore and open up the area of sexual difference without people deciding that it isn't about them': she is not a didactic writer, but says that if her writing has a 'message' she wants that message to be 'not open-ended, but able to take in as many interpretations or people . . . as possible'. In common with Galford, however, Smith sees coming out as having had a significant impact on her work: before, she had known that she was a writer, but didn't have a subject. For her, the ability to be open in and about her own identity and sexuality 'has been to do with moving south [to Aberdeen as an undergraduate and then to Cambridge] . . . and at each stage it's been easier . . . to be honest with *myself*.' Moving south also brought new developments in her writing: as a postgraduate in Cambridge, she began for the first time to write plays, three of which were produced at the Edinburgh Fringe.

All the parts in Smith's plays are for women, although she is unsure how far that was or was not determined by being able to write for already existing women's theatre groups. The plays present identity as both ritualised and unstable. In *The Dance* (1988), the same actress plays three roles, designated as Maiden, Mother and Hag (the traditional Scottish labels for the three aspects or stages of female identity): at the end of the play, the Hag leaps grotesquely into the position occupied by the Maiden at the start, completing the cycle. *Comic* (1990), described by one Cambridge don as 'Godot for girls', has two characters: Verity Venture, a stiff, black-and-white figure from a schoolgirl comic who has to talk about herself in the third person; and Jinny, whose apparently more fully rounded identity is also exposed as a series of fictional constructions, repeated every bit as ritually as Verity's third-person narratives. In *Trace of Arc* (1991), the figure of Conscience watches in amazement as 'the same woman' reappears under different names to go through a bizarre, formulaic process of shopping: the supermarket staff's apparently personal but in fact rigidly patterned questions about her health and family; the woman's own replies in the form of unconnected advertising slogans, which the staff treat as if they made perfect sense; and the check-out worker's final report to the manageress of what the woman has bought – always the same recited list, no matter what the actual purchases have been. Conscience herself undercuts the conversations between the two supermarket workers with her narratives of saint's lives: the inarticulate Trace, fulfilling the play's title, responds by becoming a martyr through political protest, while Jackie, 'Too Clever For Her Own Good' as she ironically says of herself, remains trapped within the carefully packaged and standardised identity she mistakenly believes will save her from burning.

Alison Smith responds with instant recognition to Ellen Galford's comment that 'I was living somebody else's life'. For her, 'somebody else's life' was not marriage but academia, and leaving it had similarly revitalising effects on her writing. She began writing prose fiction for the first time, has just had a first collection of short stories accepted by Virago and is working on a novel, a new experience which she describes as 'a very unmapped state'. That metaphor corresponds to another significant change in her thinking and writing: 'When I came away from academia I began to think spatially instead of logically . . . it was like learning a different language'. She no longer writes poetry, but sees some parallels between that genre and her short stories: 'Short fiction, for me, works on a momentary image of something which is spatial again, which allows something to radiate out from it.' The first story in the collection, 'Free Love', in which the narrator recalls her first sexual experience with a prostitute in Amsterdam and the beginning of her first love affair with another woman, centres on just such an image: 'I stopped there and leaned on the railings and watched the late sun hitting the water, shimmering apart and coming together again in the same movement, the same moment.'[20]

Smith describes her prose fiction as mainly 'love stories for girls . . . quite obviously in a clearly stated gender base', but would like to work on more 'things which are not gender-designated', in which 'whoever you are, it can be anything you want'. In her explicitly lesbian writing, she constantly returns to the problems of 'how immediately you're put down, how [lesbianism] is socially contextualised all the time . . . You're always up against the limits that other people make for you.' She relates her general concern with limitation to 'coming from a small Highland town where writing about sexual difference would still be very difficult', but says that in Scotland 'sexual discussion, and discussion of issues particularly about sexual difference, now is something which people are beginning to be able to do'. In her own work she hopes to 'open up . . . rather than close down' a sense of sexual difference, but to do so from the kind of 'humanist' perspective she sees as exemplified by Sally Potter's film, *Orlando*:

> I really think deep in my soul that categorisation in the end will let people dismiss you as a category and that it's very important to avoid it in exactly that humanist spirit, exactly the notion that everyone has – ought to have – rights to tolerance, rights to exist in the way which he or she chooses . . . and to be as pluralist as he/she would like to be.

Despite her interest in 'non-gender boundary things like [Jeanette Winterson's] *Written on the Body*', they are not exactly the model for what she wants to do: 'To be humanist is to be of the world as well and to be more rooted than something which is divided in two, and so I hope to make the play between those difficulties work out and reconcile.'

At the opposite extreme from Smith and Crow, with their desire to subvert and resist categorisation, is Paula Jennings, a white English-woman in her mid-forties who has lived most of her adult life in St Andrews. Jennings has a strong positive sense of the power of names and labels – poet, feminist, lesbian – and the part these have played in the formation of her own identity. The process of coming out for her was closely linked to naming: she had 'no name for it' at nineteen when she felt attracted to another woman who, like her, was in a heterosexual relationship; at a later stage, which lasted five years, she called herself 'bisexual', while still relating to men because she couldn't find any lesbians. Historically it was a time of supposed openness and tolerance of sexual experimentation, but 'I felt I needed to find a lesbian to be lesbians with'. In the formation of her identity both as a poet and as a lesbian, she feels that an unconscious need has been followed by a stage of intellectualising, almost the adoption of a pose, before the final synthesis.

Jennings emphasises the importance of feminist politics in her development, saying that she probably wouldn't have thought of lesbianism but for the historical accident of being in her twenties in an era of questioning: 'A lot of the lesbians I know were feminists first.' Whereas Galford and Smith both speak of their personal coming out as vital to their development as writers, she sees feminist politics as having been the liberating force which enabled her and others like her to write: 'We didn't have to identify as writers to write feminist theory.' Of her involvement in the 'Political Lesbian-ism' debate she says that she felt part of 'a community of revolution-aries', for whom 'writing and love relationships were both part of what we did'. There was a strong sense of network and communica-tion ('tons of badly duplicated newsletters') and of excitement: 'I was in love with the Women's Liberation Movement'.

Asked whether coming out had changed her writing, Jennings replies that she has written very few overtly lesbian poems: the first one, 'Lesbian', which appeared in Onlywomen's *One Foot on the Mountain* was reprinted (without permission) in the *Penguin Antho-logy of Homosexual Verse*. It's a poem Jennings now doesn't like ('the rhythm's too clompy'), but which deals very directly with nam-ing and labelling, summoning up the erotic and tender meanings 'behind the word lesbian / stinking in men's mouths, / rhyming with perversion and revulsion'.[21] She describes her poetry now as aiming for something which does not 'make sense' of her own experience, but which 'transform[s] the outer life into a dream state – condensing, outrageous, unexpected'. About her own difference of perspective from a dominant view, Jennings says: 'I look at the world through lesbian-feminist spectacles (a lesbian feminist describing a primrose!) – it may or may not be clear in what I say.' She does not feel under pressure to write for a particular external audience, but is very aware of 'the great lesbian-feminist mafia in the head, the ghost of the fierce '70s lesbian feminist (we created this!) . . . saying "Lesbian feminism must be your whole life".'

The impact of lesbian-feminist politics on poetry is something which Gillian Hanscombe and Suniti Namjoshi discuss in their reflections on the 'centralist' stage of lesbian consciousness: 'One characteristic of the flood of verse released in response to lesbian feminism was the assumption that what really mattered in poems was the content . . . [which] should reflect the authentic experience of lesbian women' (p. 162). They define this new writing as 'polemical poetry', characterised by a 'a passionate rhetoric, a content of personal narrative, and a declarative "I" who addresses the audience directly' (p. 162). The problem with such poetry, Hanscombe and Namjoshi argue, is that it 'abandon[s], to a greater or lesser extent, the principal features of lyric writing: i.e. the development of imagery; the control of shifts in tone by means of ironic distancing; and the awareness of resonances with and subversions of traditional practice' (pp. 162–3). Polemical poetry can be appreciated in terms of its function – 'the best of such work strikes an authentic polemical note because it has justice on its side' – but does not necessarily succeed as poetry in its own right (p. 163). The 'community of revolutionaries' did not have to identify as writers in order to write feminist theory, but the implication of what Hanscombe and Namjoshi say is that good poetry cannot be produced on the same terms – which is not the same as saying that poetry must (or can) be apolitical.

In his introduction to *Dream State: the New Scottish Poets*, Daniel O'Rourke borrows the title of one of Carol Ann Duffy's poems to label her as 'Poet for our Times', emphasising that 'Duffy, for all her sometimes erotic and intimate lyricism, also writes outspoken poems about the condition of the state'.[22] His comment echoes Sean O'Brien's suggestion (reviewing Duffy's latest collection, *Mean*

Time) that 'she could well become the representative poet of the present day, much as Philip Larkin came to seem for the time between Attlee and Thatcher'.[23] This representativeness has much to do with Carol Ann Duffy's sense of her own (dis)location. Duffy, who is white and in her late thirties, was born in Glasgow but left Scotland as a small child when her family moved to England: 'I spent most of my childhood in Stafford, feeling very much an outsider and trying to change my accent to sound like the English kids', she writes in *Dream State*. Although some of her poems ('Yes, Officer', 'Deportation' and 'Translating the English, 1989', for in- stance) feature those who are literally in a foreign country, such figures do not have the monopoly on her poetry of displacement. Duffy's status as a transplanted Scot and long-term resident in England places her on the boundary between assimilation and differ- ence, belonging and exclusion, familiarity and alienation – paradoxic- ally an ideal position for 'the representative poet of the present day'. For many of its natives, too, England in the '80s seemed increasingly an other country, a place of confusion, fear and loss.

Loss, nostalgia and homesickness are frequent counters in Duffy's poems. The poem 'Nostalgia' itself both draws on and ironises the Scottish threnody of displacement with its references to the clear air of the mountains and the sad music of the pipes: even those who stay put catch the sickness of loss, while the returning exile finds 'the same bell / chiming the hour on the clock, and everything changed'.[24] It's not so much that there's no place like home but that there's no such thing as home – only the word itself, echoing again and again. In 'Plainsong', the sounds of grasses and trees evoke a sudden melancholy: 'This is your homeland, / Lost One, Stranger, who speaks with tears.'[25] Homesickness can happen anywhere and about anywhere, as the conclusion of another poem shows: 'Love, later, / I will feel homesick for this strange place.'[26]

That constellation of homesickness and love is an important one for Duffy: the poem 'Homesick' asks, 'Why is our love imperfect, / music only echo of itself, / the light wrong?'[27] In 'The Way My Mother Speaks', with its incantation of two Scottish phrases, '*The day and ever*' and '*What like is it*', juxtaposed with images of childhood, of the end of the day and the end of summer, the poem ends: 'I am homesick, free, in love / with the way my mother speaks.'[28] The mother's voice, too, recurs, calling the child in from play in 'Nostalgia' and 'Moments of Grace': in the last poem in *Mean Time*, 'Prayer', it is 'dusk, and someone calls / a child's name as though they named their loss.'[29] In 'Before You Were Mine', contemplating an old photograph of her mother (the relationship is implied, although never stated), the speaker recalls and relives her childhood longing for 'the bold girl winking in Portobello, somewhere / in Scotland, before I was born.'[30] The location is important: as Daniel O'Rourke says of 'The Way My Mother Speaks', the nostalgia is 'for mother and motherland both'.[31]

O'Rourke calls Duffy 'at once a *performing* and a *confiding* poet';[32] but despite what he says about her 'erotic and intimate lyricism', the poetry gives little away in terms of sexuality. There are implicitly or explicitly woman-to-woman poems, but these are usually distanced in some way: by their setting in childhood ('The Good Teachers', 'Crush'); by a literary or artistic sense of origin ('Girlfriends', derived from Verlaine, and 'Oppenheim's Cup And Saucer'); or by the use of historical setting ('Warming Her Pearls'). There are some suggestive juxtapositions of poems – 'Girlfriends' on the page facing 'Two Small Poems of Desire', for example – and of images (fruit, seas, rose, petals, and scent in 'Till Our Face').[33] Several of the poems use mirror imagery, a trope of lesbianism: 'As she undressed me, her breasts were a mirror / and there were mirrors in the bed' ('Oppenheim's Cup And Saucer');[34] 'In her looking-glass / my red lips part as though I want to speak' ('Warming Her Pearls');[35] more whimsically, in 'Small Female Skull', the speaker stares drunkenly at her own reflection, concluding: 'this is / a friend of mine. See, I hold her face in trembling, passionate hands.'[36]

In lyric poetry, Gillian Hanscombe and Suniti Namjoshi argue,

> the gender and stance of the persona are supremely important, because the 'I', the persona in a lyric poem, controls the relationship between the 'I' and the 'you' (since the 'you' is almost always silenced) and it is this relationship between the 'I' and the 'you' which embodies in itself at least some aspect of the basic relationship between the 'human' and the 'other' and therefore lays claim to universality. (p. 158)

Much of Duffy's poetry is written deliberately from a position of 'otherness', a position which, I have suggested, paradoxically helps to make her central rather than marginal. In her love lyrics, the precise nature of that 'otherness' is harder to define. Duffy's love poetry sometimes genders the speaking 'I' as female, sometimes does not gender it at all; she sometimes writes about love and sex in the second person or the first person plural; she may cast the first-person speaker as female but refer to the desired other woman in the third person and add the other kinds of distancing which I have noted. What she does not do is to make the gender of both lovers unambiguously female when the speaker is an 'I' addressing a 'you'.

The absence of public statements by a writer about her sexuality obviously doesn't preclude the reader from tracing lesbian images or themes in her writing. The presence of Christine Crow's work in this chapter should suggest that 'lesbian writing' is a category which is not confined to writing by lesbians, and that it need not exclude those who find the label 'lesbian' generally problematic as well as personally inaccurate. Even when a writer's sexuality is known, however, it's hardly the end of the story: I recall an incident from my first year as an incomer to Scotland, a few months before I came out. A heterosexual male lecturer discusses a genderless love lyric beginning 'Lay your sleeping head, my love, / Human on my faithless arm'. At the end of the lecture, he tells the students that the poet, W. H. Auden, was homosexual, and that they have just been appreciating and studying a gay love poem. It's a neat trick and it serves the purpose, but is it a true statement about the poem? By keeping to the 'human' and 'universal', Auden produces a poem which will fit any coupling, not The Love That Dare Not Speak Its Name, but the love that lets you fill in yours. This ungendered poem doesn't 'open up' the question of sexual difference; rather it evades it altogether. It becomes a classic because difference has been elided, leaving the lovers 'human' and safely undefined. 'Universal' status here depends on the poet's *not* asserting homosexuality, on *not* writing 'a gay love poem'. In any case, the assumption runs, those who 'know' will be able to read it in, and those who don't know don't need to.[37]

In 'Visibility Eighties Rising', written in the wake of Clause 28/29, Iona McGregor concluded:

> Our strongest weapon is that we are convinced of our right to an open existence. We have become visible to ourselves. Those of us who are old enough to have lived through these changes should be mildly hopeful.[38]

The rise of 'lesbian chic' has, one might think, increased our visibility to others, but Ellen Galford voices a scepticism shared by many:

I can't wait until 'lesbian' stops being a trendy subject for the mainstream, you know, *Vanity Fair* covers! It'll be great when it's no longer flavour of the month because then it'll be interesting in its own right again as opposed to 'Oh no, we did lesbian culture *last* month, we're all on to something else now'. Like 'Nobody eats Thai any more, we all eat Vietnamese' – this kind of consumer, throw-it-away approach to art and culture both.

Heterosexuals, meanwhile, remain largely invisible as themselves members of a category. The students I asked to list things, words and people under two headings, 'Homosexual' and 'Heterosexual', came up with plenty of suggestions for 'Homosexual' people (mostly male and mostly flamboyant, public figures past and present), but the only 'Heterosexual' people to appear on the lists were Mel Gibson and Mrs Thatcher – make of that pairing what you will. As Iona McGregor says, the dominant class never sees its own boundaries.

This is the state we're in: a state in which some will 'label themselves when forced to band into a tribe for protection', as McGregor puts it, while others will opt for camouflage or the 'Designer Closets' which Galford envisages in *Queendom Come*. In the introduction to Polygon's second collection of gay and lesbian writing from Scotland, *The Crazy Jig*, McGregor asks: 'Must gay writers assert their identity in order to avoid being deconstructed into the heterosexual majority?'[39] For an answer one might look to Maud Sulter's comment about 'the need to name oneself, for oneself, rather than accept easy categorisation by other people' and add to all those easy categories the one labelled 'invisible'. While 'universal' and 'lesbian' remain incompatible terms, hopelessly skewed in favour of the former, lesbian writers who sink their differences will disappear into the mainstream, leaving their lesbian readers at a loss. If, as Alison Smith suggests, 'to be Scottish is to be separate', Scotland's lesbian writers must all the more assert their 'other forms of difference', drawing and redrawing their own boundaries in this often 'very unmapped state'.

NOTES

I would like to thank all the writers who agreed to be interviewed: Christine Crow, Ellen Galford, Paula Jennings, Iona McGregor and Alison Smith. Their comments and responses not only provided the basis for this chapter but often suggested new directions which the research might take; Paula and Alison also lent me copies of published, and in Alison's case unpublished material. Thanks to Bloodaxe Books for their co-operation in sending me material about Jackie Kay. I am also grateful to the following people for encouragement, stimulation, and sometimes for help in tracking down material: Carol Bagnall, Florence Germain, Gillian Hanscombe, Jennifer Kerr, Janet Martens, Alison Reeves, Christopher Whyte and Liz Wilson. Finally, my thanks to Alison Hennegan for the use of her library and for her generous intellectual and emotional support throughout.

1. As Carol Anderson notes, Scots dictionary definitions of 'debateable ground' 'suggest such ideas as "ground, literally or figuratively, over which there is contention; borderland"': see her 'Debateable Land: The Prose Work of Violet Jacob' in Caroline Gonda ed. *Tea and Leg-Irons: New Feminist Readings from Scotland* (London, Open Letters 1992) pp. 34–5.

2. The question of whether only lesbians can produce 'lesbian writing' is discussed by Alison Hennegan in 'What Lesbian Novel?', *Women's Review*, no. 1 (November 1985) pp. 10–12. See also her more recent general statement for the Lesbian Landmarks series which she devised and edits. (The first four titles launching the series for Virago in 1994 included one by the heterosexual, married Han Suyin.) Other positions in the debate are taken up by Patricia Duncker *Sisters and Strangers: An Introduction to Contemporary Feminist Fiction* (Oxford and Cambridge, Mass., Blackwell 1992) and Bonnie Zimmerman *The Safe Sea of Women: Lesbian Fiction 1969–1989* (Boston, Mass., Beacon Press 1990; London, Onlywomen 1992). See also Paulina Palmer *Contemporary Lesbian Writing: Dreams, Desire, Difference* (Buckingham and Philadelphia, Open University Press 1993).

3. Gillian Hanscombe and Suniti Namjoshi, '"Who Wrongs You, Sappho?" Developing Lesbian Sensibility in the Writing of Lyric Poetry', in Jane Aaron and Sylvia Walby eds *Out of the Margins: Women's Studies in the Nineties* (London, Falmer Press 1991) pp. 156–67. All references will be incorporated in the text.

4. Gillian Hanscombe *Sybil: The Glide of Her Tongue* (Melbourne, Spinifex Press 1992) p. 14.

5. Sarah Schulman 'Troubled Times'. Interview by Andrea Freud Loewenstein, *Women's Review of Books* (July 1990); reprinted in Betsy Warland ed. *InVersions: Writings by Dykes, Queers and Lesbians* (Vancouver, Pressgang Publishers 1991; London, Open Letters 1992) p. 222. Warland's anthology is a rich source of material on the relationship between

sexual identity/sexuality and writing as articulated by 24 very different lesbian writers, most of whom are based in North America.

6. For discussion of McGregor's detective fiction, see Palmer *Contemporary Lesbian Writing* pp. 67–70, and Margaret Elphinstone, this volume pp. 107–36.

7. Iona McGregor, in Bob Cant ed. *Footsteps and Witnesses: Lesbian and Gay Lifestories from Scotland* (Edinburgh, Polygon 1993) p. 44.

8. Paulina Palmer writes that *The Fires of Bride* 'creates an original interplay of discourses, interweaving materials drawn from such varied and apparently incompatible sources as Scottish myth, Gothic romance and lesbian theory' (*Contemporary Lesbian Writing* p. 105). Palmer also discusses Galford's third novel, *Queendom Come* (London, Virago 1990), in terms of its satirical response to Section 28 of the Local Government Act (*Contemporary Lesbian Writing* pp. 89–90).

9. Maud Sulter, interviewed by Rebecca Wilson, in Rebecca E. Wilson and Gillean Somerville-Arjat eds *Sleeping with Monsters: Conversations with Scottish and Irish Women Poets* (Edinburgh, Polygon 1990) pp. 28–9.

10. Ibid. p. 30.

11. Ibid. p. 30; p. 33.

12. Ibid. p. 127.

13. 'So you think I'm a mule?' appears in *A Dangerous Knowing: Four Black Women Poets* (London, Sheba Feminist Publishers n.d.) and in *Sleeping with Monsters*; 'In my country' appears in Kay's latest collection, *Other Lovers* (Newcastle upon Tyne, Bloodaxe Books 1993).

14. 'A passport to revisit the future': interview with Jackie Kay by Jackie McGlone in *The Herald*, 16 October 1993.

15. *Sleeping with Monsters* p. 127.

16. Christine Crow *Miss X, or the Wolf Woman* (London, The Women's Press 1990) p. 223.

17. Ibid. p. 188.

18. Lucy O'Brien 'Xual Healing', *City Limits*, 22 November 1990; *The Pink Times*, Oxford, Autumn Edition 1990, p. 20: both quoted in Mary Orr, 'Crossing Divides: *Miss X, or the Wolf Woman*' in Gonda ed. *Tea and Leg-Irons* pp. 158–9. For discussions of lesbian genre fiction, see Palmer *Contemporary Lesbian Writing*; Duncker *Sisters and Strangers*; Gabriele Griffin *Heavenly Love? Lesbian Images in Twentieth-Century Women's Writing* (Manchester and New York, Manchester University Press 1993); and Gabriele Griffin ed. *Outwrite: Lesbianism and Popular Culture* (London, Pluto Press 1993).

19. 'Crossing Divides', p. 160; Nicki Hastie, 'Lesbian BiblioMythography' in Gabriele Griffin ed. *Outwrite* pp. 68–85, p. 85.

20. Alison Smith, 'Free Love', unpublished manuscript.

21. Paula Jennings 'Lesbian', in Lilian Mohin ed. *One Foot on the Mountain: An Anthology of British Feminist Poetry 1969–1979* (London, Onlywomen Press 1979) p. 202.

22. Daniel O'Rourke ed. *Dream State: The New Scottish Poets* (Edinburgh, Polygon 1994) p. xx.

23. Sean O'Brien, writing in *The Sunday Times*, quoted on back cover of Carol Ann Duffy *Mean Time* (London, Anvil Press Poetry 1993).

24. *Mean Time* p. 10.
25. Carol Ann Duffy *Selling Manhattan* (London, Anvil Press Poetry 1987) p. 60.
26. Ibid. p. 55.
27. Ibid. p. 19.
28. Carol Ann Duffy *The Other Country* (London, Anvil Press Poetry 1990) p. 54.
29. *Mean Time* p. 52.
30. Ibid. p. 13.
31. O'Rourke *Dream State* p. xx.
32. Ibid. p. xxii.
33. For a discussion of 'natural' imagery and its uses, see for example Griffin's chapter, 'Wet caves and roses: representations of lesbian sexuality in women's writing', in *Heavenly Love?* pp. 135–58, especially pp.146–8.
34. Carol Ann Duffy *Standing Female Nude* (London, Anvil Press Poetry 1985) p. 48. On mirror imagery and lesbianism, see for example Gillian Spraggs, 'Hell and the Mirror: Jane Rule's *Desert of the Heart*' in Sally Munt ed. *New Lesbian Criticism* (Hemel Hempstead, Harvester Wheatsheaf 1992) pp. 115–31, and Toni A. H. McNaron 'Mirrors and Likeness: A Lesbian Aesthetic in the Making' in Susan J. Wolfe and Julia Penelope eds *Sexual Practice, Textual Theory: Lesbian Cultural Criticism* (Cambridge, Mass. and Oxford, Blackwell 1993) pp. 291–306.
35. *Selling Manhattan* p. 58.
36. *Mean Time* p. 25.
37. On this, and related difficulties in the attempt to make literature 'come out', see Alison Hennegan 'On Becoming a Lesbian Reader' in Susannah Radstone ed. *Sweet Dreams: Sexuality, Gender and Popular Fiction* (London, Lawrence and Wishart 1988) pp. 187–8.
38. Iona McGregor 'Visibility Eighties Rising', in Toni Davidson ed. *And Thus Will I Freely Sing: An Anthology of Gay and Lesbian Writing from Scotland* (Edinburgh, Polygon 1989) p. 15.
39. McGregor, introduction to Joanne Winning ed. *The Crazy Jig: Gay and Lesbian Writing from Scotland 2* (Edinburgh, Polygon 1992), p. 4.

2

And Woman Created Woman

Carswell, Shepherd and Muir, and the Self-made Woman

ALISON SMITH

Take a look at a choice selection of recent fiction, fiction of over the last decade or so, by Scottish women. Start, say, in 1981 with Anne Smith's *The Magic Glass* and Stella Ross, one of our first urban working class heroines to be created by a woman, in a novel that takes as its subject seeing clearly, not blinding yourself to a Scotland that's far from the ideal of the nostalgic psyche. *The Magic Glass* is rebellious and intelligent like its young heroine, setting out to challenge and rewrite the great stream of (mostly male) narratives of Scottish childhood. It deals with child sexual abuse long before it became easy or fashionable to do so; it deals directly, for what I think is the first time in our literature, with what it's like for a girl to fall in love with another girl in a societal structure which has nothing but contempt for anything 'other' than itself and its inbred rules. It's about what it's like to be born and grow up a girl rather than a boy in a world whose society rejects girls as less important.

Next, take the fiction of Janice Galloway, whose first novel, *The Trick is to Keep Breathing* (1989), is a perceptive study of the terrifying stasis of a woman's breakdown, ostensibly because of the death of her male lover, essentially because this rips the surface off the everyday world to reveal nothingness and fear beneath the acceptable construction of female identity. Galloway's short stories in *Blood* (1991) examine contemporary society's hostility to women, often focusing on women who have been silenced by this hostility.

Or take A. L. Kennedy's fiction. Her novel, *Looking for the Possible Dance* (1992) deals, among other things, with the pressures on its heroine to accept or reject marriage, to remain independent yet open to those close to her, to leave or stay in Scotland. In the end, personal and communal responsibility are what force the issues of place and partnership, and in a way communal responsibility replaces marriage as the binding force between the man and the woman in this novel.

All of this was foreshadowed in the work of Scottish women writers sixty to seventy years ago, at the other end of this enlightened century. Willa Muir's writing reveals her to be very interested, like Anne Smith, in how societal, religious and sexual norms condition, limit and reject women and girls. She examines, like A. L. Kennedy, the urge to escape Scotland. There's room for a book to be written on the links between Catherine Carswell's and Janice Galloway's fiction; both portray women trapped into passivity yet attempting to fight against being silenced by conventional views of what they should be or do; both examine states of breakdown, the roots of it, the outcome. One of the main themes in Nan Shepherd's fiction is the accepting of personal and communal responsibilities; she explores, like A. L. Kennedy, the notion that women need not follow conventional patterns to fulfil responsibilities that are nothing to do with gender anyway.

There are great differences, of course. Though Smith, who's writing about growing up in a Scotland of the 1940s and 1950s, still has to deal with the influence of religion, Galloway and Kennedy are young enough to have been relatively unscathed by the Calvinist and Presbyterian scourge that overtly haunted much of our literature until very recently. Carswell, Shepherd and Muir still have to deal with religion as a very real pressure on what women can or cannot do, and they all reject the notion that women are responsible to a God who created them for childbirth and a subservient existence – only Carswell is tempted to try to reinstate religion as a needed discipline, and she uses an eroticised notion of nature to help her back to Eden. Nature, of course, has little to do with the erotic or the holy in women's writing in today's environmentally soiled and endangered world, whereas all three earlier writers can still use the natural world as a liberating erotic or anti-domestic landscape for their heroines (though Muir is keen to reject nature as a helpful ally for women).

With the creation of their various heroines, all three writers studied in this chapter work hard to foreground the notion that women have a great deal of power in the making of their own destinies, regardless of the ways of gods, or men.

*

At one point in Catherine Carswell's *Open the Door!* the heroine, Joanna Bannerman, finds herself waiting to meet up with the married man whose illicit lover she will soon become, the artist Louis Pender. She's waiting at the bottom of a hill and at the other end of the street from where Pender stands impatiently waiting for *her*; they're waiting at the wrong places for each other. There's an implicit metaphor in this, and not just the one Carswell emphasises, on the level of the mismatch of their particular relationship. The larger metaphor, of man and woman out of synchronisation with each other, can be found in both of Carswell's novels, *The Camomile*, published in 1922 and this one, published in 1920.

Some of the possible reasons for this mismatch are suggested by the communication that follows when Joanna and Louis each eventually work out where the other might be on the hill and finally meet up:

> He was not interested in their talk, nor in what she was about to say: but he liked to see her face thus serious. She looked now, he thought, like an early Gothic Madonna, rather faultily carved perhaps, but with inspiration.[1]

'Do you know what I was doing up on the hill there while I was waiting for you?' Pender asks her. 'I was trying to draw the lines of your face from memory against the sky as if it were a canvas' (p. 206). As he tells her how pleased he is with his aesthetic version of her Joanna is reduced to silence, a blissful silence, but none the less a having of 'nothing to say.' This process of being reduced (albeit sometimes quite pleasurably, she notices) to and by another's version of her happens repeatedly in the novel as she moves from stage to stage, from relationship to relationship.

In *Open the Door!* it's not clear whether it's Carswell or her heroine who's torn between the attractions of convention and the flouting of it. Spawned of an uneasy mating of Lawrentian influences[2] and middle class Glasgow respectability during the years of the first world war, Joanna Bannerman becomes a model of sustaining convention at the same time as challenging it, poised between the attraction of being an all-martyring essence of woman and an autonomous individual.

The novel has no plot as such; it follows Joanna's progress through several relationships with different men until she finds, by trial and error, the one for her, the ideal husband/partner, and consequently her fulfilled feminine self. But it's clear that the heart of the book really lies in one of her errors in this scheme, her impassioned love affair with Pender the married artist. Certainly this is the affair to which the book's title, its key scene of passion and its key image refer, and there's much less of a sense of doors opening in Joanna's life after it, when she settles for the 'natural' choice, her 'natural' mate. There's a war in the novel between what we're given as the more powerful experience and what we're asked to accept in the conventional end, and though the book sets out to explore and especially to resolve the issue of relation between the genders, in the end it reveals gender deadlock, which it resolves at the cost of believability.

At the core of this novel is the notion that the genders are in trouble. Not that Carswell would admit this – on the contrary, she wants to persuade us that Joanna is at her most completed when she finds her 'natural' place alongside man, and 'natural' here is an important notion. Two possibilities face each other in the novel: that woman can find and fulfil herself best in isolation from man, and that woman cannot be complete without man. It's a battle with no clear winner as Carswell dares herself nearer and nearer the autonomous self only to pull away at the last moment into the conventional and rather unconvincing satisfaction of the ideal and 'natural' match.

In Joanna we have a heroine who could be remarkably interesting in her own right. She's an artist and a designer, she's highly intelligent, articulate and spirited, she earns her own living from her art and moves from Glasgow to London to take a studio of her own and live on her own – very daring, and very independent in terms of the possibilities of lifestyle available for women in the first decades of the century. Yet we get no real idea of the kind of work she does, we get little notion of Joanna herself outside the ebb and flow of her emotions for whichever man is her love of the moment, Bob, Mario, Louis or Lawrence. Carswell is aware of the irony and the attractive romanticism of Joanna's desire to be 'great in love' (p. 66), the terrible urge 'of her being to give itself utterly' (p. 88) though to what or to whom she's not quite sure. Late in the novel she has a momentary glimmering of autonomy and freedom between leaving Louis and finding Lawrence; this she finds healing at first, and then simply confusing. As soon as she declares herself a 'free woman' she finds that she is lost as to what to do with herself: 'quite, quite free . . . but I know nothing . . . and I am so weak. I know nothing, nothing! I can't tell what I should do. I'm blown by any wind' (p. 384). Luckily, the conventional end of the novel comes to her rescue.

Carswell gives us a sense very early on in the novel of the unsatisfact-oriness, particularly sexually, of male–female relationships in the delineation of Joanna's parents' marriage: her father prefers public speaking to the 'curbed enjoyment of his wife's virginal freshness', and this leaves his wife, who wants 'utter union' 'dimly ashamed' (as he is too), when she feels the 'stirrings of passion' (pp. 15–16). This is, after all, a book very much about the stirrings of passion, the guilt and the freedom which passion visits on you, and, most importantly, the lack of a suitable figure on which to lavish it. Bob, the first man to whom Joanna is engaged, isn't 'virile' enough for her, doesn't kiss her with the passion she imagines a great love to have; Mario, the sultry Italian she marries, is too concerned to keep her trapped as a good little wife rather than an equal companion or a woman in her own right. He reduces her to a martyrdom, 'let him kill her if that was his way,' she thinks, quite happily (p. 120).

Pender is the great love and the lost cause of the book. The real centre of *Open the Door!* lies in its daring to explore the territory of the morally questionable extra-marital affair – the having, not just of sex, but of sex with a married man. This is where she recalls the central romantic image of the Italian door opening in the wall to let the secret lover through. But it leaves Joanna at the mercy of the very convention it challenges, easily shrugged off by Pender as he returns at the end of the day to his marriage. Finally, and all along, there's Lawrence, the rather insubstantial character with the very meaningful name, whom Carswell insists throughout is the 'natural' partner for Joanna. Lawrence carries a great symbolic weight in the novel, too much for his thinly drawn self. Carswell inscribes him with 'instinctual' imagery, imagery which is supposed to remind Joanna and the reader of her first love for nature and which is there to set up a sense of inevitability – in the end, *of course* Joanna will meet Lawrence in the very spot where she found her 'essential' self in childhood, and know him to have been the only partner for her all along, seed to her soil, 'Adam to her Eve' in their new innocent Eden, (handily absolving her of all the moral soul-blackening of her affair with Pender the married man).

But Carswell's 'natural' ending is another trap for her heroine though neither Carswell nor Joanna give any hint of being aware of this. The 'instinctual' memory she has while dancing a reel with Lawrence, one of her first moments of recognition of his suitedness to her and a moment reminiscent of the dance sequence in chapter 29 of D. H. Lawrence's *Women in Love* (1917), takes her back beyond the origins of her being and wipes her identity out altogether as she becomes instead woman as nature, woman as earth:

> From the outset he caught Joanna up into something of his own dignity, winning her surprised acknowledgement. Then, as the reel progressed, she began to lose all sense of identity. Every moment she became less herself, more a mere rhythmical expression of the soil from which they both had sprung. The memory dawned in her of some far back ancestress . . . Fresh, dim, sweet like dawn, she could see the Stirlingshire farmer's daughter carrying the milk-pails at sunrise . . . could smell the spilt, clover-sweet milk, while the farmer's daughter gave her lips to the young, unknown Welsh soldier who kept the draw-bridge. *She* was that lass, that meeting, without which her being would not have been. And soon she was not even these. Beneath the candid darkness of Lawrence Urquhart's face, soon she was no more than a field of barley that swings unseen in the wind before dawn. (pp. 169–70)

A Lawrentian undertow surfaces occasionally in the novel, in mentions of 'essential maleness' and 'essential femaleness' that are never fully developed or explored; here it wipes out individuality just as surely as do Louis's and Mario's reductions of Joanna to aesthetic objectivity. But this is the end which Joanna accepts as her destiny, the natural end. This seems to be what Carswell wants.

Carswell's treatment of sex is interesting. Her heroines lust after it, know instinctively that it's good and honest to do so, but have to call it 'the final abandonment', 'the other thing'; it can't, of course, be described in anything but euphemism. Even the metaphor of opening the door is an implicit demand to let not just physical desire but the sexual act into the novel. Here's the paradox of the woman writer whose main subject is female desire at a time when women were not decently meant to voice or even to have desire. Carswell is a writer for whom decorum and decency are very important terms, terms which touched her personally; this is the writer who in 1915 lost her reviewing position at the *Glasgow Herald* for deigning to review well Lawrence's banned novel *The Rainbow* (even though she duly noted the 'revolting detail' of it).[3]

Here we have a writer used to suffering in the name of 'decorum', whose first, highly autobiographical novel sets about challenging the acceptable mores, yet who several decades later still feels that a woman writer like Virginia Woolf is showing 'overweening vanity' because she dares to claim to exceed or even equal male writers' achievements.[4] *Lying Awake*, Carswell's posthumously published autobiography, more than once reveals a block in her notion of what a woman writer can rightly aspire to or do, which she puzzles over with her usual combination of questioning acceptance:

> Is a woman writer fundamentally handicapped in a whole important sphere of verbal expression? If so, why? . . . The man can give himself (and others) away passionately, wittily, blatantly, imperfectly, coarsely, neurotically, without the reader feeling that his effort or his achievement was unsuitable to a man . . . Rousseau can say anything: so can George Moore: so can Keats in his letters, and a thousand others, English or not English, without offending any reader save on moral grounds; and morality here does not enter, because be the woman never so moral, she can still offend by the mere intimacy of her confession. Is there here a marked, an essential disparity between men and women? The woman, because she is a woman, must as an artist suppress what the man as artist or as man is entitled to reveal.[5]

Women are trapped in their art by their gender, by gender conventions of what they can or cannot say or do. Though Carswell is clear enough in the analysis, she can't find an answer for it, except within another gender role, the answer that it's only *natural* that women should want to create art too, since 'women figure one way or another in the origins of literature as in those of life'.[6] *Lying Awake* also reveals that Carswell has always been troubled by the notion that writing may not be a fit task for women. 'Writing – for women,' the woman writer says in a note to herself, has 'inherent difficulties . . . In a man there is nothing ridiculous, certainly nothing disgraceful here. In a woman there tends to be something of both.'[7]

This is a notion central to Carswell's only other novel, *The Camomile*, where Ellen, the heroine, is racked with guilt by her irrepressible urge to write her own fiction and drama, because she thinks women who write are acting irresponsibly, perhaps even blindly and dangerously. *The Camomile* is usually seen as a poor sister to *Open the Door!*, much less complex, 'much more light-hearted',[8] though I'd suggest the opposite. This is a novel much darker at the heart, much less rambling, more courageous formally and thematically than the first, especially as concerns Carswell's preoccupation with what women may or may not do. Its dilemma is clear – it's about a woman who reacts against a convention, a social expectation that is stifling her and removing her identity, it's a novel where the breaking off of an engagement, the break with convention, is paralleled with the breakdown – and, importantly, the recovery – of the self. Part of the book's bravery lies in the fact that there's no 'knowing' god of a narrator to control the procedure; Ellen, its heroine, is never cushioned as Joanna is by the safe moral judgements and the help with articulation of self knowledge that the narrator of *Open the Door!* gives her. Where *Open the Door!* has no real tension, everything spelt out in the process by the narrator, *The Camomile* has the direct liveliness of its heroine's voice, the direct contact of the reader with her discoveries and revelations about herself.

It's very important to note that the world of *The Camomile* is one that doesn't offer a suitable hero for woman or women. Instead, it shows the demise and the death from alcoholism and loss of self-control of the last worthy and superior male, Ellen's friend Don John, the elderly scholarly gentleman she much admires.

But the legacy of this death, and of the refusal to marry and the breakdown, is not the exciting possibility of Ellen finding her self-worth and writing some fiction herself at last. At the end, instead, Ellen is glad to be left with her new responsibility, not to write her own books, but to put the books of the last worthy male in order, to organise Don John's writings and get them into print, guard his legacy for the world. Perhaps any other, more self-possessed ending would have seemed too overweeningly vain of her heroine for Carswell.

In this novel art and writing act as guilt mechanism *and* liberation for the heroine (rather like sexual desire does) – something women shouldn't do, but are drawn to with a natural urge that can't be repressed without damage. Liberation is certainly one of the main concerns of the novel, as is the necessity of self-knowledge and self-change, themes throughout Carswell's fiction. *The Camomile* is fascinating in its reading of the relations between men and women, and dark in its conclusions. Its very use of the letter/journal form explores connections between the voice of the female self and other specifically female voices – more than this, it provides us with a 'disguised' work of fiction, masquerading self-consciously as something less unfeminine, achieving the end of writing Ellen's novel for her at the same time as decorously pretending not to.

For all that, Ellen *longs* for the return of the superior, the worthy man; the novel voices another D. H. Lawrence commonplace, rather worrying in the hands of a woman writer, that it's man's fault that woman has lost her direction in the world, that woman would know and love her place if man would only teach her how: 'if we would passionately insist – not merely fretfully exclaim – that women should be "kept in their place"; if all men were individually male and creative, it could be done.'[9] All of this goes against the main force of the novel in yet another Carswell war of intention. It goes against the sense in *The Camomile* that women will, under pressure of self-limiting role, undergo the pain of physical and mental break-down of the constituents of the self, so as to break from role and start the process of reconstituting that self.

In her first novel and with her first heroine, Nan Shepherd takes us a palpable step past Carswell. In *Open the Door!* the only time Joanna really considers that it might be crucial to be self-sufficient is when she ponders on death: 'it was she only – Joanna – *She, Herself* – that would be no more if her body were now to perish' (p. 358). It's the same with Ellen in *The Camomile*: 'the sooner one knows that one has to stand quite alone in the world, the better,' she says after the lesson of her breakdown and Don John's death (p. 292). For her this is a disillusioned, brave-in-the-face-of-doom statement, and it's this same lonely doom that leaves Joanna so unsure of herself when she finds she is 'free', the solitary doom that the harmonious end of *Open the Door!* sets out to refute, providing a partner who'll accept her as she is (or as Carswell makes her, nature incarnate) rather than for what he could make of her.

Martha Ironside in Shepherd's *The Quarry Wood* (1928), however, at the moment of realising that she can be a free agent, is filled with the positive knowledge of her own creativity:

> she smiled, a bitter mirth. 'I'm an uncompleted work of art. My creator has flung me aside.' But stung suddenly by the admission the thought implied, 'Good Lord!' she exclaimed. 'Am I such a slave as that? Dependent on a man to complete me! I thought I couldn't be anything without him – I can be my own creator.'[10]

The Quarry Wood is a book deeply concerned with the getting of wisdom, and this is one of the climactic moments of the novel. The central theme of all of Shepherd's fiction is that of freeing yourself from self-deception and from the power of the deceived or received views others might have of you. In both *The Quarry Wood* and *The Weatherhouse* (1930) this deception is in some way to do with marriage or sex or the relations between the genders. In her final novel, *A Pass in the Grampians* (1933), the theme of deception is even directed with an authorial sense of play quite absent from the first two novels straight at assumptions and suspicions about sexual dealings which the reader draws; here she sets up suspicions in the reader's mind concerning one particular character, only to quash them and leave you ashamed at having had them when the truth about old Durno finally comes out.

In *The Weatherhouse*, her second novel, confusion and misunderstanding arise around marriage and the promise of it. But the true casualty of desire in the novel is the blindly romantic Ellen, whose

> choicest hours were spent in unreality – a land where others act in accordance with one's expectations. Sometimes her toppling palaces would crash at a touch of the actual, and then she suffered an agony of remorse because the real Ellen was so unlike the Ellen of her fancies . . . Shortly she was 'telling herself stories' again. It might be wicked, but it made life radiant.[11]

Ellen's fantasy desire becomes her moral impetus, and this is where the trouble starts.

Shepherd knows this 'radiant' power that fiction has, and is keen to keep her own close to reality, especially to the earth – both *The Weatherhouse* and *The Quarry Wood* have undercurrent references to the responsibilities of those who make or write fictions. She fills her work with a rich sense of the weather and the soil of the real and rural world of north-east Scotland making it fiction that defies radiance with an emphasis on 'sharny boots and hacked hands seamed with dirt'. In all three novels she concentrates on the development of lively, intelligent young women, and examines what it takes for them to gain an important balance both of self-knowledge and knowledge wider than the self; all three also explore characters who have deceived themselves into thinking they are acting on and for truth with some kind of moral mandate or superiority. To some extent all three, *The Weatherhouse* especially, explore how this self-deception can end darkly, in self-destruction, violence or, as in Carswell's work, breakdown.

But there is always a redeeming feature, even in the darkest moments of *The Weatherhouse*. There is always an open mind, either that of the narrator or of a carefully placed character, which promises understanding. If Shepherd herself has a moral mandate it can be said to be her emphasis on how we should be at least generous in our versions of others, comprehending and accepting this human need for making versions of the self, recognising where and why they're made. Shepherd never harnesses the reader to any single narrative, keen to spread the structure of a story as wide as possible so that central characters are only central in relevance to and with reference to their communities and their communal responsibility.[12] At the end of *The Quarry Wood*, Martha, who was reluctant to see herself as part of any community or family which challenged her vision or version of herself, has accepted exactly this relativity in a way which, far from disempowering her, actually allows her to 'create herself'. In the end, Martha can even 'get' a child for herself *by* herself (completely without the participation of a man) simply by telling stories the right way.

Shepherd sets out to compare educations, the one got by books and the one got by the novel's own farcical process of Martha's de-mystification. Her real education is in where the ideal and the actual meet. For instance, Martha discovers that 'the crux of a spiritual adventure' is that it's an intensely physical adventure too. This is a book keen to point out that women do after all have minds *and* bodies – and any objectification of women as simply physical or spiritual is at best laughable, at worst deeply damaging. In fact, the balance of outer and inner existences is the most valuable thing Martha can learn. It's a process begun by her Aunt Josephine on the very first page of the novel; Josephine, with something of the impersonality of the weather about her, knows that 'trees is awfu' gweed for ye' and first walks Martha through the quarry wood where 'the quiet generosity of the visible and tangible world sank into her mind' (p. 6); she starts off the education which will end in Martha's being truly ready for the education of others.

Shepherd's main attack on self-delusion lies in her debunking of the fantasies suspended between the genders. Luke and Roy Rory Foubister act as opposite poles of the same problem in their response to Martha. Luke's first comments show that he objectifies everything: a visit to his wife's childhood home is 'a holy pilgrimage', Aunt Josephine becomes 'that wonderful Aunt Josephine' (pp. 43–4). Soon he is objectifying Martha, reading what he wants to hear into her silence, pleased with the simile he makes of her, deciding what she is and what form she'll take. He romanticises her until he forgets 'that her nature might be other than he had perceived,' and sees her 'only in his own conception of her' (pp. 74–5). This conception spiritualises her, creates her as an aesthetic construction, a Beatrice figure and something with a semblance to the Virgin Mary all at the same time – it turns her into the vessel of his making. 'I don't worship you . . . But I have learned through you to worship flame. The flame of life,' he tells her (p. 76). 'He saw her face, held straight ahead and as though she walked without seeing where she went' (p. 77). Martha humbly accepts the roles given to her and sure enough they leave her with a kind of blindness, wandering through life in a dwam, feeling formed by his 'very words' about her: 'if the spirit had chosen her for shining through, she would be crystal clear. Crystal clear! Luke had used the very words' (p. 79).

Martha creates Luke too, he becomes 'her imagined perfection' in her head (p. 98). Shepherd takes witty advantage of the ironies that arise when the 'perfect' world of the imagination collides with the real vulgar world. Martha, still thinking of herself as a mythical Artemis or Diana, is plunged straight into pure physical desire for Luke, and the rest of the book's plot revolves around the various misreadings of a kiss in the woods as the author ironises 'the spiritual mysteries' (p. 112) of basic physical lust and leaves Martha at the terrible and mentally exhausting mercy of unrequited passions, almost to the point of physical breakdown.

Foubister, like Luke, finds Martha attractive because she listens to him; he objectifies her too, sees her not as a spirit, however, but as a sturdy horse to be tamed and ridden. When he hears one of the more vulgar readings of the kiss in the woods he is outraged – his property has been cheapened by belonging to another, he won't be the first to ride his horse. Shepherd shows how this brings Martha to her senses, leaves her laughing at Foubister's ridiculous bluster about her being his property, and at herself, knowing the truth now about her 'sheerly spiritual' love for Luke:

> And what was love really like? Not so sheerly spiritual after all. She recalled the frenzy of her June desire. That was what had driven her to the wood. In intent she had been just what Roy supposed . . . And what madness there was in the world's morality! She had given herself utterly – all save the one thing that the world condemns a woman for giving. Was she any whit less guilty – if it were true that there was guilt in love – than

the woman who gave her flesh? Or Luke less guilty in taking
her soul than though he had taken her body? (pp. 159–60)

What's more, after this clear-sightedness Martha's preoccupations
take on a 'sudden change of theme' (p. 180); she becomes interested
in what happens to people who come under the pressure of society's
'versions' of them, particularly other women. Most importantly, she
faces out a false rumour about her own bearing of an illegitimate
child, adopts the child people commonly believe to be hers (one of
her mother's adoptives), and lives unmarried with the child she
might so easily have given birth to. Shepherd has her give the lie to
this image to remind us of the difficult relationship between the
truth and versions of it, the theme throughout the book.

By the end we're shown that she has learned generosity and
responsibility on many levels; she's learned particularly that 'the
shattering of her selfhood' is what allows for 'the condition of
growth' (p. 199). Roderick Watson, in his essay, '"To Get Leave
To Live": Patterns of Identity, Freedom and Defeat in the Fiction
of Nan Shepherd' sees Martha's 'future' beyond what's given in the
novel as quite 'ambiguous': 'where are all the ideals of freedom and
knowledge and the finer things in life which she had as a young
student,' he asks; 'has she gained something, or has she been defeated?'[13] Shepherd suggests, I'd argue, that she's gained a great
deal, not least the ability to judge the worth of such 'ideals' and
judge what 'freedom and knowledge and the finer things in life'
actually are. She's gained the wisdom of truth despite appearance,
living regardless of and as a constant challenge to social codes and
others' versions of her. In the one moment Shepherd allows us to
project into Martha's future, Martha is shown to have the self-
possession to give 'a steady and smiling refusal' when Roy Rory
Foubister returns from the war to ask her to marry him after all (p.
179). She turns down the prospective husband who would make
her an 'honest' woman in other folk's eyes, but create yet another
dishonest image of her.

Both Carswell and Shepherd know how to persuade readers to
think about the power and the trap of social convention, and both
were careful to circumnavigate the larger problem of making their
heroines unattractively brazen to their contemporary readers.
Although Martha feels she may as well have given herself bodily to
Luke it's quite significant that she hasn't; Shepherd's heroine has
her child without actually 'having' it in the same way (though much

less awkwardly and with a great deal more centrality to plot) as Carswell has Joanna marry Rasponi in *Open the Door!* only to kill him off with a timely exploding motorcycle. This leaves her heroine an 'experienced' married woman who already and legitimately has the sexual knowledge she needs when it comes to the real passionate affair of the book, not quite as shocking, not quite as extra-marital as it might have been.

But both Carswell and Shepherd are determined to show their women characters as refusing the given roles of wife and child-bearer. These are courageous works, particularly in their emphasis on women's desires – it's easier to remember just how courageous even Carswell's hooded references to 'the final abandonment' were when you consider that only fifteen years later Naomi Mitchison's *We Have Been Warned* was 'delayed by timorous publishers because of its alleged outspokenness on sexual matters, chiefly the mention of contraceptive rubber goods,' as Isobel Murray notes in a recent essay.[14] In these novels, and in Willa Muir's *Imagined Corners*, sex is for the satisfaction of love or desire, and only the Victorian monster of Muir's second published novel, *Mrs Ritchie*, thinks the one justification of sex is childbirth. Childbirth as a purpose for existence is volubly rejected by Carswell's two heroines, and the only thing Martha actually gives 'issue' to in the *The Quarry Wood* is the 'cataclysm' of a new self 'cracked within her' (pp. 121–2), the shattered self which will provide the painful basis for the knowledge that she can go ahead and create.

From the fragmented selves of the work of Carswell and Shepherd, we can come to the radical self-making of Willa Muir's first novel, *Imagined Corners* (1931). Elizabeth Shand is a heroine who is actually two women, not just one – that is, there are two Elizabeth Shands in a novel which deals with her/them in a structure of two halves, concerned with finding a complementary balance between opposites. Here the fragmented or split self reconstitutes itself before your very eyes, and Muir suggests that at least for the moment the answer to this completion lies in the support of the right woman, rather than the wrong man.

Like Shepherd's *The Weatherhouse*, *Imagined Corners* has a structure which embraces the stories of several individuals at once. Its aim is very much to talk about living within the community constraints of its small east coast Scottish town, Calderwick. In the end, however, the only way forward for the Elizabeths is to 'run away', to leave the claustrophobic Calderwick and head for the liberality of Europe. From the opening pages Scotland is shown as a mental construct as well as a geographical one; these women eventually leave this behind for a place of less constriction, and there's a question posed at the end of the novel as to whether in doing this they have left men behind too.

The young Elizabeth, clever and passionate, just married to boorish, philandering and immature Hector Shand, comes to live in Calderwick where her name and something about her calls up memories in her new brother-in-law, John, of his spirited sister, the other Elizabeth. The other Elizabeth was, it seems, a 'wild thing' who 'behaved scandalously' and ran away some years earlier with a married man, worse than that, a foreigner.[15] John remembers her as the liveliest thing there has ever been about Calderwick, and decides to invite her back; halfway into the novel back she comes, lively and irrepressible as ever.

Into this basic plot line Muir also builds the story of another brother/sister family, attached to the parish church, and through them she studies the dark influence of Calvinism in warping and destroying the sensitive; *Imagined Corners* calls for the rejection of Calvinist dogma for humane liberalism. She suggests the harm there is in believing 'the body in itself is evil' – throughout her work, from *Women: an Inquiry* in 1925 to *Belonging* in 1968, there's a forceful rejection of the notion of original sin, which she sees as guilt about sex being palmed off on women as a controlling measure. For Elise in *Imagined Corners*, God 'was merely an enforcer of taboos, and a male creature at that, one who had no sympathy for little girls and did nothing for them' (p. 185). The watchful eye over this novel, the narrator, is the opposite of this God in every way in a book that explores both female and male identity with a positive emphasis on the former.

Later in the novel Muir even suggests that the effects of Elizabeth's marriage to Hector are as bad as the stifling effects of religious dogma ('in marrying Hector Elizabeth had entered upon a discipline that was to bruise her much as the discipline of the Church had bruised the minister' (p. 251)) and the first half of the novel examines the effect of the marriage on her. Having married because they both seemed equally passionate in love and spirited about life, Elizabeth soon finds herself hopelessly trapped and unhappy, unwittingly made responsible for Hector's childish actions by the other women in her new Calderwick family and by Hector himself, who believes that 'good women existed to keep in check men's sensual passions . . . if she could not do her duty as a woman he would leave the rails and wreck himself fatally' (p. 77). Hector, as miserable and lost as his wife is in this arrangement, does what Muir suggests the men of his family and of Calderwick would generally do under pressure of stereotype, spends his time feeling sorry for himself and relying on 'his precious wife to help him not to make a bloody mess of his life' (p. 94) while he has an affair with his brother's wife and makes plans to escape his responsibilities.

Muir takes time to present Elizabeth as a character painfully torn in two, between taking back her own name and leaving Hector and Scotland, and believing she's only unhappy and dissatisfied because she's not being a good enough wife. The latter wins over. 'Give up the old Elizabeth Ramsay, she told herself, emotion sweeping her away, and became Elizabeth Shand' (p. 66). For Carswell, emotion was what provided individuality. For Shepherd, emotion provided the possibilities for farce. Muir's book, in the very analytical tone of the narration (the narrator almost has the voice of a patient lawyer for the defence, explaining and arguing for her characters at every turn), is a book about the analysis of emotion, and when Elizabeth tells herself in a rush of nostalgia and emotion for Hector that 'she must learn to be a good wife', we're made aware that being swept away by any emotion is precarious. 'I'm not me,' she finds herself thinking when she accepts the role of 'Noble Wife' and 'perfect lady' (p. 134). Certainly, before Elise enters the story, Elizabeth has begun to feel like 'two separate persons', one confident in giving herself to her husband and marriage, the other lost, disappointed and fearful. 'I feel that myself has let me down,' she thinks (p. 123).

Muir presents Elizabeth as having suffered a deep identity crisis in her marriage, having lost herself to her role. She creates her as

> a victim of her upbringing as well as of her temperament. From her earliest years she had been subjected to the subtle pressure of the suggestion that a husband is the sole justification of a woman's existence, that a woman who cannot attract and keep a husband is a failure. That some such theory should emerge in a society which regarded the sexual act as sinful was inevitable; one cannot train women in chastity and then expect them to people the world unless the sinfulness of sex is counterbalanced by the desirability of marriage. (p. 120)

The escape Muir allows Elizabeth in the novel, an escape with an older, wiser Elizabeth, is a redemption from the expected roles of wife and mother and from years of such conditioning.

Imagined Corners suggests in its title a paradox of possibility and limitation, the cornering of the imagination as well as the sense that being cornered is only an imaginary constraint, the freeing sense that this novel presents only one tiny corner of the possibilities of the imagination. It's a fiction aware that 'we're all reared on fictions from the breast up' (p. 206), unimaginative fictions, fictions which naturally constrain us, and it sets out to expose some of the fictions of conventional expectation and some of the limits of imagination as far as women are concerned. At one level it shows as laughable the stuffy Calderwick disapproval of Elizabeth's 'running about without gloves and saying damn, and screaming with laughter in the street like a mill-girl' (p. 75), or saying hello to her maid when she meets her in the street when the decorous done thing is to ignore your servants. But this transforms into quite another challenge to convention, when in the end 'why shouldn't you talk to your maid in the street' has become something unimaginable on Calderwick standards, why shouldn't you run away from your husband, and with another woman at that.

One of the important questions the novel asks is put by Elise. 'To what end do we live?' she asks herself in a room full of women boring her with the triviality, the 'soft strangling' of their social preoccupations (pp. 232–3). The end to which Elizabeth has been living has been Hector, and the smooth running, the management of a marriage by its Noble Wife. By the end of the first half of the novel, before the strong and subtle substance of Elise enters to change the chemistry, in both the main plot and the subplots the people of the novel are out of control, a society of social and religious turmoil. The answer, at least for Elizabeth, comes in the shape of the second half – her other, Elise. Even before she has met Elise, the concept of another version of herself is deeply exciting to her: 'just think of meeting another Elizabeth Shand! . . . it gives me the queerest feeling. It's like seeing yourself in a mirror for the first time' (p. 78). The fact that another version of the self is possible outside the constraints of marriage and the small town leaves her excited and open (her opposite self, the already free Elise, reacts with predictable individualist annoyance that another woman should have her name).

Elise, Muir suggests, is exactly the woman for Elizabeth, she emphasises that Elise is the nearest possible thing to another Hector, but a female version of him. And she stresses the ambiguity, the freedom from social constraint and the space for interpretation created by this new gender relationship:

> Elizabeth was looking for her other self. Had it been a man whose arrival she was expecting with so much interest, she would have been embarrassed by that interest; had it been a man who now came into the room she would have been afraid of her own emotion; but since Elise was a woman Elizabeth did not know that she actually fell in love with her at first sight. (p. 165)

The knowing narrator has, with a modicum of irony, allowed Elizabeth some space here, the space to define herself outside the norm. Because Elise is a woman, Elizabeth has no language with which to saddle herself with closed definitions of how to behave, or how to feel. And significantly, the first discussion that the two women have is on gender, language and definition. They both dislike the neutralising effect of the German article *das* on the words *Mädchen* (girl) and *Weib* (woman), they both dislike the control of the terms of definition of a gender which, after all, is made up of individual women, individual selves (pp. 169–70). Elizabeth is delighted with Elise and with their discussion, and as the plot progresses Elise is surprised to find herself becoming open to and keen to help Elizabeth, 'the most interesting woman I've met for years,' particularly for her 'lack of any social sense' (p. 217). Muir repeatedly presents them in dialogue which sets up opposing mirror images of them, making 'one damned fine woman between us,' as Elise eventually puts it. 'We're only separate like waves rising out of the one sea,' says the younger. 'I maintain myself in the teeth of all indeterminate forces,' says the elder, 'this wave-top, this precariously held point of separateness, this evanescent phenomenon which is *me*, is what I live to assert' (pp. 192–4). The younger teaches the elder to take responsibility for others. The elder promises to teach the younger a sense of herself, and of self-survival.

And the plot culminates in one woman buying off the other's husband, giving him enough money to free himself from a constricting marriage for which he has no skill, freeing his wife from her suffocating love and her responsibility for him, and then carrying 'her off like a second Lochinvar,' as Elise thinks in the final chapter, returning to Europe not just with a version of her younger self but 'with a brand-new daughter, or sister, or wife, or whatever it was' (p. 279).

What *is* the younger Elizabeth in this relationship? She's all of these things, and none of them. There's subtle play made by Muir here between her new role being so fluent in, even lacking in definition, and the 'carrying off' being a romantic redemption. Does Muir think the genders survive best apart, that women survive best under the care of other women? 'Have you then given up men?' asks the friend Elise meets on the boat taking them to Italy. It's the last page of the novel, and the question is left radically open. For the elder Elizabeth it's a moral question and almost a career choice; Muir has charged her novel and her heroine with the responsibility to 'clear away stones of prejudice and superstition so that other girls might grow up in a more kindly soil' (p. 281), and the only way she can do this is to take the still wounded, numbed and confused younger heroine far from the hurtful sense of role that ate her alive in Calderwick and marriage.

What Muir has insisted on throughout is that women should not rely solely on their emotional responses. In the mid-1920s, when she was writing the first drafts of the earlier half of this novel, she also produced her pamphlet for the Hogarth Press, *Women: an Inquiry*, where, she remembered afterwards, 'I was thinking out the implications of my inability to detach myself from emotions, which I suspected might not only be a peculiarity of mine but a characteristic of most women.'[16] The finished form of *Imagined Corners* certainly goes against the bent of *Women: an Inquiry*, in which the romantic hope is for the achievement of an ideal state between the genders, a harmonious balancing between men and women of what she sees as their essential attributes and differences. It's an essay paradoxical in its very analytical voice, as Muir decides that women are essentially not analytical, are stronger in the 'unconscious life', 'essentially emotional, spontaneous and irrational,' and can match men and complete them by complementing their essentially analytical, 'conscious' and logical attributes.[17] 'Creative love is the fundamental attribute of womanhood, as perhaps creative thought is of manhood.'[18] Women feel, men think, she suggests, in an essay which at the same time splendidly hits out at the forced subserviency of women in a male-dominated society, and comments very sharply on the traps of conditioning and role. By the time she finished *Imagined Corners* some six years later, it seems that she had discovered that sometimes the gender balance, the harmony, couldn't be found. Or perhaps that it simply didn't apply to, or that Scottish society didn't yet have a place for, women who feel *and* think.

Imagined Corners also demands that women (and men too) must have a different relationship with what was Carswell's final saviour, nature. Elise sums it up in an earlier discussion with Elizabeth:

> one should ask only: Is this intelligent? and never: Is this natural? People who urged intelligent men and women to go 'back to Nature' were merely imbecile, in Elise's opinion . . . civilized mankind . . . might develop in the most unexpected directions if it were encouraged to trust its intelligence and to outwit Nature wherever it could . . . Nature was too strong, too cunning; one had to filch from her the energy for one's own purposes. Especially if one was a woman. (pp. 255–6)

This couldn't be further from Carswell's creed, from her resolutely happy and Edenic ending of *Open the Door!*.

But Muir, in her outwitting of the feminine 'Nature' with her analytical other Lochinvar in *Imagined Corners*, is highly ambiguous, in fact quite flirtatious. There is clearly a seduction of sorts happening here. It's the promise of other things; it's the romantic rescue of the self by the self from false role, from slow death by stereotype, the rescue of the emotional, naive and passionate by the experienced, analytical and articulate, and it's an attractive statement of strength. It's a strong thumbing of the nose at what was expected of women. And it's the providing of a metaphorical language, a set of terms for the beginning of a positive, much needed and clearly gender-specific education of the female self.

Muir wrote in her memoirs, nearly forty years later:

> As a schoolgirl I shrugged my shoulders at the gap between the self I knew and the female stereotyping expected of me, but when I moved to the university I began to find the discrepancy comic . . . The patriarchal Law rated us as second-class citizens (we could not vote) and the patriarchal Church assumed that we were second-class souls (being suspect daughters of that Original Sinner, Eve) . . . And yet we females were strong natural forces deserving a status of our own as free citizens. The theory of female inferiority did not square with the actual strength and courage of women.[19]

Belonging also covers Willa's visit to Europe in the 1920s and 1930s with Edwin, her husband, and the subtle rise of fascism which she records here is also very much present in her second published novel, *Mrs Ritchie* (1933), a novel where the Victorian closed, sure mind meets the modernist shell-shocked mind. It emphasises the importance of cause and effect. Read alongside *Imagined Corners* it can be seen as a work examining what happens when there's no alternative self available, no romantic 'other' to help you escape Calderwick, so that the self, trapped by tradition, convention, religion and conditioning, grows embittered, grotesque and in the end, deadly.

Muir's novels scan the social structures of Scottish life of the first decades of the century, and call for a complete reassessment of the relations between the genders. This is true of all three writers surveyed here, writers who now make up our alternative modernist canon. It's an alternative only recently rediscovered; it's a commonplace that although each of these writers was remarkably successful, well known and well reviewed for her fiction at its time of publication, each was subsequently forgotten as a novelist for decades. Carswell was famous for her biographies of famous men, Burns and Lawrence especially. Shepherd was remembered as a lucid critic of MacDiarmid and a correspondent with Neil Gunn before the reprinting of her own novels was a reminder that not only was she another of our finest novelists but she was a clear forerunner of Grassic Gibbon. Muir was Mrs Muir, Edwin's wife, who helped him with translations. The novels I've just been discussing were lost to us for over half a century, reprinted in the late 1980s by Virago (Carswell) and Canongate (Shepherd and Muir) and even so some of them are still not available. There are, incredibly, three unpublished novels by Willa Muir in the University Library of St Andrews, 'reputedly inferior to the two which attained print'.[20] I'll end on a sobering thought from one of today's most highly successful writers, with whom, of course, the writers of the past have much in common:

> there is no real reason to think the present wave of interest in women's writing will not be allowed to go 'out of print' like the forerunners; no evidence to suggest this present honeymoon with publishers won't pass abruptly when women's writing stops being flavour of the month and there's a less immediate way to make money out of it.[21]

Anne Smith's *The Magic Glass* had already been out of print for ten years by the time Janice Galloway sounded this warning bell. The warning might be summed up like this. Sustain the alternative, because the alternative isn't just an alternative, it's been the real issue all along. From one end of the century to the other the gender debate has been central to women's writing, and it still is, still relevant, still raging.

NOTES

1. Catherine Carswell *Open the Door!* (London, Virago 1986) p. 205. All subsequent page references are to this edition.
2. Carswell's friendship with D. H. Lawrence and his substantial influence on her life and work have been well documented, particularly readably by Carswell herself in *The Savage Pilgrimage*, her 'narrative' biography published in 1932, two years after his death.
3. This review of *The Rainbow*, which Carswell made sure reached the newspaper uncut by its editor, can be read in *The Glasgow Herald* of 4 November 1915, p. 4.
4. Catherine Carswell *Lying Awake: An Unfinished Autobiography and Other Posthumous Papers*, ed. John Carswell (London, Secker and Warburg 1950) p. 116.
5. Ibid.
6. Ibid. p. 117.
7. Ibid. p. 118.
8. John Carswell, Introduction to the Virago edition of *Open the Door!*, p. xiii.
9. Catherine Carswell *The Camomile: an Invention* (London, Virago 1987) p. 269. Readers interested in this point will find Lawrence's 1928/9 essay, 'Give Her a Pattern' of particular interest: 'a pattern [women] must have, or they can't exist . . . The fact of life is that women *must* play up to man's pattern. And she only gives her best to a man when he gives her a satisfactory pattern to play up to.' D. H. Lawrence *Selected Essays* (Harmondsworth, Penguin 1950) pp. 19–23.
10. Nan Shepherd *The Quarry Wood* (Edinburgh, Canongate 1987) p. 184. All subsequent page references are to this edition.
11. Nan Shepherd *The Weatherhouse* (Edinburgh, Canongate 1988) pp. 8–9.
12. Shepherd's structuring of her novels, particularly *The Weatherhouse* can be likened to the structures of the work of recent women filmmakers like Penny Marshall (*A League of their Own*) and Allison Anders (*Gas, Food, Lodging, Mi Vida Loca*). 'I really believe that if the narrative structure of films had been invented by women, there wouldn't be this neatly driven three act formula,' Anders says in interview with Lizzie Francke, 'Greasy Hamburgers and Cheap Cassettes', *Second Shift*, Spring 1993, p. 41.
13. Roderick Watson ' "To Get Leave To Live": Patterns of Identity, Freedom and Defeat in the fiction of Nan Shepherd', *Studies in Scottish*

Fiction: Twentieth Century, eds Schwend and Drescher (Frankfurt am Main, Peter Lang 1990) pp. 207–18, p. 211.

14. Isobel Murray 'Novelists of the Renaissance', *The History of Scottish Literature* Vol. 4, ed. Cairns Craig (Aberdeen, Aberdeen University Press 1987) pp. 103–17, pp. 107–8.
15. Willa Muir *Imagined Corners* (Edinburgh, Canongate 1987) p. 25. All subsequent page references are to this edition.
16. Willa Muir *Belonging: a Memoir* (London, The Hogarth Press 1968) p. 114.
17. Willa Muir *Women: an Inquiry* The Hogarth Essays, no. 10 (London, The Hogarth Press 1925) p. 15.
18. Ibid. p. 28.
19. *Belonging* pp. 140–1.
20. David S. Robb 'The Published Novels of Willa Muir', *Studies in Scottish Fiction* pp. 149–61, p. 155.
21. Janice Galloway, Introduction to *Meantime* (Edinburgh, Polygon in association with Women 2000 1991) p. 5.

3

Fishy Masculinities

Neil Gunn's The Silver Darlings

CHRISTOPHER WHYTE

*'. . . our scholarship always reflects our selves however
hard we try to objectify it . . .'*

Philip Brett

For as long as I can remember, the work of Neil Gunn has irritated
and even angered me. I feel like the child in the fable of the emperor's
clothes. It would be going too far to claim that Gunn walks entirely
naked. But whatever clothes he does wear strike me as rather thread-
bare and, in any case, insufficient to conceal the unpalatable realities
beneath.

The child in the fable blurts out its surprise and amusement
without any thought for the reactions of other people in the crowd.
I have hesitated rather longer before articulating my misgivings
about Gunn's work. His reputation has stood the test of time better
than those of MacDiarmid or Muir, two other giants from the first
wave of the Scottish Renaissance Movement. MacDiarmid's allega-
tion that Muir was a quisling has stuck, if only to the extent that
the theses contained in his infamous polemic *Scott and Scotland*
(1936) are no longer the object of serious debate.[1] The multiplication
of voices in Scottish writing over the last two decades has caused
MacDiarmid's undoubted achievements to be both contextualised
and actively challenged in a way that, in the long run, can only
improve our understanding of him.[2] But the formidable body of
critical work on Gunn is uniformly eulogistic, so much so that it is
hard at times to accept it as critical in any valid sense.

Hart and Pick, the authors of the definitive biography *Neil M. Gunn: a Highland Life*, refer to their subject throughout by his first name.[3] He is quite simply Neil, an honorary member of our family as of theirs. His claim to respect, intimacy and tenderness is axiomatic. He was in there at the very start. Kurt Wittig's *The Scottish Tradition in Literature*, first published in 1958, is by now a somewhat outdated text. But it played an important part in constituting the tradition. Wittig writes that with Gunn 'modern Scottish fiction reaches its highest peak'. He is 'so far the only Scottish novelist whose work in some measure embodies all the ideals of the Scots Renaissance'.[4] In other words, he epitomises the movement and can even be taken as emblematic of it. Nothing that matters in the Scottish Renaissance is absent from his writing.

Such an established reputation is not to be questioned lightly. Could a whole phalanx of venerable critics have got it wrong? Had they failed to notice certain crucial aspects in his work? Could it be that because of those aspects, rather than praising his work fulsomely, they should have hesitated before praising it at all? Surely the wise thing to do was to keep silent. And yet my misgivings about Gunn refused to go away. I tried to convince myself that the elements in his writing which disturbed me were marginal. I told myself I must be missing the point. Side issues were blinding me to his effective strengths.

The issues in question were his treatment of Gaelic and his treatment of gender. Perhaps it will be easier if I start with Gaelic. Scottish critics have only recently acknowledged gender as a significant factor in their readings. On the other hand, it has been obligatory more or less since the Renaissance Movement was first launched in the early 1920s to pay at least lip service to Gaelic. It would of course be taking this veneration to excessive lengths to actually learn the language. In this respect Gunn was no more industrious than his critics. J. B. Caird writes that

> Until comparatively recently Gaelic was spoken in the southern part of Caithness, where Dunbeath [Gunn's birthplace] is situated. Gunn's father and some of the members of the crew of his fishing-boat were Gaelic speakers, but Gunn himself, as he admits in his travel book, *Off in a Boat* (where he refers to his 'sparse Gaelic') had only a smattering of the language.[5]

According to his biographers, he 'even tried briefly to learn some Gaelic' (p. 14). (Whether the 'even' expresses his or their surprise at such a rash course of action is uncertain.) So far, so good. Wittig's attitude is more puzzling. The German scholar, one of Gunn's most vigorous champions, believes that

> The Gaelic basis of Gunn's style is apparent in the rhythms, sentence structure and idioms of the dialogue, and also, though less obviously, of the narrative. Many of the similes . . . are clearly of Gaelic derivation; and Gaelic is for him the unique expression of the working of his people's mind. (p. 335)

If Gaelic is indeed 'unique', irreplaceable, I asked myself, and Gunn is denied access to it, what can be his chances of evoking that 'mind', or representing the culture associated with it? By some mysterious sleight of hand, Gunn had come to be acclaimed as the novelist of Gaelic Scotland, as the man who encapsulates 'the essential Highland experience' (the title of the second section of McCulloch's 1987 monograph) in his fiction.[6] Yet it had escaped general attention that, almost without exception, the critics who gave him this accolade knew no more Gaelic than Gunn himself.

I do not wish to be misunderstood. I am by no means suggesting, in moralistic fashion, that Gunn was under some kind of obligation to master Gaelic. What bothers me is that such interpretations promote a false idea of Gunn's relationship to Gaelic culture (whatever the latter may be or have been). By misrepresenting what his writing does they prevent us isolating the processes which are in fact at work. As I became more and more conversant with the language, I could not help noticing how great a gap separated the culture associated with it from the images made available in Gunn's fiction. The gap does not invalidate the fiction. It does invalidate certain ways of interpreting it.

His handling of specific incidents puzzled me. At the very beginning of *Butcher's Broom* (1934), whoever Dark Mairi of the shore encounters on her way

> might say in greeting, 'It's the fine day that's in it,' as though he were setting the day in the hollow of the world so that they might with courteous detachment regard it. There was always this detachment, this reserve of the person, removing the world to a slight distance and permitting it to be addressed or discussed in a grave and pleasant voice.[7]

Here Gunn uses a rather clumsy rendering of a typical Gaelic phrase to draw conclusions about the world view of Gaelic speakers. He gives a syntactical pattern first a spatial and then an emotional significance. But would those using the pattern be aware of its implications? Why translate 'in it' when 'in him' would be just as accurate a rendering of Gaelic 'ann'? Gaelic, after all, has no neuter gender. What about the fact that 'in it' is in Gaelic one word, and not two? Or that Gaelic has two verbs for 'to be' as against English's one? What effect would the choice between these have on the speaker's world view at this particular moment? Should not all these factors be taken into consideration? Gunn is clearly predicating his Gaelic world view on the English translation rather than on the characteristic structures of the language itself.

So it would be a mistake to believe that Gunn could act as an intermediary between a Scottish, or an English audience and a Gaelic culture from which they were separated by barriers not just of language. He was in no position to do so. Rather he filled the void labelled 'Gaelic' in the minds of his readers with a construction of his own making, one that had precise ideological and philosophical implications.

And now for gender. I have always found Gunn's erotic (or pseudo-erotic) writing ham-fisted. There is little point in attempting to relate this to the man himself, or to make deductions about the effect on his style of the affair with Margaret MacEwen, a 'scrupulously concealed relationship' which ran parallel to Gunn's apparently happy marriage for some thirty years.[8] It is fairer, and more instructive, to look closely at the texts. I still cannot help smiling at the pressing need to remind each other of their names which afflicts Gunn's characters at moments of sexual arousal. Here are Colin and Elie in *Butcher's Broom*.

> Colin gave a small nervous laugh and began talking of the piper's odd humours. Elie did not answer. He tried to see her face. Touching her cheek, his fingers got wet. Her glimmering smile came at him on a moon wave; he crushed into it. 'Elie! Elie!' he said. And 'Ah, Colin!' she answered as the wave sank. (p. 63)

Roddie and Catrine in *The Silver Darlings* run into roughly similar problems:

> 'Roddie, no!' she said, feeling the dark force of his body coming at her, pleading wildly out of the weakness that was melting her flesh.

'Yes,' said Roddie, enfolding her. 'Yes, Catrine.'[9]

Gunn's erotic writing was so uniformly chaste that almost any of his books could have been laid in the hands of an adolescent boy or girl before the war without any danger of corrupting knowledge. Or was it? Tactile realities risk breaking through the surface of the text in the first of the extracts quoted. If the pun on 'humours' is unintentional, are we obliged to ignore the implications of 'Touching her . . ., his fingers got wet'? How then are the 'moon wave' and its crushing to be interpreted? Am I the only reader to be intrigued when Finn is 'oddly moved by an access of quiet manhood' in *The Silver Darlings* (p. 345)? Or were there others who wondered whether Gunn was trying to tell us his hero had a hard on? After all, according to the previous sentence, the men in the fishing boat were now 'preparing to shoot, as if some silent common intelligence had been at work'. Are these unlooked-for delights the consequence of mischievous misreading? Or do they offer a better understanding of Gunn's writing, what it reveals and conceals?

Representation is of course always also interpretation. The erection (if that is what is meant) is not merely a physical sensation Finn can be left to enjoy. The text insists on its social implications. It makes him more of a man, adding to his growing but still insufficient stock of 'manhood'. In this way both the character and the reader are reassured that Finn's metaphorical voyage will end in the secure harbour of an unquestioning and unquestionable masculinity. The hunting instinct has its part to play in this process. Long before puberty affects him, Finn chases after a butterfly and comes upon a larger prey, a trout.

> If he got a stick and gave it one sharp prog under the stone! What a fright the trout would get, and maybe it would kill him! And then he would catch the trout and take it home and his mother . . . (p. 91)

The syndrome is there, waiting to be activated. He will kill a wild thing and take it home to the trapped, expectant female, who will both praise his achievement and cook it so that it can be eaten. Where was the syndrome waiting? According to Gunn, in Finn's blood. Where else? In their discussion of *Second Sight* (1940), a novel in which hunting plays a crucial part, Gunn's biographers cite this journal entry for 4 July 1939:

> At one time I was quite fond of shooting. In fact the hunting

instinct is one of the strongest in my blood. I know nothing so
exciting, so health-giving, so full of the very glow of life, as
stalking game – fish or feather or fur . . .[10]

They quote the entry more extensively, showing that Gunn experienced a certain distaste for blood sports and was aware of the
problematic social and political background against which these are
practised in Scotland. What interests me is the rhetoric being used.
Any mention of blood in Gunn's prose not capable of literal interpretation merits close attention. This rhetoric implies that, through
the agency of blood, patterns of behaviour we would see today as
cultural rather than innate are transmitted from generation to generation. Blood is the site where an ideology of race intersects with an
ideology of gender. If the urge to hunt resides in the blood of men
but not in that of women, then men's blood and women's blood
must, in terms of this rhetoric, differ in significant ways. The two
do not have the same content.

Personally, I suspect some primitive men may have undertaken
the daily hunting expedition rather as a contemporary commuter
undertakes the daily journey to work. It is a necessity which has to
be gone through in order to free time for more rewarding pursuits.
What puzzled me was that Gunn should consider the hunting instinct
so relevant to Scotland and Europe in the decade leading up to the
Second World War that he gave it a privileged place in his fictional
world. Was he totally out of touch with his time? Or did current
political events on mainland Europe make the exhumation of the
hunting instinct peculiarly topical?

Again I tried to persuade myself that I was being unfair. I told
myself that I was personally unsympathetic to negligible aspects of
Gunn's fictional world. They must be negligible, given that his
critics' silence about them was virtually unbroken. But the niggling
doubts persisted. They became overwhelming when I realised that
gender is not a side issue in Gunn's fiction. More often than not it
is *the* issue.

This is especially true of *The Silver Darlings*. His critics hover
close to the point without ever actually making it. For Richard
Price the plot is 'basically the biography of its central character,
Finn'[11] while for John Burns the focus is 'Finn's "journey" from
childhood, through adolescence, to maturity' or, in other words,
'the archetypal journey made by each of us in the course of our
lives'.[12] It is worth pointing out the tell-tale intrusion of 'archetypal',

a key word in Gunn criticism. Its use denies any possibility of dissent. The archetypal is always already present in each individual psyche (or bloodstream). Individual denial is pointless. If you lack the hunting instinct then by that very token you are not, or are less than, a man. Neither character nor reader has the option of being or acting differently. The rhetoric of the archetype, on both Gunn's and his critics' lips, is a coercive rhetoric.

Burns also makes a swift and deft but perceptible move across gender boundaries, from the young male Finn to 'each of us in the course of our lives'. What happens to the young male, to this young male, happens to everyone. Alexander Scott has a more limited scope when he comments that, here and elsewhere in Gunn's fiction, 'the principal protagonist is at once individual and archetypal, at once a particular boy . . . and a representative of all boys'.[13] There is the obligatory reference to an archetype. It comes as no surprise when Burns, further down the same page, writes that

> full development and maturity only come when a man can retain his own individuality while losing his selfishness. Within the circle of his own experience each person has to find his own place, a position in which he is perfectly balanced . . .

The mention of the 'circle' shows Burns, like so many who write about Gunn, reproducing his terminology rather than seeking to gain a critical perspective on it. Notice the slippage from 'a man' to 'each person', the subsuming of humanity under the male gender which permits Burns to describe Gunn's fiction as preoccupied with maturity. *The Silver Darlings* is not about the maturing of a human being. Its theme is the construction of a masculinity (one of many possible, although it seeks to be mandatory). The novel propounds a *myth of masculinity*.

Douglas Gifford performs a slightly different slippage when he makes Finn the embodiment of a Scottish spirit:

> Finn, in mastering self, in reconciling himself with mother, community, and his role as husband and father, is Gunn's final and finest exemplar of Scottish spirit triumphing over forces within and without Scotland.[14]

Much of Finn's energy goes into combating his mother's influence and eventually breaking free of it. Does this mean that Catrine is within Scotland, but somehow outside the Scottish spirit?

All these manœuvres help to camouflage the novel's essential preoccupation with masculinity, its construction and safeguarding. Hart and Pick show greater perceptiveness when they speak of *The Silver Darlings* as not just a 'folk epic' or a 'panoramic chronicle' but a 'dark, desperate examination of the roots of male pride'.[15] And while taking part in the general eulogy of the novel, Alan Riach admits the presence of 'troublesome aspects to its depths and magnitude'.[16]

I decided it would be a mistake to underrate my own misgivings when I understood that Gunn's treatment of the two issues, of Gaelic and of gender, is closely linked. He invokes his version of Gaelic society before the Clearances to validate the gender ideology that underpins his fiction. The tactic is blindingly simple. How did he carry it off so successfully, especially since many of the Gaelic trappings in his work can be shown to be fake?

Gunn exploited not just his own but, more seriously, his public's ignorance of Gaelic culture. He had illustrious precedents for doing so, not least in the work of James Macpherson (1736–96), the compiler and/or fabricator of the epics *Fingal* (1762) and *Temora* (1768). Macpherson's construction of an ancient Gaelic world was so powerful as to have a rebound effect on literature in Gaelic, something that cannot be said of Gunn. In the opinion of Derick Thomson

> James Macpherson had some influence on subsequent Gaelic writing, almost always a pernicious or trivial influence. This produced poems like '*Miann a' Bhàird Aosda*' ('The Aged Poet's Wish'), John Smith's *Sean Dàna* (*Ancient Lays*) and archaized poems such as '*Mordubh*' and '*Collath*'. These have some place in a history of Gaelic poetry, but need not detain us here.[17]

Macpherson's work, and in particular the translation into Gaelic of his English texts, spawned a bogus Ossianic literature which significantly affected the taste of a nineteenth-century poet such as William Livingston (Uilleam MacDhunlèibhe 1808–70).

Gunn's strategy had more subtle and less notorious consequences. He purports to give an account of gender arrangements at a particular time and place. If he is merely a recorder, he cannot be accused of bias or prejudice. Here as elsewhere, his critics have collaborated in the hoax. Richard Price considers that in *Butcher's Broom*

> Gunn's authorial voice [is] occasionally foregrounded to supply anthropological detail which could not be shown incidentally.

This occurs, for example, when the author explains the strict work and activities differences between men and women.[18]

The passage in question supplies virtually no anthropological detail. It is concerned not with anthropology but with ideology. Gunn uses an imagined retroactive vision of Gaelic society to underpin a gender ideology based on division, polar oppositions, and the safeguarding of a masculinity he evidently felt to be endangered. We have to abandon the comforting illusion that passages in his fiction can be read as instances of detached, objective truth (whatever that might be) about the Gaelic world (whatever that might be). Rather than charting a growth in personal maturity, *The Silver Darlings* is a rearguard action in defence of a threatened gender identity.

The passage from *Butcher's Broom* is among Gunn's most outspoken pronouncements about gender roles. It comes early on in the novel and is worth quoting in full:

> The women were the more persistent and fruitful workers, and found the males frequently in their way. Many of the tasks about a house they would not let a man perform – even if he had wanted to, which, of course, he did not. In this matter of work there was so strong a custom that if a man did a woman's work, where a woman was fit to do it, the feeling of shamed surprise would be felt stronger by the woman than by the man. The system worked very well, for the man in his sphere and the woman in hers were each equally governing and indispensable. Thus the difference between a man and a woman was emphasised and each carried clear before the other the characteristics and mystery of the male and female sex. Men were not knowing with regard to their women. They left them their realm and could thus on occasion meet them like strangers and even make a verse or a song about them. In life's major dealings, like cattle-droving, marketing, hunting, and war, women would have felt helpless without their men. Yet more than their usefulness, men were to them their final ornament, and their secret pride in them, when worthy, was complete. (p. 64)

Although Price wants to give an almost scientific validity to this passage, its fictional context encourages us to read it expressively. Remarkably little information is conveyed. We are told that there is a sharp division of roles but not where the dividing lines occur.

Were the cows milked and the stables cleaned out by the same or by different persons? Which tasks connected with the house were considered appropriate for a woman and which for a man?

Gunn has no interest in answering these questions. Far from being detached or balanced, the passage is carefully weighted so that the women have an excess when compared to the men. The situation is described from their viewpoint and the speaker praises them as if he were championing them. They were 'the more persistent and fruitful workers'. The sense of shame at an infringement of gender roles was 'felt stronger' by the women. They valued men 'more' for their ornamental than for their practical purposes. While each sex has its 'sphere', only the women have a 'realm'. However, by the end of the passage it can be seen that this apparent advantage of the women is deceptive. When it comes to matters such as 'cattle-droving, marketing, hunting and war', they are helpless without men. And if these are 'life's major dealings', then those in which women have a relative autonomy must be minor. The speaker lends enthusiastic support to these arrangements in a way that must invalidate an anthropological reading: they 'worked very well'. The cultural distance which might cause both the observer and his audience to be puzzled, or even dismayed, by the customs of the Gaelic-speaking peasantry before the Clearances, is collapsed.

The passage is symbolic rather than factual. It describes a world where the separation of genders is continually brought to awareness. Indeed, men and women carry 'clear before the other the characteristics and mystery of the male and female sex', like a priest showing the body of Christ to his congregation in a golden monstrance. A cynic might comment that they carried the mystery of their sex between their legs. But Gunn is not referring to anatomy or biology. His seductive paradox of revealing and concealing, of indicating while at the same time hiding, has an almost sacramental quality. It comes as the culmination and mystical justification of the gender arrangements he is describing. The Gaelic peasants can see what it means to be female and what it means to be male. After all, they carry it around in front of them every day in the course of their duties. Only we, craning impatiently over the author's shoulders, fail to make out what it is they hold in their hands. And although he can see it, he does not put it into words.

I have already commented that Gunn's critics tend to adopt his terminology rather than clarifying its implications. According to Gifford, Gunn saw the Clearances as the time of the spiritual deformation of the Highlands, when women took over the guardianship of the communities from men, since the forces which are destroying the community have drained them of men and of their essential manhood.[19]

The idea of an 'essential manhood' which is somehow fluid and can be 'drained' away is kin to the 'access of manhood' Finn experienced. For women to assume guardianship is a symptom of 'spiritual deformation'. It is a usurping of power inevitably accompanied by a fall in the quantity of 'manhood' possessed by each man. I am more sympathetic to Alan Bold's view that the 'magical world' which for Gunn lies beyond 'everyday reality' is

> recognisable as the earthly paradise associated, in Gunn's imagination, with the Gaelic world that obtained before Culloden. Gunn constantly recalls the pre-Culloden paradise lost . . .[20]

The Gaelic world the Clearances destroyed acquires an Edenic quality, as if the evictions were a kind of fall exiling the people to a harsh existence along the Sutherland coastline. They also disrupted gender arrangements which had a transhistorical, atemporal rightness about them. The world that disappeared had a degree of sexual innocence, given that 'men were not knowing with regard to their women'. This Utopian aura helps to validate the gender arrangements imputed to it. Perhaps if we could reinstate them, the lost Eden might return.

They are further validated by Gunn's manufacturing of a fake Gaelic heritage. The third chapter of *Butcher's Broom* describes a combined waulking and ceilidh in the house of Angus Sutherland. The host recites (though one would have expected him to sing) the poem of the Ancient Bard, 'who was a man like Angus'. The magic of his performance enchants his circle of enraptured listeners:

> Behind the Aged Bard was the eternal earth and over it the Sun. In instinct and in heart they delighted and worshipped there. What they knew as God and religion interfered with this spontaneous worship and love. The Aged Bard had no Hell. They had no God of Vengeance to fear in those days. But yes now. Therefore when they slipped back with Angus, their hearts opened like flowers and the muscles of their bodies grew fluent with immortal health. (p. 57)

We have, of course, already encountered a reference to this poem in a quotation from Derick Thomson. Price remarks, 'as a reminder of Gunn's limitations', that it is the only poem in John Mackenzie's 1841 anthology to appear in both Gaelic and English.[21] The note Mackenzie supplies may well have prompted the poem's exploitation in *Butcher's Broom*:

> This is a curious and valuable relic of antiquity. It affords internal evidence that the doctrines of Christianity were either wholly unknown to the poet, or had no place in his creed. The Elysium of bards upon Ardven, the departure of the poet's shade to the hall of Ossian and Daol, his last wish of laying by his side a harp, a shell full of liquor, and his ancestors' shield, are incompatible with the Christian doctrine of a future state.[22]

Or as Gunn has it, the 'Aged Bard had no Hell'. Derick Thomson has explained that the poem actually dates from the second half of the eighteenth century and is one of a spawn of compositions which mimic the pseudo-epic world shown in Macpherson's work. This late eighteenth-century fabrication is an important source for Gunn's evocation of Gaelic culture before the Clearances, even though it could hardly have been more than twenty years old at the time he writes of and is not likely to have been in oral circulation.

The poem takes Angus's guests back to a past which antedates, not only Calvinism, but Christianity. Gunn establishes a tension between the natural, life-enhancing tendencies of traditional culture and the crippling effects of the grim religion which will now be forced on them:

> The Aged Bard, then, lived in days before St. Columba came to Iona and came to Inverness; he lived maybe before the Saviour Himself was born. That explains why there are certain things in the poem, and why the Paradise of the Aged Bard is not God's Paradise . . . Their hearts turned in them with love of the old man who loved the primrose and the streams and prayed to the Sun by which all things grew. They understood him. His words ran like a soft fire in their blood. In their bones they knew him. Their flesh was warm with desire of him. (pp. 54–6)

A verbal text courses through the blood of the listeners like fire. The poem enables Gunn to depict Gaelic as an ancient language, linking its speakers to a time before history, before records. The passage precedes that on gender by only some ten pages. Five pages further on he stresses the importance of the chief to each man in the community. His manliness is nurtured on 'all his history in descent from the Aged Bard, writ in the one blood and spoken in the one tongue' (p. 71). Of course Gunn does not mean that this (oral) history was literally transcribed in letters of blood. It was transcribed within the blood, carried there and transmitted as text. Language and culture are inscribed almost genetically, a kind of racial patrimony.

In the remainder of this chapter I will concentrate on *The Silver Darlings*. My choice of such a limited range of material – only two novels – is motivated by a desire to ground my case in a word-for-word reading of Gunn's actual texts, given the importance of unmasking his seductive style of writing. And since I have a sense of taking on an entire critical establishment, caution must be the order of the day. But there are other reasons.

In *The Silver Darlings*, the divisive gendering of Gunn's world becomes so explicit as to verge on the obsessive.[23] The novel depicts a gendered universe where it is impossible to tread on land or set out to sea without being reminded that the first is feminine, the second masculine. So pervasive is the technique that one is tempted to take it perhaps further than Gunn intended. The House of Peace is a masculine location. Roddie presents it to Catrine (p. 61), and Finn takes refuge there just before we first see him interacting with Roddie (p. 95). During the plague episode he glimpses a monk there (p. 218), and at the close of the novel he again escapes there, to the 'heart of the circle' (p. 580). Conversely, it is tempting to connote the plague as feminine. True, it is brought to Dunbeath by a fisherman, David, who goes to visit his wife's relations near Wick and contracts it from her mother. When he returns he is haunted by the 'taint', although he reminds himself that 'he had not touched the body' (p. 199). He dies, and seven days after him, his wife dies too. He has merely acted as an intermediary between two women, respectively source and destination of the contagion that passes through him. In the most memorable scene from this section of the novel, Finn and Roddie wait helplessly outside a cottage while inside Catrine, who will survive, nurses a sick Kirsty, who will die (pp. 266 ff.) Catrine refuses to let either of the men enter this feminine, domestic enclosure for fear they may be infected.

Another reason for privileging *The Silver Darlings* is the importance Gunn's critics have attributed to it. For Scott it is 'the greatest' of Gunn's novels, 'a triumph-song of the Gael'. Gifford goes one better, asserting its 'claim as the greatest of all Scottish novels'. Alan Riach enthuses, in rather tortuous syntax, that *The Silver Darlings* is 'his most memorable book, still an underrated masterpiece, standing in relation to all his other work as *Moby-Dick* to Melville', while for McCulloch 'in its universality the book stands at the summit of Gunn's narrative achievement and is a unique contribution to the novel in Scotland'.[24] This is where the enigma of Gunn criticism becomes most acute. Can all these scholars have praised the novel so highly while failing to realise *what it was actually about?*

The ceilidh chapter in *The Silver Darlings* has significant parallels with the one in *Butcher's Broom* as far as its support for a gender ideology is concerned. There are warning signals in the presentation of North Uist, where the scene takes place. It is reduced in scale, a kind of Lilliput. Finn is journeying back not into history, but beyond history:

> The crops looked healthy enough, but the patches of land were tiny for the number of houses squatting about them. From a slight eminence, it was a world of sea-inlet and fresh-water loch and peat. There were moments, then and afterwards, when to Finn it seemed a forgotten place that had lived on. (p. 536)

Burns tells us

> that the significance of North Uist in the story of Finn's development is that there he comes into direct contact with a culture that is wholly integrated . . . This sense of wholeness and integration had been destroyed in his own society by the Clearances . . .[25]

According to Gifford

> Finn, in North Uist, learns from and participates in the seamless garment of the community's commentary on itself through its three nights of ceilidh.[26]

This place beyond history, beyond the world is the repository of a privileged truth: a truth about gender, about what it means to be a man or a woman.

The catalyst is another song, sung (presumably in Gaelic) by Matili, a teenage girl who is 'very old, archaic, a dark one out of the old race'. Her voice 'had in it the innocent note of the child, and surrounding it the primordial innocence of the mother' (pp. 542–3). Her song evokes in Finn 'the withdrawn fatality of the mother' but it is not until he is back at sea, reliving the experience, that he understands how 'the girl, not teaching, but singing the experience of the race of women in tradition's own voice' has shown him that his mother is 'a woman under the spell of her own destiny. And that somehow was eternally right' (pp. 549–50). As before, the language of the passage is indicative. Gunn speaks of a 'race of women', explicitly making a kid of ethnicity of sexual difference. He repeatedly uses a definite article where one might not expect it. This implies that what he writes of is already known to his readers and is also unique, agreed to be one only. He pre-empts our assent to the concepts he is formulating. And so we have '*the* innocent note of *the* child', '*the* primordial innocence of *the* mother', '*the* fatality of *the* mother' and '*the* experience of *the* race of women'.

Finn has a revelation of what I will for the moment call a female icon, a gender epiphany, a privileged insight into the meaning of womanhood and into the destiny to which women are subject, their 'withdrawn fatality'. It has been foreshadowed in an incident near the start of the novel where Roddie glimpses Catrine through a window. The feminine is identified with the landscape in accordance with the wider gendering of the novel's world. Catrine is not herself, but a type of all women that have ever been or will ever be:

> Slowly he brought his head past the side of the window. Catrine was sitting beyond the fire, one hand, with elbow resting on knee, stretched towards the peat, arrested by thought or reverie in the very act of smothering the live embers. He saw her features against the red glow, warm and soft, not only with her own beauty, but with all women's beauty. It was a picture a man might glimpse once in a lifetime, and have a vision of women afterwards in his mind that time or chance, good or evil, would never change. Like the still landscape that had troubled him a moment, when he first looked up at the cottage. (pp. 101–2)

Gender is a binary system and, as one would expect, Finn's epiphany at the novel's climax is a double epiphany. The icon of the masculine corresponding to his icon of the feminine has also been carefully foreshadowed. Mr Gordon speaks of Roddie as 'one of the old Vikings' (p. 281) and, as their ship approaches Roan Island off Tongue Bay on its way to the Outer Hebrides, the sight of Roddie 'upright, his eyes ahead, drawn in on himself, solid and emotionless' makes Finn think of the illustration of a Viking longship's carved head in one of the books he studied at school (p. 286). Now a

more disturbing image intervenes. During a religious meeting in
Leurbost Finn remembers his recent confrontation with Roddie in
a pub. The novel does nothing to contextualise or distance this
outburst of male violence, Roddie's 'terrible magnificence . . . the
flattening of lower lip and flesh over the jaw, the rocking power of
the body, the roar'. A moral reaction is clearly excluded. This figure
comes from 'another place and time', somewhere 'beyond the littleness of man today'. It is neither evil nor good but 'imminent and
terrible' (p. 368).

However, it is to the static icon of the figurehead, to Roddie 'at
the tiller, upright as if carven' that Finn turns after his revelation of
Catrine 'under the spell of her own destiny'. The two icons have the
same visionary quality. They match each other like the two halves
of a diptych, occupying the entire space of the possible. Gunn
makes characteristic use of the definite article. Finn has learned '*the*
ultimate companionship of men', has seen '*the* gentleness . . . at *the*
core of male strength' (p. 550). He adds at once that 'Finn experienced this far more surely than could ever be thought out or expressed
in words', using the same strategy as in the *Butcher's Broom* passage.
At the very moment of manifestation, the thing manifested is withdrawn from our vision. It is beyond language, axiomatic, not open
to question.

Gunn's narrative of the journey towards masculinity is complete.
This privileged, double vision of Finn's marks the culmination of
the internal side of the process. Its more external side had already
climaxed in the previous chapter, in a strangely chilling paragraph.
It is just possible that Gunn intended the last sentence ironically. If
not, then there can be no doubt that he saw achieved masculinity as
involving, not self-knowledge, self-criticism or self-doubt, not an
acceptance of relatedness, interdependence and vulnerability, but
the conscious acquisition and retention of economic and material
power:

> Why not? There was a coldness of revenge in the question. He
> would take these possessions. They would be his. His own
> croft, his own house, his own boat. He felt them surround
> him and give him power. At that moment, a cool shiver cleansing
> his skin and his mind, Finn entered with clear consciousness
> upon the estate of manhood. (p. 502)

I have deliberately spoken of 'icons' where most Gunn critics would
prefer to use the term 'archetype'. I want to indicate briefly why I

consider the use of the latter term to be not just tendentious but dangerous. The underlying reference is to a vulgarised form of Jung's psychology and to the collective unconscious in particular. If you like, it gives a spurious intellectual respectability to Gunn's rhetoric of the blood. The former is seen as the conceptual equivalent of the latter, a store of images and behaviours waiting to be activated. Just as the Gaelic heritage and the Gael's sense of his manhood is passed down through the blood, so the understanding of what it means to be a man or a woman lies waiting in Finn's unconscious for the appropriate moment of revelation. According to Jung, the collective unconscious

> has contents and modes of behaviour that are more or less the same everywhere and in all individuals. It is, in other words, identical in all men [sic] and thus constitutes a common psychic substrate of a suprapersonal nature which is present in every one of us.[27]

While the collective unconscious contains archetypes, the personal unconscious is chiefly composed of 'feeling-toned complexes'. Indeed, it seems to be in the nature of an archetype to remain unconscious. It is

> essentially an unconscious content that is altered by becoming conscious and by being perceived, and it takes its colour from the individual consciousness in which it happens to appear.[28]

Archetypes are not necessarily, or exclusively, personal in form. Jung speaks at length about the archetypes of transformation, 'typical situations, places, ways and means . . . ambiguous, full of half-glimpsed meanings, and in the last resort inexhaustible . . . they are in principle paradoxical . . .'[29]

While it might be unfair to project what is said of the archetypes of transformation back onto the more personal archetypes, the last passage points to the problem with Gunn's critics' use of the term. The archetypes they indicate are far from being paradoxical. They are static, transhistorical and prescriptive. There is an enormous leap from unconscious contents which may reach individual consciousness in the course of an encounter with another human being, or in a particular situation, to characters presented as fully-fledged individuals with their own psychologies as part of a realistic fictional narrative. Even if archetypes could be embodied in an artistic verbal text, the traditional novel would not offer an appropriate framework.

Catrine may activate or shape Finn's dormant mother archetype. She cannot on any account be a transpersonal embodiment of that archetype having a broader range of validity. The passage quoted above implies that it would be inconceivable for any transformed archetype to assume the same quality in the consciousness of two different individuals.

I suggest that when these critics speak of 'archetypes' they really mean 'stereotypes'. This is the word with which I would replace the term 'icon' used above. It is significant that they do not speak of archetypes of the shadow or of the anima, but limit themselves to what are effectively social roles: woman, man, mother, boy. In line with the general practice of the critical literature on Gunn they have adopted his viewpoint unquestioningly. If one chooses to see from someone's position, it becomes extremely difficult to see what that position is. More seriously, by calling the role models he presents 'archetypes' they have given them a bogus psychological validity which conceals their strongly political nature.

And the last point I will make is a social and political one. There can be little doubt that Gunn's gender ideology, with its strict separation of domains, its women trapped in the domestic sphere while men go forth to fight, explore and hunt, its young men who attain maturity by disowning the feminine and distancing themselves from it, was closer to that of European fascism than to any other contemporary ideological conformation. This is not to say that Gunn was a fascist. But it does mean that the time has come to look honestly, with the perhaps wiser eyes of the 1990s, at the political implications of his seductive rhetoric of blood, ethnicity and gender stereotypes, and to find it an appropriate place among the range of cultural nationalisms, both progressive and reactionary, practised and preached in Scotland in the course of this century.

NOTES

1. Edwin Muir *Scott and Scotland* with an introduction by Allan Massie (Edinburgh, Polygon 1982).
2. Two papers from a seminar on 'Destabilising MacDiarmid' held in Edinburgh in February 1993 appeared as Aileen Christianson 'Flyting with *A Drunk Man*' and Christopher Whyte 'Gender and Sexuality in *A Drunk Man*' in *Scottish Affairs* 5 (Autumn 1993) pp. 126–35 and 136–46 respectively. The remaining papers by Cairns Craig and Catherine Kerrigan are unpublished.

3. F. R. Hart and J. B. Pick *Neil M. Gunn: A Highland Life* (originally 1981) (Edinburgh, Polygon 1985).
4. Kurt Wittig *The Scottish Tradition in Literature* (Edinburgh, James Thin 1978) p. 333.
5. James B. Caird 'Gaelic Elements in the Work of Neil Gunn' in *Studies in Scottish Literature* XV (1980) pp. 88–94, p. 89. The passage in question indicates a difficulty in understanding idiomatic speech, though Gunn remarks that 'certain nouns were known to me in both tongues' (Neil Gunn *Off in a Boat* (originally 1938) (Glasgow, Richard Drew 1988) p. 32.)
6. Margery McCulloch *The Novels of Neil Gunn: A Critical Study* (Edinburgh, Scottish Academic Press 1987).
7. Neil Gunn *Butcher's Broom* (London, Souvenir Press 1977) pp. 13–14. Subsequent page references are to this text.
8. Hart and Pick pp. 128–35.
9. Neil Gunn *The Silver Darlings* (London, Souvenir Press 1969) p. 478. Subsequent page references are to this text.
10. Hart and Pick p. 171.
11. Richard Price *The Fabulous Matter of Fact: The Poetics of Neil M. Gunn* (Edinburgh, Edinburgh University Press 1991) p. 90.
12. John Burns *A Celebration of the Light: Zen in the Novels of Neil Gunn* (Edinburgh, Edinburgh University Press 1988) p. 70.
13. Alexander Scott 'Folk Epic: *The Silver Darlings*' in Alexander Scott and Douglas Gifford eds *Neil M. Gunn: The Man and the Writer* (Edinburgh, Blackwood 1973) pp. 123–40, here quoted from pp. 124–5.
14. 'Neil Gunn and the Mythic Regeneration of Scotland: the Two Great Epic Cycles' in Dairmid Gunn and Isobel Murray eds *Neil Gunn's Country: Essays in Celebration of Neil Gunn* (Edinburgh, Chambers 1991) pp. 75–111, here quoted from p. 98.
15. Hart and Pick p. 176.
16. Alan Riach 'Neil Gunn: the Shadow of the Other' in W. N. Herbert and Richard Price eds *Gairfish: The Anarchy of Light* (Dundee, 1991) pp. 13–27, here quoted from p. 17.
17. Derick Thomson *An Introduction to Gaelic Poetry* (London, Victor Gollancz 1974) p. 216.
18. Price p. 56.
19. Gifford p. 92.
20. Alan Bold *Modern Scottish Literature* (London, Longman 1983) pp. 139–40.
21. Price p. 60.
22. John Mackenzie *The Beauties of Gaelic Poetry and Lives of the Highland Bards* (Edinburgh, John Grant 1907) p. 19. In this connection see also Derick Thomson 'Bogus Gaelic Literature c.1750–c.1820' in *Transactions of the Gaelic Society of Glasgow* 5 (1958) and '"Ossian", Macpherson and the Gaelic World of the Eighteenth Century' in *Aberdeen University Review* Vol. 40 (1963).
23. An often quoted passage from *The Atom of Delight* (originally 1956) (Edinburgh, Polygon 1986) indicates that this perception had an autobiographical background: 'As his existence had two parents, so it had

the earth and the sea. If his mother was the earth, his father was the sea . . .' (p. 79).
24. Scott p. 140; Gifford p. 99; Riach p. 17; McCulloch p. 96.
25. Burns p. 81.
26. Gifford p. 98.
27. C. G. Jung *The Archetypes and the Collective Unconscious* transl. R. F. C. Hull (*Collected Works* Vol. 9 part 1) (London, Routledge and Kegan Paul 1969) p. 4.
28. Ibid. p. 5.
29. Ibid. p. 38.

4

Men, Women and Comrades

JENNI CALDER

Naomi Mitchison's first novel *The Conquered* (1923) begins in 58BC.[1] A brother and sister of the Veneti tribe of Gaul go fishing together. They are on the edge of adulthood, Fiommar soon to marry, Meromic to test himself in war. They are very close, physical contact flowing naturally from shared activities, loyalties and emotions. Fiommar worries that marriage will distance her brother. The adult world threatens their easy intimacy.

In particular there is the threat of Roman invasion. Shortly after this opening episode, which establishes this emphatic and empathetic brother and sister relationship, the Veneti have been defeated in battle. As the Roman fleet approaches Fiommar dreams of escape. Her fantasy has room only for her brother and herself. 'After the war, we'll run away together and find an island all by itself somewhere, and make a home out of stones, and thatch it with whin, and have a fire in the middle and heaps of fern to lie on and tell stories; and you'll be king and I'll be queen . . .' (pp. 68–9)

But the realities of defeat change everything. Faced with the prospect of slavery, Fiommar chooses suicide. She tends her wounded brother, hunts and kills a kid to feed him, and then turns the knife on herself. She feels Meromic has a better chance than she has of coping with captivity. '"You're a man: life may hold something for you still"' (p. 81). And as if to confirm this, Meromic 'still felt intensely alive, conscious of his strong, unused body . . . there was something in oneself that went on through it all, something that would make even suffering more worth while than death' (p. 82).

So Meromic chooses captivity, and gives himself up to the Romans.

It is clear to Fiommar that, though marriage may acknowledge a brother's emotional value, slavery attacks every kind of human relationship. But Meromic, freed from sibling bonds, goes on to establish new relationships, and it is these that become the axis of the novel. This introductory sequence is both powerful and paradoxical, and establishes issues and themes that Mitchison returns to again and again. In creating a spirited and self-determining female character and then so quickly destroying her, there is the suggestion that Mitchison did not yet know how to fit a heroic female figure into her fiction. Yet that is too simple an interpretation. There are complex issues here, of sibling attachment, choice, different levels of freedom and captivity, which move into an examination of relations between men. The suicide of Fiommar can be seen both as blood sacrifice – one of the themes that recur in Mitchison's work – which liberates Meromic (to become a slave) and as an escape from negative options for women, a concern that is rarely absent from her fiction.

Three-quarters of *The Conquered* explores Meromic's relations with his owner Titus, a sympathetic Roman officer, and with Lerrys, a fellow captive. They are comrades, who share dangers and develop their own loyalties. Meromic and Titus, though slave and master, are mutually respectful and sustaining. Although there is no specifically sexual intimacy, support and understanding are physically expressed.

The Conquered is in many ways an extraordinary novel for a young woman in the 1920s to have written. It does not deal with 'conventional' social or emotional relations; it hints at incest and homosexual love; it lingers over details of violence and is absorbed by the effects of violence; it explores ideas of power and powerlessness, in the context of both gender and politics. And all of these features recur in the novels and stories that followed, in quick succession. The concern with destruction is identified by Mitchison herself as a direct result of her experience of the First World War. Many of her male friends were killed, and she was still a teenager when she joined a Voluntary Aid Detachment at St Thomas's Hospital.

> becoming acquainted with all that pain did something so drastic that I had to write about it, to externalise it on to paper, in order to get it out of my mind: hence the blood and pain in *The Conquered* and my earlier stories.[2]

The war's legacy marked her writing deeply, expressed both in the violence she depicts and in the urgency with which she addresses the need for kindness.

In later stories heroic women are not destroyed but are allowed 'male' roles, either disguised as men, like Gersemi in 'When the bough breaks' (*When the Bough Breaks* 1924) who becomes a soldier, or freed from all the conventional limitations of female lives, like Erif in *The Corn King and the Spring Queen*. In both cases, these women are able to form comradely relations with men. This does not mean a denial of their own sexuality, rather an extra dimension in the pattern of response and affection between women and men. It is echoed by the currents of male responses to men which are also strongly present. This freedom goes beyond freedom of action: indeed physical activity is often politically curtailed. It enters and explores emotional and psychological territory which in many respects becomes the trademark of Mitchison's fiction. Her almost matter-of-fact tone and colloquial style mask the genuinely experimental nature of what she was doing, and few recognised it at the time. When she was praised, it tended to be for the freshness of her historical narratives rather than for the challenge she offered to social and sexual norms, so very differently expressed from those of, say, the more influential Lawrence or her friend Aldous Huxley.

Mitchison's story 'The wife of Aglaos' (*The Delicate Fire* 1933) begins with a woman losing both her husband and her brother. Kleta is sold into slavery. She is raped by her owner, escapes, becomes the 'wife' of a band of outlaws, and is eventually reunited with her husband. She has three children – the results respectively of marriage with Aglaos, of rape, and of her collective relationship with 'the gang'. The story is really about motherhood, about how Kleta's maternity not only survives but strengthens in a climate of flux and violence, and provides a pivot through which she can to some extent control her own life. The title is both ironic and affirmative. Kleta never ceases to think of herself as the wife of Aglaos, but this does not in any way change or diminish her experiences, or her sense of herself as the mother of her children – and as a provider of a maternal kindness to many others. That kindness is offered through sex, but it is essentially both motherly and comradely. It is something she can contribute to the welfare of the group, without the erosion of her feelings for her husband.

Kleta is relating the story to a younger woman. 'Nothing very sudden or very frightening has ever happened to you,' she says.[3] The events she relates are set in Greece in the fourth century BC, but this could be any voice of experience talking to a younger, more protected generation. Kleta goes on:

> But sudden and frightening things have happened to me, so now I find it very hard to remember – to remember, that is, with my blood and body, for I can remember well enough with my mind – what I was like before they happened, when I was a girl, or a young wife as you are now. It seems to me that perhaps, if these sudden and frightening things do not happen, it is very hard to grow up, very hard to become a wise man or woman.[4]

Part of this wisdom, this growing up, involves moving beyond conventional categories of identity or experience. Extremes force this: the slaughter of loved ones, betrayal, slavery, sacrifice both physical and moral. This is the context of Kleta's story, and it is this location of human need and human response in the laboratory of 'sudden and frightening things' that releases new possibilities. One of the possibilities is the movement away from the female as victim. Kleta's wisdom derives from her surviving loyalty combining with a pragmatic generosity.

Most of Mitchison's novels and stories of the 1920s and 1930s deal with the rivalries and conflicts of the Grecian city-states, or of Greece and Central Asia, and with the Roman conquest of vast areas of Europe, and the challenge to Roman authority from rebels and Christians. In the sixteen years between the publication of *The Conquered* in 1923 and of *Blood and the Martyrs* in 1939, she was writing with the First World War unforgettably vivid, and the growing understanding that another major conflict was brewing.

The literary response to this climate involved crossing sexual and social frontiers, some of which had been quite successfully negotiated some decades earlier and before the moral dislocations of the Great War. As I have suggested, Mitchison's approach to these frontiers has its own distinctiveness, and strongly reflects her personal responses to the familial, social and political circumstances she encountered, as well as specifically to the war. Although she set her fiction at a distance in time and place, she has never made any attempt to distance herself from what she creates. Her books, she says, are expressions of herself at the time of writing. 'All my life I have been very much in the hands of the books I was writing' and 'any of what I did was also part of a book', she said in February 1992.[5] She explores emotions and tests possibilities that are directly a part of her own life. These recur throughout her fiction, and include relationships between brother and sister, mother and child, comrades of either sex, as well as lovers – of either sex and within and outwith marriage.

The Conquered is dedicated to her brother Jack, J. B. S. Haldane. As children, Naomi and Jack conducted scientific experiments and observed genetic changes in guinea pigs. Running through all her fiction is an uninhibited curiosity, a spirit of experiment that informed her life as well as her writing. Kleta in 'The wife of Aglaos' is worried that she may be unable to remember 'in the blood' the experience of violence and rape, but, whatever the emotional horror and confusion, she has retained the past with a mental clarity which echoes Mitchison's own alertness to experience and experiment. Nothing is not valid. No doors are closed. The encouragement of easy judgments by externally imposed rules is likely to be irrelevant. Mitchison's attitude to human behaviour is informed simultaneously by an objective curiosity and a passionate involvement.

Her fictional treatment of human relations is free both of conventional categorisation and of the self-conscious rebellion present in some of her contemporaries. Fiommar and Meromic are physically close and there are undoubted hints of incest, but this is handled with no sense that this is either unusual or unnatural, or that the suggestion of incest is in some way daring. Fiommar runs her hands over her brother's naked body, 'admiring the faint ripple of movement that followed her under the smooth skin' (p. 13), helps him to bathe and to arm. Mitchison is able to lift her characters out of the boxes social conditioning has provided.

It is possible that Mitchison understood best the relationship between brother and sister. It is certain that her relationship with her own brother was formative, rewarding and competitive. Jack was five years older than her. As a young girl she clearly both cared for him deeply and admired him greatly, and he in his turn seemed genuinely to enjoy her company and respect her considerable abilities. When Jack went to Eton, Naomi burned with indignation when she discovered he was being bullied. Even after her marriage to Dick Mitchison, a school friend Jack brought to their Oxford home, brother and sister went on holiday together. Naomi herself went to a boys' school – 'I was for all practical purposes a boy'[6] – until puberty, when she was rapidly removed. It was no longer possible for her to have brotherly and comradely relations with the other boys, to climb trees, play conkers, compete at Latin. But, her early marriage and numerous children notwithstanding, Naomi Mitchison clearly continued, and has continued throughout her life, to want to climb trees and play conkers with the boys. One way in which she was able to do this was to write fiction.

In *The Conquered* she sacrifices Fiommar and frees the narrative to focus on brotherly or comradely relations. The implication is that Fiommar is an intrusion, that because she cannot be a man (although she can fish and hunt and is physically strong and active) she cannot provide as much for Meromic as Meromic seems to provide for her. Although his relations with Titus and Lerrys are not sexual, or not overtly so, they have a sympathetic physicality. There is mutual respect between Titus and Meromic, which grows into genuine affection, though one is conqueror and the other slave. The tension between Meromic's unfreedom, his loyalty to his own people, and his recognition that Titus is a just and decent man, representing the potential if not the reality of the Roman state, brings a shift in the novel's critical dynamic. This shift, away from a sibling relationship which cannot offer the same comradeship that can exist between men, is underlined by the mutual support and understanding between Meromic and Lerrys. Again, there is a strong physical bond with a sexual undercurrent.

Many of Mitchison's early stories are concerned with tensions between the personal and the political. These are manifested through clashes between the individual and the state, and between personal imperatives and social norms. Sparta offered her fertile territory, and in the context of the increasingly insistent realities of European dictatorships it was particularly apt. In Sparta, the individual was subservient to the collective need, and the collective need was determined through a narrow authoritarianism. The cultivation of group loyalty was critical, and the acceptance – if not the encouragement – of sexual attachments between men was part of a structure that sustained a military ethic. Marriage was a necessary prop of the social fabric, but an amalgam of male attachment and male competitiveness nourished the values that helped men to fight.

These tensions form part of the concerns of the novel *Cloud Cuckoo Land* (1925) and the stories in the collection *Black Sparta* (1928).[7] In the title story of the latter the contradictory pulls of the state and the individual, public and personal loyalties, are explicit. But they are not straightforward. In choosing to free a captured helot who had shared his childhood, Phylleidas is challenging the authority of the state. Because his wife puts loyalty to the state above loyalty to her husband, he is also relegating marriage to a less important sphere than comradeship. His wife Theano has been tutored to accept that the personal and the political are not only compatible, but mutually supportive. Phylleidas as a soldier owes his primary duty to the state; his marriage exists in interludes.

> This going back to camp was all part of it, the wholeness that she had tried to make clear to herself and him. It would have happened in no other state in Hellas. But yet it worked out in the arithmetic of love; her mother said so, and the older women. And she knew at least that kept her brave. (pp. 287–8)

But the story is about the way in which the personal has grown out of alignment with the political, with a rigid state unable to accommodate individual needs and actions. Phylleidas makes an individual choice dictated by an idealism and personal loyalty that he cannot force into subservience to the state. '"Are you a better judge than the state?"' he is asked, to which he replies '"yes"'. His wife Theano comments, '"He is not mad . . . but he is singing a song of his own, against ours"' (p. 306). Theano accepts the state's authority, and in doing so her own lack of individual status. She sees herself as 'a little bit of the whole thing' (p. 287). Yet Phylleidas's challenge is almost unwilled, and *his* sense of littleness excludes him from the whole: 'he felt very little and helpless and knew she was right about the trouble he would be in, and suddenly he saw his state as a vast, menacing black thing that he could never even try to appeal to if his rights were not its' (p. 286). The projection of marriage as an interlude is underlined by the child-like nature of husband and wife together: 'she threw her head back and laughed and jumped with both feet like a child, and then tugged his hand so that they both started running.' (p. 284). It is not that sexuality is absent, rather that the emphasis is on a boy-and-girl (brother and sister?) almost pre-pubescent physicality.

The relative weakness of marriage enables the force of male loyalty to override its demands, and, in the case of Phylleidas, those of the state as well. Male comrades celebrate by oiling each others' bodies and bathing together, considerate of each others' wounds and scars. Although it is Theano who saves the situation, deflecting the wrath of the Krypteia, mollifying the climate of punishment and retribution, she watches, outside the magic circle. Her feminine influence is valuable, but she is not a comrade.

Paradoxically, relationships between men seem to offer more ways of operating outside the state, whether Spartan oligarchy or Athenian democracy, than those between men and women, especially if the latter are safely regulated by marriage. A soldier falls for a prisoner and helps to set him free ('The lamb misused', *Black Sparta*); a Spartan slave is caught in the rivalry between Athens and Persia ('Nuts in May', *Black Sparta*). The desire to compete with and to impress other men is often more powerful than any wooing of women. Above all, the mutuality between men, the communal activities and the feasting (excluding women), the exchange of poetry and praise – this, with or without love-making – creates a circle of independent and comradely intimacy. A passage in 'O Lucky Thessaly!' (*Black Sparta*) captures this:

> They went into the feast; the curtains were pulled back now and the place filled with shallow level sunlight. But by the time everyone was wreathed and happy and settled down with food and drink, the sun had set and rapidly more and more stars came out over the apple trees and the dark river. There was a mixed smell of things to eat and drink, and people, and sweet herbs. (p. 50)

Women are excluded, physically and emotionally. The bonds between men, of shared goals and shared dangers, give them an intimacy which the Classical world recognised but which Judaeo-Christian culture denied. In militaristic Sparta, tenderness between men is part of an ethic which helps to sustain a warlike competitiveness because it offers mutual support and consolation. Women cannot share in it. In democratic Athens – no less dependent on warfare – there is more space for individual voices, both male and female (although women are excluded from citizenship). And there is perhaps more space for individual expressions of emotion, but in Mitchison's portrayals, for example in *Cloud Cuckoo Land* (1925), the climate of affectionate and comradely exchange is absent.

Many of these threads can be traced in Mitchison's own experience, in a growing-up process where she was 'one of the boys', first at school, then with her brother and the school and student friends he brought to their Oxford home. Oxford offered a liberal environment, up to a point, though her Scottish background and, in particular, her mother were a constant reminder of class traditions and expectations. She would confront those at a later stage of her writing career.

In the meantime, Mitchison's preoccupations were drawn together in the novel that represents the summation of her achievement in this first phase of her work, *The Corn King and the Spring Queen* (1931).[8] It is a remarkable novel, bold in its scope, both geographical and psychological, vivid in its implementation, and dynamic in its narrative. It creates a fictional country, Marob, on the edge of the Black Sea, and a people based on the Scythian culture of south-east Europe. At its best, the writing is both skilled and sensuous, conveying a sympathetic and often excited response to the natural world, to animals, to season and climate, and to artefacts. Mitchison savours the texture of fabrics, the colour of ornaments, the workmanship of things fashioned by the human hand. And all these play a part in sexuality and its expression, in the way men and women come together and break away, lose themselves in mutuality and fracture intimacy.

At the narrative's shifting centre is a triangular relationship, and at the apex of that triangle Mitchison's hero-heroine, Erif Der. At the other two angles are Erif's brother Berris, an artist and craftsman who never quite fulfils his aspirations, and Tarrik, the Corn King, Erif's husband, magnificent in the early parts of the novel but whose pre-eminence leaks away as the narrative progresses. As Tarrik's presence diminishes, Erif's grows more complex and substantial. It is this growth, painfully achieved, that drives the narrative. When they ultimately come together again, Erif and Tarrik achieve, or perhaps rediscover, an essential balance.

Between them, power and gender generate both creative and contradictory currents which have an almost tidal effect, ebbing and flowing, crossing each other, setting up eddies and whirlpools. This tidal flow is sustained through the novel's nine sections, though occasionally it dwindles and wavers. We see the cross-currents in operation from the first pages. Erif is young and immature, but vigorous, with the gift of magic. She influences her brother's creativity, and the Corn King is ineffective without the Spring Queen. The welfare and future of the community depend on the agencies of male and female. Yet there are limits to her influence: she cannot enable Berris to overcome his self-doubt, nor free herself from the weighty paternalism of her father, nor protect herself against the prideful demands of Tarrik.

The enhancement of male power is strongly conveyed: indeed, part of the female function is to provide this enhancement. Berris, the artist, beats out silver and gold at the forge (though Erif pumps the bellows and fans the flame – Erif Der backwards is 'red fire').

Tarrik subdues wild horses and wild bulls, and it is a horse that gives him the power to carry Erif off and rape her: 'she was fascinated by the twitching, jumping body of the horse, the pawing of its hoofs on the dry mud'. Tarrik picks her up 'like a rabbit' (p. 37) and gallops off. The horse is both tamed and tamer. Erif cannot fight against her role, but comes to see herself less as victim than as the essential catalyst of power.

This power, real and symbolic, is at the very heart of Erif's world, enshrined in its mythology and beliefs, its family structures, its expectations of men and women. Erif with her witchcraft can play with it a little, and as Spring Queen she can complement the Corn King's assertive grip on the seasons' productiveness. There can be no harvest without the spring's fertility, yet the spring is handmaiden to the crop, not the crop itself. If there is complementarity, there is also tension, and it is tension that makes the Erif–Tarrik axis interesting. Mythology defines the male and female roles and tradition enshrines and decorates them. Ritual, costume and ornament are all a vital part of confirming both the influence and the limits of the female.

Objects are closely associated with both power and sexuality. Erif has inherited her magic from her mother, and when her mother dies she takes some of her things – 'an embroidered coat, a pair of shoes, and a little box full of cowrie shells, some painted red, and small loose pearls' (p. 48). These objects transmit and represent her inheritance and her responsibility. She cannot deny her inheritance, and such objects are defined by gender. Tarrik wears 'crown and sword, bronze rings on neck and arms, and a round gold shield like the sun' (p. 80), accoutrements that spell action and authority. Female ceremonial gear is a stiff, felt gown and tall hat, encrusted with embroidery, which confine movement. The definition of male and female roles is insistently conveyed in Mitchison's description of the spring festival.

Erif as Spring Queen wears 'a white dress with hundreds and hundreds of little coloured wool flowers fastened on to it all over by long wool stalks. As she walked slowly over the fallow field she was almost shapeless with the hanging mass of them, dropping over her fingers and down from the hem nearly over her feet.' Tarrik, on the other hand, is almost naked, wearing only 'long strips of coloured stuff . . . from neck to knee, belted at the waist, but splitting everywhere as he moved' (p. 209). He is active, unencumbered, moving with plough and oxen. 'Tarrik pressed on the plow-beam, in, in to the hard, sticky, reluctant earth' (p. 210). The sexual metaphor is obvious. '"I am the plow,"' Tarrik says. '"It is my body. It is hard and strong."' The Spring Queen's sexuality is covered by her shapeless dress. There is something neutral and ambivalent as she sits, passive and waiting, in the middle of the field. She represents the cold, resisting earth, while the crowd begs her to be 'kind', to submit to the plough. However crucial her magic, her presence is a symbol, there to be looked at and to submit to action, rather than to act.

It is fertility that releases the Spring Queen. Erif is both pregnant herself and the essential vehicle for bringing fertility to the earth.

> If everything else about her was appearance, if she grew so uncertain of her own existence that it became no difficult or unlikely step between life and death, then this thing which was her and not her, anchored her, nailed her down to some kind of reality. It was good to feel secure, good to be part of the seasons, budding and ripening with them. (p. 212)

Fertility is power, but its ambivalence has already been conveyed – dependent, outwith personal control, and limited. With the approach of the plough, Erif 'leapt to her feet, ran under the horns of the oxen, between their panting flanks, and leapt the plowshare itself as it made the last furrow right through the centre of the fallow field, tearing apart the warmed, flattened grass where she had been sitting' (p. 212). It is an orgasmic release of tension, triggered by the Corn King, and the collective 'dance of courting' that follows reiterates the intensely sexual nature of the episode. But it also reiterates the essentially submissive role of the female. 'He leapt at her. She gave at the knees and all along her body . . .' (p. 213). Both personally and ritually, Erif must submit. She cannot, as Erif or as Spring Queen, choose not to receive the plough or Tarrik. And later she has to lie still as the people of Marob pull the woollen flowers from her dress. 'The Corn King turned her over for them to pluck the flowers from her back . . . she was the sacrifice' (p. 214).

The tensions here are sexual, but they are also bound up with Erif's equivocal feelings about her destined role and responsibilities, her relationship with Tarrik, motherhood, and perhaps above all the clash between tradition and choice. In killing her father, she offers the classic challenge to tradition, but it is usually the son who makes it. Daughters are more conventionally the ritual sacrifice. Erif is symbolically both. Berris, her brother, is not able to confront tradition. His uncertainties are bound up with the aesthetic possibilities offered by his own culture and with the attractions of Hellas. As an artist, he is less conventionally male than Tarrik. Erif, in a sense, is more of a son than Berris.

Throughout the novel, the personal is enmeshed in the political. Erif's father engineers her marriage to forward his own political ambitions. She is instructed to use her magic first to entrap Tarrik, then to contrive his death. Erif as a character is hugely ambivalent (this is what motivates the narrative) and her feelings towards Tarrik reflect this: can she allow herself to soften towards the man she has been instructed to kill, can her pride allow her to love a man who is so arrogantly dominant? There seems to be no means of escape from this dilemma or from the limitations of her influence. '[Tarrik] stirred himself and everyone else to prodigious energy. They swirled around Erif in a sea of life and action. She was just left in the middle of it, half dead and small and useless' (p. 91). Nor can she, at first, throw off the authority of father on the one hand, husband on the other. A sequence of events, including the killing of her own father who is responsible for the death of her child, releases her from these bonds. From this point in the narrative she leads a nomadic existence, exploring and testing as she goes. But although she gains more control over her life, Tarrik and Berris shadow her everywhere, if they are not actually physically present.

The independent relationship of Tarrik and Berris with each other operates outside Erif. When Tarrik leaves Marob, Berris, on impulse, leaps onto the departing ship. They are both lured by the sophistication of Greece, but the bond between male friends is a significant factor, and stronger than that between husband and wife, or brother and sister.

> Erif was alone in the Chief's house. She had all the lamps alight in her room, and the shutters open too; it was still enough for that. She sat on the edge of her bed, undressed, with a fur rug pulled round her, clutched under her chin. There was no one in the room, nothing to hurt her. But she still sat there, quite quiet, watching and listening, very white. (p. 97)

The scene shifts to Sparta and another line of the narrative, which concerns Philylla, the young Spartan girl whose story now begins to intertwine with the triangle. Philylla, though not yet fully mature, is too much of an individual for the state to allow to live. Like Erif, she wants to contribute more. She is confined by the state, Erif by tradition. As a child, Philylla can play and compete with the boys. As a woman the possibilities narrow, defined and constrained by the needs of men and the collusion of women. Erif's challenge to patriarchy gains in definition and strength, but the reality is that most women who attempt such a challenge are destroyed. And although Erif gains in stature and self-knowledge, in the end she accepts the role which has been thrust upon her. Mitchison's projection of women's entrapment in *The Corn King and the Spring Queen* is uncompromising, although it is also richly exploratory.

Many of Mitchison's stories concern nomadic women, exiles and wanderers, separated from home and family. Tradition offers numerous examples of men, moving in search of symbols and solutions, or sometimes just of adventure. But Mitchison examines again and again the woman who is freed by exile, whether the separation from home is voluntary or forced. Erif is parted from Marob and her husband. Her first child dies, her second she has to leave behind. This distance is an essential part of her journey of discovery. She has to free herself not only from the bonds of family, but from the constraints of continuity which define her as Spring Queen. In the end, she does not succeed. She has magic, but it cannot redirect the established way of things, which allot her an identity delineated by gender. There can be no Spring Queen without the Corn King. Away from Marob she finds other delineations. A woman does not have to be defined in terms of mate or mother. She can be solitary. She can be a sister, or a comrade. But she cannot escape for long the network of human need which provides the lifeline of human nature. She returns to Marob, and the novel ends with the next generation's Corn King and Spring Queen making their entrance.

Women are the vehicle of fertility, and by implication the guardians of human nature. But it is not only Erif who balances the aggressive maleness of Tarrik. Berris has a critical part to play. His bending to varying influences, depending on where he is and who is with him, can be seen as weakness. But this 'weakness' balances both Tarrik and the straining independence of Erif. He contains something of each of them, he is fluid, restless, dissatisfied. As an artist, he is reaching beyond his abilities, and as a man of action he is not decisive enough. When he gets the chance to prove himself as a warrior, he kills the enemy leader – but he is just the man whom it would have been politically useful to keep alive. He is a foil to the more vigorous Erif and the god-like Tarrik, but he is more than that. He provides for both of them sympathetic, uncompetitive comradeship, and they each respond to him with affection and encouragement. He is sibling and companion to both, but neutralised. It is safe to be fond of Berris. There is much affection but no danger in the sexual electricity that occasionally sparks between Berris and Erif.

The relationship between Erif and Tarrik is never neutralised, but it does mature. Their magnetism, partly sexual, partly a recognition of their symbolic juxtaposition, becomes healing rather than hostile. There is both magic and sacrifice involved in their final acceptance of who they are and what they must do, but the protectiveness and humility of Tarrik's vigil over Erif on the edge of death indicates the possibility of an equal partnership. While their sexual roles and the demands of the seasons require dominance and submission they can now also relate to each other as comrades.

Erif moves from Marob to Hellas to Egypt. She, like each of the main characters, is looking for some kind of fusion, of identity and action, of creative and political fulfilment, of the spiritual and the practical. It is an unusual quest for a woman, and because of that illuminates the springs of female action with particular vividness. What Mitchison seems to be saying, not only here but in most of her fiction, is that existence is tension and ambiguity, at best momentarily resolved or released, whether by sex, physical or mental prowess, or sympathetic companionship. And although that tension and ambiguity are by no means solely female, she suggests that women experience them with unrivalled intensity.

She continues her exploration of sympathetic companionship in later novels. In *The Blood of the Martyrs* (1939) inspiration and support comes from the 'love-feast', *agape*, 'a breaking of barriers and setting free of resentments and complexes', as she explained in *The Kingdom of Heaven* (1939), 'the meal of common love'.[9] The early Christians gather and literally break bread together. *Agape* is as much the source of their strength as faith.

> [They] came to the breaking of bread and they learnt how in the love-feast all those eating together could be sure of the temporary experience of the kingdom and got from it enough faith to go on in a world which seemed utterly against them.[10]

This notion of sharing, whether as a group or a couple, is central to Mitchison's life and work, and transcends gender. 'I like any of the kinds of basic sharing, work or food or bed (no doubt)', she wrote in her wartime diary (unpublished manuscript: p. 473). The essential factor in the fictional relationships she describes in a positive or celebratory fashion is this sharing, for which I suggest the word comradeship. Comradeship can be part of a sexual relationship but sex does not need to be a part of comradeship. Sexuality can enhance and invigorate comradeship, whatever the gender of those involved and regardless of whether there is sexual activity. Mitchison catches the sexual currents that run between Erif and her brother, between Philylla and her women friends, between soldiers. These currents in themselves generate warmth and creativity, which do not necessarily require a sexual outlet.

Until 1935 Mitchison located her fiction in a time and place distant from between-the-wars Britain. It was a time of social and sexual experiment, in which Mitchison herself played a part, but she did not in her earlier novels attempt to investigate this in a contemporary context. By going back to the ancient world, she gave herself more freedom to explore issues of gender and politics and to write with considerable and straightforward frankness about both homosexual and heterosexual love. When she did turn her attention to the contemporary scene, in *We Have Been Warned* (1935) she ran into trouble with her publishers, Jonathan Cape, who had not balked at scenes of tunics slipping from naked bodies but had a problem with trousers being unzipped. In fact, the novel is disappointingly raw, too literal a translation of 1930s sex and politics to succeed as fiction. But it highlights the achievement of her other books.

In *The Conquered, Black Sparta, Cloud Cuckoo Land, The Corn King and the Spring Queen* and her other fiction of the 1920s and 1930s Mitchison is crossing frontiers. She is taking women and men away from the well-known territory of British narrative, away from the home and the social and political arenas which her better-known fellow novelists continued to occupy, and watching how they behave in situations of threat, war and terror, of exile and uncertainty. In recording what she observed, she peeled away many of the familiar wrappings that are our usual aids to recognition. She offers portrayals of men and women which in their probing and questioning of conventional boundaries still challenge the reader. At the heart of her portrayals is her belief in connection, however it is expressed. And by far the most subtle connection, she suggests, and perhaps the most sustaining, lies in comradeship.

NOTES

1. Naomi Mitchison *The Conquered* (London, Jonathan Cape 1923). All subsequent page references are to this edition.
2. Naomi Mitchison *Small Talk: Memoir of an Edwardian Childhood* (London, Bodley Head 1973) pp. 127–8.
3. Isobel Murray ed. *Beyond This Limit: Selected Shorter Fiction of Naomi Mitchison* (Edinburgh, Scottish Academic Press 1986) p. 106. The story originally appeared in Naomi Mitchison *The Delicate Fire* (London, Jonathan Cape 1933).
4. Ibid.
5. Interview with the author of this chapter, London, 7 February 1992.
6. Naomi Mitchison *All Change Here: Girlhood and Marriage* (London, Bodley Head 1975) p. 11.
7. Naomi Mitchison *Cloud Cuckoo Land* (London, Jonathan Cape 1925); *Black Sparta: Greek Stories* (London, Jonathan Cape 1928). Subsequent page references are to the latter edition.
8. Naomi Mitchison *The Corn King and the Spring Queen* (London, Jonathan Cape 1931). Page references are to the 1990 edition (Edinburgh, Canongate) with an introduction by the author.
9. Naomi Mitchison *The Kingdom of Heaven* (London, Heinemann 1939) pp. 119, 122.
10. Naomi Mitchison *The Blood of the Martyrs* (London, Constable & Co. 1939), here quoted in the 1988 edition (Edinburgh, Canongate) with an introduction by Donald Smith, pp. 41–2.

5

Angry Young Masculinity
and the Rhetoric of Homophobia and Misogyny in the Scottish Novels of Alan Sharp

BERTHOLD SCHOENE

'You can't love a man unless you're a poof.'

Alan Sharp's Scottish novels were originally conceived as the first two parts of a trilogy which was left incomplete when in the late 1960s Sharp left Scotland for a film-script writing career in Hollywood.[1] In *A Green Tree in Gedde* (1965; winner of the Scottish Arts Council Award in 1967) and *The Wind Shifts* (1967) Sharp's central subject is the quest of four young people, three men and one woman, for identity and a meaning in their lives:

> Moseby, the eternal student, uneasily married: Gibbon, the crypto-homosexual: Cuffee, for whom the search is by way of being a sexual odyssey: and Cuffee's sister Ruth, with whom he has had a long-standing incestuous affair.

This is how the promotional blurb on the cover of the 1985 edition of *A Green Tree in Gedde* describes the four main protagonists. The clearly sexist bias of the summary reflects the novel's tendency to depict heterosexual men much more favourably than women and homosexual men, often directly at the latter's expense. Edna, for example, to whom Moseby is said to be 'uneasily married', does not even find marginal mention here as a young individual herself; similarly, Ruth is described solely in terms of the positions she holds in her elder brother's life: sister and ex-lover. In an equally discriminatory manner, Gibbon, the only man in Sharp's books who – at least initially – seems seriously interested in exploring his sexuality, is called a 'crypto-homosexual', suggesting a twisted and secretive personality. In contrast, Cuffee's relentless and egocentric pursuit of women for his sexual satisfaction is described in rather more positive terms as 'a sexual odyssey'.

The sexist rhetoric of Sharp's novels has completely eluded Scottish critics to date. Douglas Gifford counts Alan Sharp among those novelists of the 1960s whose books constituted a 'reappearance of what I feel to be the highest and finest endeavour in fiction, that attempt to celebrate and ennoble man's life in art'.[2] Not once in his appraisal does Gifford mention the issue of sexuality which is a central and urgent issue in Sharp's novels. Glenda Norquay likewise eschews a discussion of sex. It is furthermore conspicuous that, as a woman critic, Norquay should display a greater sympathy towards men than towards women, taking Moseby's side when he refuses to discuss an adulterous affair with his devastated wife and simply walks out of 'his constrictingly conventional marriage' and what 'he perceives as an equally sterile environment: Scotland itself'.[3] Against the backdrop of such an androcentric, clearly pre-feminist interpreta-tion, Edna's genuine hurt and despair over Moseby's marital betrayal become synonymous with what Norquay perceives as the moral restrictiveness, political pettiness and generally unfulfilling atmo-sphere of Scotland as a whole. In Sharp's novel Edna embodies 'all that's normal and stupid and lasting and sane' (*Wind Shifts* p. 51); she appears as a negative Chris Guthrie figure, not as a real-life woman but an abstract symbol of intellectual dullness and emotional conventionality.

With respect to the character of Cuffee, Norquay also chooses not to question Sharp's unwaveringly positive presentation of straight male behaviour, calling him 'the most anarchic figure in the novel, the one who appears to offer the best chance of escaping and who most obviously challenges conventions in his extreme behaviour'.[4] However, Sharp's portrayal of Cuffee is far from unproblematic. This becomes most evident in his relationship with Uta, the first woman Cuffee meets on his 'sexual odyssey' who – although obvi-ously amused at his attempts to act the irresistible *homme fatal* – adamantly rejects his amorous overtures.[5] To her flirtatious teasing Cuffee responds with steadily increasing aggressiveness, starting harmlessly enough, as it were, with a twisting of arms (*Green Tree* p. 277) before culminating in a vicious attack on Uta's face when she refuses to elope with him from her foster-father's castle. Surely, Norquay cannot mean this when she says almost admiringly that 'Cuffee makes things happen'?[6]

> He hit her very hard in the stomach, just below the buckle of the belt, his fist sinking into her unprepared body and driving all the wind from her so that her eyes opened wildly and as she sat down slowly her mouth desperately sought air. Cuffee caught her by the hair with his left hand, low down near the nape of the neck, and twisted her round so that she was looking into the wall. He lowered his mouth to her ear. All the while her body tried convulsively to draw air into it.
>
> 'See that wall? That is the wall of no choice. It's your turn to go to it,' and saying that he drove her, open-eyed, against the stone, once, then again; then coldly, leaving no room for remorse, twice more. When he let loose her hair from among his fingers she slid down the wall, leaving a red smear on its whiteness from her destroyed face. (*Wind Shifts* pp. 338f.)[7]

Cuffee punishes Uta for 'teasing' him, assuaging his need for revenge in an act of wilful destruction. What he destroys is what attracted him to Uta in the first place and made him helpless with desire for her: her beauty. Obviously, on a more abstract level, Uta is punished for something else, namely her autonomy as a sexually inaccessible woman. Unlike Ruth, Uta does not consider it an honourable distinction to succumb to Cuffee's 'greater spirit':

> [Cuffee] could sound curt and hard. It meant he had decided something and wanted her [Ruth] to agree so that it could sound mutual. But it never was. She had been playing this game long enough to know. Still, it was only her he played it with. That meant something. (*Green Tree* p. 52)

Sharp manages to mitigate the impact of Cuffee's violence against Uta by leaving his readers in uncertainty about whether or not – even in the fictional reality of the novel – it is meant to have ever happened at all. In parallel to Sharp's reduction of the authenticity of Edna, Moseby's wife, to that of a symbolic cipher, the character of Uta becomes ever less realistic and more mysterious during the third, strongly allegorical part of *The Wind Shifts*.[8] When Cuffee batters Uta in the windowless ex-bunker student house in Bonn, we are not sure if she is still meant to represent a real-life woman.

Maybe, the reader is led to wonder, there is some truth in Cuffee's speculation that the bunker is 'perhaps just the spatial extension of his mind' (*Wind Shifts* p. 327) and Uta his *Doppelgänger* – 'an apparition' (*Wind Shifts* p. 337), spectral, and hence ultimately immaterial and unreal. What comes to light in this context is the sexist rhetoric inherent in Sharp's tendency to devise women characters solely as expedient figures of contrast employed to characterise more poignantly the angry young hero on his quest.

A particularly irritating example of Sharp's unabashed misogyny is to be found in the telephone conversation between Cuffee and Merle Curvis with whom he has had an affair and who is now pregnant by him. Merle's contributions to the dialogue are fitted with terse, scornful stage directions, describing her way of speaking as 'angry', 'hard boiled' and 'venomous'. Instead of sympathising with Merle's understandable outbursts of fear, anger and despair Sharp disparages and ridicules her as a 'silly bitch'.[9] In contrast, Cuffee emerges as an admirably self-possessed hero, successfully maintaining his freedom against the attempt of a pathetically predictable and conventional woman to capture him and bind him to her.

> There was a delay before she came to the phone. Behind her voice a chintz of female talk.
> 'Hello, Merle Curvis speaking' – a groomed distant voice.
> 'Peter.'
> 'Darling, where are you phoning from?'
> 'The station.'
> 'The station?' – her tone pitched a little up.
> 'I'm leaving Manchester.'
> 'When, Peter?'
> 'Now.'
> 'Peter, darling, why, where are you going?' thinner now, anxious.
> 'Away.' A pause, then the edge.
> 'You're, what about me –' her voice got ready to rise, then caught and angry, came low – 'what about this –' pause and the hard boiled – 'baby of yours?'
> 'You're going to get rid of it.'
> 'And you're going to clear out.'
> 'That's right.' . . .
> 'Stop playing the cool bastard' – genuine exasperation. Then

switch, 'Peter, let me go with you. I could get a job in London easily, it's London you're going to, isn't it?'

'Passing through.'

'Look I could have it done there better, safer, can I come with you, you know how much I hate it here.'

'Get out then. But not with me.'

'You don't love me' – accusation.

'No.'

'You said you did' – after a little choke, hollow.

'I lied' – silence. Then venomous.

'You lousy cruel bastard. You never cared about me, never, did you?'

'I could have gone in the night.'

'You just think all you have to do is run, don't you?'

'Most problems are problems of geography. A problem in Manchester is not a problem in London.'

'Well my problem isn't geography, what am I going to do?'

'Look after yourself.' He put the phone down and stepped out. (*Green Tree* pp. 90f.)

In the course of Sharp's two novels it transpires that in the author's eyes Cuffee's sense of personal freedom and quest for fulfilment are indisputable values that need not be explained or justified at greater length. Both his freedom and self-fulfilment are threatened by the counteractive, eternally waylaying magnetism of female desire, ready to confine Cuffee to the dead end of a single, pre-programmed place and purpose in life: home and family. It is significant in this context that Cuffee's quest should consist of a series of split-ups from women: Ruth, Merle and Gerda.[10] Only when he falls in love with Uta does his journey momentarily come to a standstill which he, however, resents and from which, characteristically, he tries to free himself by violence.

There is no doubt that within the context of Scottish literature *A Green Tree in Gedde* constitutes a major literary innovation. Against the wider background of British fiction, however, it follows the pattern of *angry young man* literature, a movement of English writers of the 1950s and later who are said to 'manifest hostility toward the traditions, standards, and manners of what has come to be called "the Establishment".'[11] Famous *angry young men* are Jimmy Porter in John Osborne's *Look Back in Anger*, Arthur Seaton in Alan Sillitoe's *Saturday Night and Sunday Morning* and Kingsley Amis's *Lucky*

Jim. With respect to 'the awful business of getting on with women',[12] these forerunners of Peter Cuffee share their Scottish counterpart's misogynous stance, alternately either despising women for their lack of intellectual integrity[13] or fearing their alleged sexual insatiability and man-eating dangerousness.[14] It is interesting to see how the much acclaimed rebellious anarchy of all angry young men unfolds entirely at the expense of less privileged groups, such as women and – as we shall see later – homosexual men. As Lynne Segal states with respect to the writings of Osborne, Sillitoe and Amis, 'in these bestselling books . . . women are never to be trusted. They are part of the system trying to trap, tame and emasculate men . . . While male protagonists see themselves as opposing all authority . . . in reality the battle is with mothers and wives alone.'[15] This is particularly true of Sharp's two novels: in what looks like a tedious perpetuation of the battle of the sexes Cuffee's quest very soon turns into an obsessive attempt to conquer the 'fortress' of Uta's sexual inaccessibility. In a conversation with Gibbon, Cuffee declares himself as follows:

> 'All the women who are choking all the men to death in all the suburban houses in the world, all the silent struggles that go on in all the bedrooms for supremacy. This [his, Cuffee's, relationship with Uta] is it. Reduced to its very essence. And it's exciting. And I want her, Harry. That body she flaunts, I want to hear her begging me not to stop. No, Harry boy, this is it.' (*Green Tree* pp. 279f.)

As far as Cuffee is concerned, princess and dragon, wicked king and turreted castle have merged into one and being a 'knight's no job at all nowadays, they all need chopping' (*Green Tree* p. 345), a conviction cruelly implemented in his assault on Uta.

But not only is the angry young men's attitude towards women sadly conventional,[16] their failure to deal responsibly with sexual matters is universal. Fatalistically – often conveniently – they stick to 'the rules'. When asked by his father how he could possibly get a girl with child and then leave her to have an abortion and cope with it on her own, Cuffee retorts: 'I didn't make the rules. It's the rules that women have children. They should know this' (*Green Tree* p. 176). Similarly, Moseby and Gibbon quote 'the rules' when their friendship is at stake after Moseby has got married and cannot spend as much time with Gibbon as before. They blame women in general and Edna, 'who wanted it that way' (*Green Tree* p. 73), in particular for their dilemma. Due to certain, purportedly overwhelming outside forces, which they refer to as 'the rules', their feelings for each other seem doomed to wither:

> They shook hands and Gibbon went down the hill. Moseby watched him until, as predicted, he turned and waved. Moseby had the desire to rush after him and make him see, make him understand. But what. Did he not understand only too well. What would he say that would alter the rules. Would he say 'I'll come with you Harry', or 'you come and live with us'. There was nothing to say. It was the way things were. The way things were. Mantra for the disenchanted. It's the way things are. (*Green Tree* p. 75)

As I shall argue in the following, Moseby's and Gibbon's problem is not caused by anonymous outside forces; rather, it derives from the way in which men in our society define their identity as men. Unlike the often lifelong, laborious process of finding one's identity in an unfavourable, prejudiced world – shared, to a certain degree, by women and homosexual men – the identity of heterosexual men is only rarely a result of profound reflection, let alone a painful mental struggle. As heterosexual masculinity is still commonly regarded as 'the normative gender'[17] and heterosexual men are still widely believed to be the only adequate representatives of our species – with everyone else as deviants from the ideal – straight masculinity is a given that has hitherto remained undefined. As Lynne Segal argues, it is generally considered the highly desirable opposite of homosexuality and femaleness: 'To be "masculine" is *not* to be "feminine", *not* to be "gay", *not* to be tainted with any marks of "inferiority" – ethnic or otherwise.'[18] A definition of masculinity in positive and non-sexist terms that would refrain from pointing fingers at others has not been formulated yet.[19] It seems as if Segal's assumption that 'a "pure" masculinity cannot be asserted *except* in relation to what is defined as its opposite' is correct. 'It depends upon the perpetual renunciation of "femininity"' and 'the forced repression of the "feminine" in all men'.[20] As it currently manifests itself, the identity of heterosexual men is firmly based on a habitual, often institutionalised detachment from women and gay men, frequently expressing itself in crassly misogynous and homophobic attitudes. Moreover, by invariably equating male homosexuality with 'effeminacy', women and gay men are polarised into *one*, allegedly inferior, opposite group which the golden ideal

of masculinity is believed to outshine by dint of its natural superiority.[21]

The seemingly irresolvable dilemma in which Moseby and Gibbon
find themselves is that of two men torn between their natural homosocial desire on the one hand and a socially inflicted acute homophobia on the other. In Moseby's own words:

> You can't love a man unless you're a poof. The irony was that
> if they had been working class then there would have been a
> well-defined institution in which they could have met, the
> 'mate', the boon companion, all those away trips with the
> Morton Supporters Club and the smokers and darts matches.
> Instead they had early morning walks and odd evenings in the
> 'Rowan Tree'. (*Green Tree* p. 22)

As David Cohen says, the problem 'isn't that our [i.e. men's] feelings
are less intense than those of women but that certain feelings are
shameful'.[22] The fear of being mistaken for a 'queer' is so great that
the manly courage of angry young men dwindles drastically when
they come to realise the 'dubious' intensity of their own emotional
attachment to other men. At the heart of this fear lies the common
straight male panic that their natural enthusiasm for homosocial
contacts might be wrongly interpreted by the outside world as the
expression of a latent, if not fully developed, homosexual desire.
Homophobia becomes fully understandable as a socio-emotional
phenomenon only when it is realised that, as a term, it is essentially
a misnomer. Homophobia has only very little to do with actual
fear, or 'horror', as Sharp would like us to believe.[23] Gregory M.
Herek has pointed out that, whereas 'its -phobia suffix suggests
that individual prejudice is based primarily on fear and that this fear
is irrational and dysfunctional . . . homophobia is tenacious partly
because it is very functional for individuals who manifest it':

> homophobia serves to deny one's own homoerotic attractions
> and 'feminine' characteristics; . . . it defines group boundaries
> (with gay men on the outside and the self on the inside); . . . it
> defines the world according to principles of good and bad,
> right and wrong (with oneself as good and gay men as bad).[24]

Gibbon's friendship with Norman Kimber, an American homosexual
poet whom he gets to know in Paris, incites Cuffee to a typically
straight male display of homophobic sentiments, confirming Herek's
assumption that 'friendly interaction with gay men is likely to . . .

incur the disapproval of friends, and call into question a man's virtue'.[25] Cuffee warns Gibbon of Kimber's allegedly depraved, over-sexed nature in terms of 'watch your brownie, boy' (*Green Tree* p. 280) and 'he's after your bakey old son' (*Green Tree* p. 342). In this context it is particularly interesting that what Cuffee pretends to abhor so much in Kimber is in actual fact his own behaviour. Repeatedly Cuffee submits women – complete strangers, everyday encounters – to uncomfortable lecherous glances and overtures (*Green Tree* pp. 149, 192, 343). But whereas Cuffee's behaviour is portrayed as potent and wildly funny, homosexual desire is – in homosexual Kimber's own words – pathetic and intrusive: 'We're all the same when it comes down to it. We can't leave anybody alone' (*Green Tree* p. 308).[26] Should Sharp's women dare display an unequivocal interest in sex and even go so far as to take the initiative, they are referred to as 'nymphos' – sex-crazed, undignified profligates (*Green Tree* pp. 152, 311).

Sharp perpetuates many trite, yet none the less highly offensive, homophobic clichés and oppressive stereotypes, particularly detri-mental to the general reputation of lesbians and gays because of the common inclination to view minorities largely as homogeneous. Clichés employed by Sharp are the inevitable 'warm damp hand' (*Green Tree* p. 80) and the obligatory lisp accompanied by a pair of flopping wrists, the absence of which in a homosexual man is con-sidered a great relief. Cuffee comments on Kimber: 'nice enough chap for a poove, I mean he didn't lisp or let his wrists flop' (*Wind Shifts* p. 132). Telling in this context are also Moseby's implicitly misogynous description of a homosexual, whose presence he finds uncomfortable, as 'a very queer young man . . . with menstrual eyes' (*Wind Shifts* pp. 79f.) and Gibbon's initial shock at Kimber's astonish-ing manliness, his 'agreeable, modulated voice, a contralto that was not at all effeminate' (*Green Tree* p. 222). The ultimate masterpiece of Sharp's homophobic rhetoric, however, is to be found in his creation of the character of Sammy, Moseby's gay neighbour in *The Wind Shifts*. Embodying the male counterpart of Sharp's prototype lesbian represented by mentally disturbed, socially inept and, of course, spitefully ugly Yani – Uta's adoptive sister, a 'poor little creature' (*Wind Shifts* p. 290) – Sammy is yet another offensively distorted caricature of homosexuality. Sharp portrays him as utterly repulsive in all physical, psychological and social respects:

> Sammy was a semi-illiterate Catholic-convert Communist crypto-homosexual Scottish working-class playwright sort of guy in addition to being an inveterate beggar, borrower and reluctant returner. He had breath like an old dog and a tendency to psychosomatic skin ailments that had his hands constantly at one another or on his face, picking and scratching. He had improbable red hair, quite long but thin so that the scalp showed, flaky with dandruff. (*Wind Shifts* p. 18)

Repeatedly correlating homosexuality with amorality or crime and forms of behaviour that are widely regarded as gross sexual perversions, Sharp's rhetoric often verges precariously on that of tabloid journalese, especially when he presents homosexuality not only as a vice but the worst vice of all. What is said with respect to Moseby's suspicions concerning his mother-in-law, whom he resents, is particularly pertinent:

> Moseby, who had never considered his mother-in-law a charitable woman, wondered often why she brought Agnes Davidson [her widowed sister-in-law] into her well-groomed house and watched carefully for instances of domestic sadism or even for a lesbianism to go with Mrs Davidson's large handsome appearance. (*Green Tree* p. 96)[27]

Sharp's creation of the character of Kimber, a self-loathing homosexual, is another clearly homophobic device. Kimber, the pathetic prototype of how many an uninformed heterosexual may envisage a gay man, is cautiously apologetic about his sexual orientation: 'Does it bother you that I'm a homosexual?' (*Green Tree* p. 223). Meant to speak for 'us queers' in general (*Green Tree* p. 341), Kimber is in actual fact a mouthpiece of straight homophobia, deeming sex between men unnatural and finding it 'surprising just how acceptable it can become . . .' (*Green Tree* p. 271). His ex-lover, now dead, showed him 'how it was possible to live as a homosexual, not happily mind you, but with some dignity' (*Green Tree* p. 282). While explaining how pathetic and frustrating it is to live the life of a homosexual, Kimber denies that it is society's oppression, stigmatisation and ostracism of gay people which render homosexuality an ordeal. The reason why homosexuals are doomed to unhappiness is not to be found in the hostile heterosexual environment in which they live but in the homosexual psyche as such which, according to Kimber, is innately warped and feeble. It is 'one's fellow queers' who are to blame for the necessity of leading a double life, making long-term relationships extremely difficult to sustain, if not altogether impossible. Answering Gibbon's naive question 'You wouldn't rather be, well, normal?' Kimber says:

> I'd rather be happy. The real difficulty about being queer, I've found anyway, is that all one's fellow queers are the most volatile of people, relationships, which are hard enough at the best of times, are almost impossible among all the distracted bastards one meets. I've known a lot of queers who were mad for respectable family men, and I think it's this desire for permanence, an escape from the tantrums and camp of so many of the lads, that explains it. If 'true love' is a rarity in the 'normal' world then it's virtually impossible on the other side. One is doomed to a series of demented liaisons, or straightforward seduction, and neither is the answer. (*Green Tree* p. 237)[28]

Sharp's novels contain many more instances of blatant homophobia. There is, for example, Kimber's assertion that for a homosexual 'not very much matters except art', emphasising the essential emptiness of a homosexual life while at the same time perpetuating the common prejudice that homosexuality is particularly widespread among artists: 'I'd hate to be a queer if I wasn't committed to the idea of being a poet, I don't know how the ones that aren't keep their balance' (*Green Tree* p. 238). Finally, the very way in which Stolleman, a friend of Cuffee's, chooses to explain to Gibbon 'how homosexuality happens' reveals Sharp's total lack of insight into the nature of human sexuality:

> '[Kimber] became this man's secretary and this man was queer all right but he wasn't one of the kind who have to have every man they meet. I think Norman [Kimber] just admired him and his work but of course he kept meeting a lot of homosexuals and a few real queens among them. So somewhere along the line he must have jumped overboard.' Gibbon shook his head.
>
> 'Still don't understand it, I mean how it happens.'
>
> 'It's difficult if you think of them as freaks. When you've been with them for a while, well . . . it all changes Harry, . . . you meet some of these boys and I mean boys, hipless dark-eyed pieces and after a time you have to admit that as objects, as things, they are just as beautiful as women will ever be. And after that, well it just depends on how you were brought up,

how much pleasure you get out of women, whether they fancy you.' (*Green Tree* pp. 164f.)

In *A Green Tree in Gedde* it is initially quite tempting to regard Gibbon as the blueprint of a 'new' kind of man who is genuinely interested in exploring his sexual identity. Gibbon seems aware that, to a large extent, everybody's identity is determined by the way they are accustomed or inclined to view themselves sexually. He seems also prepared to overcome his acquired inhibitions and prejudices, boldly facing emotional as well as intellectual confusion. After numerous conversations with his new friend Kimber, his attitude towards questions of sexuality and gender appears promisingly progressive when he says, for instance, that 'before anything that wasn't man and woman was queer, now I know it's not as straightforward as that' (*Green Tree* p. 285). Unfortunately, this positive development, that might have led Gibbon to an acceptance of his own latent homosexuality, is cut short by the bland prejudice of the people who surround him. It is repeatedly intimated to Gibbon, who in Stolleman's words looks 'about as queer as bull' (*Green Tree* p. 165), that he cannot possibly be gay because he is broad-shouldered and hairy-forearmed as well as amiable and unaffected. Finally, Gibbon comes to believe this himself, sadly falling victim to what among the gay community is known as the 'fallacy of choice':

> In a way it's been you, Norman [Kimber], that's made me realise it. I mean about, about homosexuality. Before I got to Paris I was starting to worry about it, about how I didn't really bother about women, whether I had them or not, and how I was attracted to Cuffee and about Moseby, and I was just sort of open to any sort of suggestion. And when I met you and then I realised that for some people there is a choice, a genuine choice, I mean Peter has no choice, he's male and even if he had it away with men, well he'd still be normal and heterosexual, and those boys you see with no hips and mascara, they've got no choice, there's nothing they can do. But you had a choice and you chose, I don't think you are very happy about it but you chose. I'm one like that. I can choose, and that is something I never really had clear before. I want to go back to Manchester and see this sister of Peter's, see if I can make it work with her. (*Green Tree* p. 299)

Unsurprisingly, Gibbon does not choose the social stigma of homosexuality. Instead, he embarks on a heterosexual picture-book relationship with Ruth who, however, soon senses that 'there was something about Harry, he did not seem somehow fully committed to the sexual act' (*Wind Shifts* p. 108).[29] Naturally, after all that has been said about the dissipated nature of gay men, Sharp will not allow Gibbon, one of his heroes, to come out and declare himself. Rather, the whole problem is 'solved' by Ruth deciding to leave Gibbon and move in with Moseby.

Ruth, the only major female character in Sharp's two novels, is a hackneyed stereotype rather than the serious fictional rendering of a real-life woman. From the outset of *A Green Tree in Gedde* Ruth is depicted as a conventional female, perfectly content with her fate that 'she should wait until Mr Right came along to rescue her' (*Green Tree* p. 53). She spends much time day-dreaming about Mr Right's arrival in her life and where it might lead her. Never does it occur to her that she could take the initiative herself.[30] As Glenda Norquay maintains, Ruth's behaviour stands 'in marked contrast' to that of her brother: the young woman 'remains rooted in one place, feeling both the static environment and her loneliness closing in on her'. However, Norquay's comment that 'escape is offered for Ruth, at least temporarily, by her beginning a relationship with Harry Gibbon after his return from travel' is hardly tenable.[31] First, it is evident that Gibbon only uses Ruth to prove that he is a fully adequate heterosexual man. There is no mention of, let alone room for, 'escape' or 'self-fulfilment'. Gibbon tries to make Ruth his dependant, dissuading her from looking for a job and telling her point-blank that '[she] should be pregnant' (*Wind Shifts* p. 231). He attempts to set in motion the ancient dynamics of heterosexual family life that climax in the reproduction of children and constitute, not only according to Jon Snodgrass, 'the historical basis of women's oppression'.[32] Secondly, it is doubtful if Ruth will ever be able to escape from anywhere as long as her quest for identity consists of a series of 'join-ups' with men: Cuffee, Gibbon, Moseby. Sharp makes a clear point, I think, when on the one hand we see Cuffee and Moseby display a certain expertise in walking out of relationships with women while, on the other, Ruth cannot do, let alone achieve, anything without a man by her side.[33] Sharp's world picture is obviously based on a myth of gender which 'endows the relatively minor biological differences between males and females with major social significance'.[34] His concept of gender distinctions is thoroughly conventional, failing to question the authority of men over women as well as other men who do not live up to, or are reluctant to comply with, the rules of standard masculinity. Sharp's presentation of the angry young man's quest is rooted in the notion of a natural complementarity of the sexes which implies that the terms 'female' and 'feminine' (and gay/male is always 'effeminate') denote a socio-emotional area that is diametrically opposed to that designated by 'male' and 'masculine'. Ineluctably, this leads to a simplistic polarisation of the semantic field of gender distinctions into 'male', 'straight', 'strength', 'desire for freedom', 'quest for identity' on the one hand and 'female', 'queer', 'weakness', 'desire for security' and 'home' on the other. Instead of questioning such patterns, Sharp endorses them, perpetuating the dynamics of sexist stereotypification, such as manifest themselves in the quotidian routine of Ruth's life with Gibbon:

> The days passed mainly indoors, with trips for shopping and the twice weekly calls to pick up her charges from the dancing lessons. Then there was a meal to prepare for Harry and Stolleman if he was coming in, and she did washings, Harry's heavy, work thick clothes, and ironing and a dress she was making herself, cut out and inching towards completion. The days passed in a monotone, trivial and full. (*Wind Shifts* p. 103)

Despite his talent for vividly depicting Ruth's everyday boredom and drudgery, Sharp never grants his heroine a chance to complain about it. Even when it gradually dawns on Ruth in *The Wind Shifts* that she may be more than her brother's spare rib, she does not rebel against her male friends' sexism. Rather, she loses herself in obscure daydreams concerning the significance, no, 'the fate of being female' (*Wind Shifts* p. 247), acting the part Gibbon has reserved for her in his vision of a blissful life among his friends in provincial Scotland:

> I used to think we'd come up here, to Greenock and we'd all get somewhere together and he [Cuffee] would paint and you [Moseby] would write and Ruth would keep house and I would work and everything would be, well right.' (*Green Tree* p. 73)[35]

In *The Wind Shifts* Ruth appears to undergo significant changes, starting with her sudden realisation that 'she had no very clear idea of what she was like, had no real image of herself' (*Wind Shifts*

p. 115). She develops a more critical attitude toward male behaviour in general and her brother's careless and cruel treatment of women in particular. However, her insights ring hollow and seem forced, much too commonplace, abstract and impersonal to be of any consequence:

> She had joined the lists, taken sides in the great civil war of the sexes . . . Before she was Peter's sister or anybody's child or Harry's mistress she was a woman, female. That was the exactest definition of her existence and the one with which she would most recurringly have to deal. (*Wind Shifts* p. 207)

Particularly illuminating in the context of Ruth's pseudo-emancipation is a scene which describes how Colin Farley, a childhood acquaintance, tries to have sex with Ruth in his car on their first night out together. Ruth is furious, expressing very clearly how frightening she found the situation in which 'somebody about three times as strong as me whom I don't know started pawing all over me in a dark country lane' (*Wind Shifts* p. 178). However, even during this impressive scene Sharp eventually swaps sides, obviously unable ever to sustain his support of a female character:

> in a way she [Ruth] knew she was teasing him [Colin], trying to tell him of the polarities of rape, inflame him with the potential of their situation. But he sat sullen, except for a swift twist to turn the radio off. The mood left her and she sank back, cold suddenly and depressed.
> 'I'm sorry,' he said. (*Wind Shifts* p. 178)

Ruth is hardly more than Sharp's alibi-woman meant to indicate his awareness of feminist issues. In actual fact Sharp's misogyny never once wavers. Judging from the large number of highly unfavourable descriptions of women in both *The Green Tree in Gedde* and *The Wind Shifts* Cuffee's outcry, 'You women sicken me' (*Wind Shifts* p. 196), emerges as a fitting motto for the whole of Sharp's literary work:

> Once with Sammy at the hospital a roomful of women, sitting splay-legged and dull, causing him [Moseby] to think of mushroom growths in the stomach. Their eyes on him with dim resentment since he could not share their internal terrors, and was in his facsimile the cause of not a few of them. The smell of women brought together assailed him, rankling in the nose,

festering in the mind and he saw women then with their slutti-
ness and the uncleanness of their ways and left with a quick
male step. (*Wind Shifts* p. 38)

It is a vital part of Sharp's sexist rhetoric that both Kimber and
Ruth, as representatives of two different oppressed groups, are
shown to concur with, and thus considerably foster, the prejudices
held against them. Ruth herself realises that women are doomed to
live 'in bondage to the phases of the moon' and that 'they could
never escape the vegetable side of their nature like men could'
(*Wind Shifts* p. 141); only then can Cuffee pick up on the imagery
and effectively develop it into something far more explicit:

> Life is a pure flame fed by the invisible sun that lies within us.
> The people who do not know of that sun must seek reflected
> light, moon people. Women are moon people, all but a few.
> (*Wind Shifts* p. 264)

Sharp's sexist rhetorical devices render his books prime examples of
misogynous and anti-feminist writing. His novels are devoid of any
instances of fruitful female bonding. Whereas Sharp's men are friends,
bonding easily with one another, even with perfect strangers,[36] his
women show only jealousy and sexual competitiveness for one another. Their lives focus on a constant vying with each other for the
favour of men. At the same time, strangely enough, Sharp insists
that women do band together against men. Cuffee, for example,
suspects that his sister blames him for leaving Gerda 'because she's a
woman and so are you' (*Wind Shifts* p. 203). Ruth is said to
experience a sudden upsurge of sympathy and compassion for her
brother's jilted girl-friend: 'The bond of being female tightened on
her sympathies and she found herself resenting Cuffee's brutal masculinity' (*Wind Shifts* p. 157). However, Ruth distrusts Gerda, feeling
her love for Cuffee to be 'improper' and 'oppressive': 'There was
something about Gerda that she felt to be false, a lie, a dissimulation'
(*Wind Shifts* p. 104). Significantly, when Gerda asks Ruth to 'please,
please be on my side', Ruth retorts: 'Against whom?' (*Wind Shifts*
p. 113). Confronted with Gerda's frantic search for a plausible
reason why Cuffee has so suddenly decided to leave her and find
Uta, Ruth's mind breaks into an interior monologue indicative of
her incapacity to have genuine feelings for another woman:

> It wasn't that which made up his mind. It was something else.
> I don't think he knows quite what himself. He's going to see

this girl in Germany. You don't know her, what she's like?'
No, except that she's not like you, you poor cow, not vulnerable
and frightened and trying to keep calm when you want to fall
down on your knees and say 'Don't, please God, don't go.'
She's nothing whatever like you Gerda with the great buttery
pats of your breasts and the overwhelming need to cling. Just
take a good long look and imagine the opposite of everything
you see. That's your rival, if rival you must have, if you need
something more than that men and women want different
things. (*Wind Shifts* p. 205)

Ruth is not the only misogynous woman in Sharp's novels who is
incapable of expressing any same-sex solidarity. The story told by
Annie, one of Cuffee's Parisian conquests, is a breathtaking concoc-
tion of misogynous and homophobic elements. While hitch-hiking
in Spain Annie and another girl are offered a lift by a group of
young men who subsequently rape the girls. Afterwards, the girls
take a room in a hotel and fall asleep. Only now does Annie's tale
reach its climax when we are told about an incident she clearly
considers worse – more unspeakable and outrageous – than the
male act of rape:

> And you'll never guess, this girl, I woke up and she was all
> over me, kissing me and all that pervy stuff. I really beat the
> shit out of her, I can tell you. I'd rather have got raped by all
> of those guys than had that lesbian at me. Strange how I never
> noticed it in her before. I hate that kind of thing. (*Green Tree*
> p. 225)

The women characters in Sharp's novels lack an awareness of themselves as 'a sex/class' which, according to Nancy F. Cott, is 'a major,
perhaps the major, contribution of recent feminist theory'.[37] Naomi
Mitchison believes that such a female sense of belonging together is
much older than organised political feminism and much simpler to
boot: 'How funny it is that women can make friends with one
another so much faster than men! It's because of the way the same
things seem to happen to them all!'[38] Be that as it may, despite male
suspicions concerning a universal female conspiracy against them,
in Sharp's books it is men, rather than women, who hold together.
Even Sharp's final description of Ruth's allegedly awakened female
consciousness is written in the form of a tirade against other women:
Gerda, Meriel (an elderly ballet teacher), Mrs Cuffee and dead

Merle Curvis. In Sharp's novels one woman's credo is another
woman's denunciation:

> As well as being who one was there was being a woman too.
> She hadn't known that before, not like she had come to, woman
> in her bondage to men and menses, to the great dragon of
> fecundity. She hated other women for their refusal to see it, to
> admit and accept it, Gerda's earth mother myth, and distorted,
> thwarted Meriel Rose, her mother's pallid plight and Merle
> Curvis' useless gesture of defiance. She hated them all for not
> succeeding, for not overcoming their female fate. Would she in
> turn fail, choose the illusion, shirk the reality, make the com-
> promise, deny the meaning. In the selenotropics she languished,
> an amazon seeking her own source. (*Wind Shifts* p. 257)

A Green Tree in Gedde was republished as a paperback in 1985 by
the Richard Drew Publishing House in Glasgow as part of their
Scottish Collection. In consequence, it has become widely accessible
to the general public; it has also become an optional item for
Scottish literature reading lists in schools, colleges and universities.
What the new edition of Sharp's novel is in desperate need of, as I
hope to have shown above, is a critically informed introduction
that would contextualise its literary value as a modern classic as well
as disclose and discuss Sharp's sexist rhetoric.[39] It ought to be made
clear that the times when a novel as crudely offensive to women
and gay men as Sharp's *A Green Tree in Gedde* could still win highly
prestigious and financially rewarding literary prizes in Scotland are
past. As it is, only furnished with a latently sexist promotional
blurb, Sharp's misogynous and homophobic novel makes dangerous
reading, particularly for young people, both straight and gay, who
are still unsure of their sexual identity and in search of adequate
role models.

In the realm of Scottish literary criticism, so preoccupied with
the issue of identity, it needs to be acknowledged that in our twentieth-century world all identity starts with the individual's definition
of him or herself. Naturally, questions of sexuality and gender make
up a crucial part in the process of finding one's identity. But whereas
women and gays – keen to reach a fulfilling definition of their place
in society – can never avoid a confrontation with the strai(gh)tjacket
of traditional gender roles, heterosexual men have so far managed
to do without such a confrontation which would involve a profound

re-consideration of all of one's attitudes towards sexuality and gender. Scotland is still waiting for the emergence and subsequent 'coming out' of a generation of angry young men who, unafraid of their own feelings, would dare contest the misogynous and homophobic rules of the 'Emotional Establishment Inside'.

NOTES

1. Alan Sharp *A Green Tree in Gedde* (Glasgow, Richard Drew 1985 [1965]) and *The Wind Shifts* (London, Michael Joseph 1967). Subsequent references are to these editions. From America Sharp published two more novels, *The Hired Hand* (London, Corgi 1971) and *Night Moves* (London, Corgi 1975).
2. 'Scottish Fiction since 1945' in Norman Wilson ed. *Scottish Writing and Writers* (Edinburgh, Ramsay Head 1977) p. 13. For Gifford's appreciation of Sharp's debut novel compare also his review of Isobel Murray's and Bob Tait's *Ten Modern Scottish Novels* which he concludes with 'Can we have volume two with the "missing" novels and perhaps . . . *A Green Tree in Gedde* . . .?' (*Books in Scotland* 15 [October 1984] p. 15).
3. Glenda Norquay 'Four Novelists of the 1950s and 1960s' in Cairns Craig ed. *The History of Scottish Literature.* Vol. 4: *Twentieth Century* (Aberdeen, Aberdeen University Press 1987) p. 259.
4. Ibid. p. 267.
5. Compare *A Green Tree in Gedde* p. 240: '"Oh it is very good to be here, now, in Paris, to be beautiful and young and awaiting the male's approach." And her [Uta's] laughter rang like silver scatter among the tables, and in the swaddle of her sweater Cuffee saw her breasts jump.'
6. Norquay p. 267.
7. This scene can also be read as an echo from *A Green Tree in Gedde* p. 295 where Yani beats Cuffee unconscious with a poker when she sees him holding Uta, her adoptive sister, on the bed after a violent altercation between the two. Sharp's depiction of Yani's overreaction contributes to the reader's impression that Yani, allegedly a lesbian, is the mentally deranged victim of her own sexuality which, we are induced to conclude, goes hand in hand with sexual frustration and violent man-hatred.
8. Compare the subheadings of Part Three of *The Wind Shifts*: 'The Journey', 'The Castle', 'The Idyll', 'The Trial', 'The Flight'.
9. *The Wind Shifts* p. 192. This is how Cuffee describes Merle when Ruth tells him of the girl's suicide after an unsuccessful abortion.
10. Cuffee's quest is mirrored by that of Moseby who leaves his wife Edna, his lover Cathy and – by the end of *The Wind Shifts* – has started an affair with Ruth. The major difference between Moseby's and Cuffee's quests is that guilt-ridden Moseby moves in circles whereas ruthless Cuffee only stops his angry crusade when, while fleeing from Bonn where he assaulted Uta, he is shot dead by a policeman in Luxemburg.

11. M. H. Abrams *A Glossary of Literary Terms* 3 edn (New York et al., Holt, Rinehart and Winston 1971) p. 10.

12. Kingsley Amis *Lucky Jim* (Harmondsworth, Penguin 1961 [1954]) p. 11.

13. Compare Amis's protagonist who observes that 'it was queer how much colour women seemed to absorb from their men-friends, or even from the man they were with for the time being. That was only bad when the man in question was bad; it was good when the man was good' (ibid. p. 142).

14. Compare what Jimmy Porter says about his wife Alison in Osborne's *Look Back in Anger* (London, Faber and Faber 1957) p. 37: 'She has the passion of a python. She just devours me whole every time, as if I were some over-large rabbit.'

15. Lynne Segal *Slow Motion. Changing Masculinities* (London, Virago 1990) p. 13.

16. In this context it is laughable to hear Michie, one of Jim's students in Amis's *Lucky Jim*, say about his female fellow students that 'being women, they're of rather more conservative temperament than ourselves' (p. 97).

17. Compare Michael S. Kimmel, 'Rethinking "Masculinity". New Directions in Research', in Kimmel ed. *Changing Men. New Directions in Research on Men and Masculinity* (Newsbury Park et al., Sage 1987) p. 11. Compare also Kimmel's definition of men's studies to which the present article is meant to be a contribution: 'Men's studies responds to the shifting social and intellectual contexts in the study of gender and attempts to treat masculinity not as the normative referent against which standards are assessed but as a problematic gender construct' (ibid. p. 10).

18. Segal p. x.

19. Multifarious attempts to come up with new definitions of masculinity have been launched in recent years by representative writers of the so-called *New Men's Movement*, all of which are unfortunately of a mythic and hopelessly sexist quality. See in this context Guy Corneau's assertion in *Absent Fathers, Lost Sons. The Search for Masculine Identity*, tr. by L. Shouldice (Boston and London, Shambhala 1991) p. 120, that '[a] man must recognize himself in the god Phallos with his erect penis; he must sense the particular kind of energy that makes him essentially different from women'. Corneau is so hyper-sensitive to the masculine dilemma that he expresses a heart-felt sympathy for killers and rapists who 'report impulses they just can't resist. In a sense, they too are victims, attacked by their own inner violence . . .' (ibid. p. 129). See also Robert Moore and Douglas Gillette, *King–Warrior–Magician–Lover. Rediscovering the Archetypes of the Mature Masculine* (San Francisco, Harper 1990) and Robert Bly's *Iron John. A Book about Men* (Shaftesbury/Dorset, Element 1991 [1990]). With reference to Bly's book Corneau points out that 'getting in touch with Iron Hans' masculine dynamism and mastering that power, is what enables a man to penetrate the world of women, literally and figuratively . . .' (*Absent Fathers* p. 131).

20. Segal pp. 16 and 114.
21. Compare Michael W. Ross who discusses the widespread tendency in society to believe that 'a male who wishes to interact sexually with another male must think of himself as, or contain attributes of, a female' ('Homosexuality and Social Sex Roles: A Re-Evaluation', in Ross ed. *Homosexuality, Masculinity & Femininity* (New York and Binghamton, 1985) p. 2).
22. David Cohen *Being a Man* (London, Routledge 1990). Compare in this context Rosalind Miles's observation concerning the enormous social pressure put on men from a very early age to live up to the standards of approved masculine behaviour: '"Boys will be boys", runs the proverb. To see a group of mothers with their sons, or a father making the first attempts at ball play with a son, is to realize that this is not an observation, but an imperative: "boys must be boys"' (*The Rites of Man. Love, Sex and Death in the Making of the Male* (London, Grafton 1991) pp. 44f.).
23. Compare Moseby's response of 'horror and pity' when Sammy hesitantly tells him about his sex-life (*The Wind Shifts* pp. 29 and 48).
24. Gregory M. Herek 'On Heterosexual Masculinity. Some Psychical Consequences of the Social Construction of Gender and Sexuality', in Kimmel ed. *Changing Men* pp. 69 and 77.
25. Ibid. p. 77.
26. Compare what Rosalind Miles concludes after commenting on the preference of some adult male homosexuals for a variety of partners: 'Yet this desire for novelty, this compulsive quest for conquest, this satyriasis even, is not confined to the homosexual male. It has been a characteristic of masculine dominance behaviour from the first of the Chinese emperors to John F. Kennedy, and has achieved mythic status in the legends surrounding Don Juan, Casanova, Errol Flynn. The heterosexual cocksman, however, becomes a hero, the homosexual . . . his polar opposite, a pervert, criminal, outcast, or "son of Cain"' (*The Rites of Man* p. 143).
27. Compare also the nonchalant remark of McIndoe, Moseby's history tutor, on Billy Wilder's famous film *Some Like It Hot*: 'Excellent example of Wilder's amorality. He's the right man to make the definitive film about poofs. And he has something that's very rare nowadays. A genuine sense of vulgarity' (*A Green Tree in Gedde* p. 117).
28. Compare also Gibbon's comment on a gay man he knows from home which testifies to his total lack of understanding for the predicament of homosexuals in provincial Scotland: 'There was a queer in Greenock but he was, well he was a pathetic wee bloke' (*A Green Tree in Gedde* p. 164).
29. Compare also Ruth's words in *The Wind Shifts* p. 228: 'It's all a bit strange. I don't really think Harry fancies me. I mean he never seems very interested in bed.'
30. See *A Green Tree in Gedde* p. 168: 'She would find a man, she did not try to think what he would be like, and she would be happy, nor did she examine happiness, there would emerge a kind of order, no matter what, and her childhood and her youth and her love for Peter [Cuffee,

her brother] would all be resolved as inevitable antecedents to the new, unimaginable content.'

31. Norquay p. 268.
32. Jon Snodgrass *A Book of Readings for Men against Sexism* (Albion, Times Change Press 1977) p. 161.
33. Compare also *The Wind Shifts* p. 131, where Cuffee talks to Ruth about Gerda, his new woman: 'Well now, Gerda is something else again. She's made for men to use. I don't mean that cuntishly. Her life is men, or a man. She's not really alive when there's no man about. She asks of you that you use her and hopes that as you do you'll come to think you can't do without it or be stricken with remorse if you try. Her generosity is tainted with latent blackmail it always seems to me.'
34. Brian Pronger *The Arena of Masculinity. Sports, Homosexuality and the Meaning of Sex* (London, Gay Men's Press 1990) p. 2. Compare also Snodgrass' definition of sexism: 'Sexism . . . is the assignment of people to dominant and subordinate orders according to gender. It is maintained by repressive sex role socialization which attempts to polarize individuals by making males masculine and females feminine' (*A Book of Readings for Men against Sexism* p. 161).
35. See *The Wind Shifts* p. 208, one of numerous scenes in which Ruth finds herself in the kitchen while the men are enjoying themselves next door – drinking, eating, talking.
36. A particularly surprising instance of male bonding is to be found after Cuffee's attack on Uta when Franz, the warden of the student house in Bonn, assists the attacker to escape instead of siding with the innocent victim, his friend. Cuffee is said to be sure that 'Franz would not betray him' (*The Wind Shifts* p. 339).
37. Nancy F. Cott 'Feminist Theory and Feminist Movements: the Past Before Us' in Juliet Mitchell and Ann Oakley eds *What Is Feminism?* (Oxford, Blackwell 1986) p. 59.
38. This is what the character of Philylla exclaims in Mitchison's semi-historical novel *The Corn King and the Spring Queen* (Edinburgh, Canongate 1990 [1931]) p. 186.
39. In the context of such an introduction one should not forget to mention gay-friendly Scottish novels like Fred Urquhart's *Time Will Knit* which has hitherto been ignored by Scottish literary criticism. It is to be hoped that Scottish critics will eventually see the challenge in what Urquhart's character Cinnamon says about 'this so-called heinous crime' of homosexuality: 'The lower classes don't understand it. Maybe, in fifty years they will. And a lot of the so-called, upper classes, don't understand it either. It's only intelligent people who understand it, and the mass of people are profoundly unintelligent. You've only got to look around you to see that' (Glasgow, Richard Drew 1988 [1938]) pp. 222f.).

6

The Quest

Two Contemporary Adventures

MARGARET ELPHINSTONE

Iona McGregor, in her detective novels *Death Wore a Diadem* (1989) and *Alice in Shadowtime* (1992), and Sian Hayton in her trilogy, *Cells of Knowledge* (1989), *Hidden Daughters* (1992), and *The Last Flight* (1993), both use the theme of the quest to examine questions of gender and sexuality.[1] However, the novels are not merely about gender and sexuality, and the journeys they represent cannot be simply translated into a manifesto on these subjects. On the contrary, the questions raised about gender serve not to focus attention on the meaning of gender *per se*, but to open up the whole issue of how assumptions about gender and sexuality dictate a world picture. If polarity and opposition are taken as immutable in terms of gender and sexuality, then the same deadening oppositions will become fixed in every attempt to reflect the human condition in any aspect at all. The critic Cixous's deconstruction of binary oppositions (based on Derrida's critique of binary logic) is a relevant yardstick here, as she argues against fixed binary oppositions as being literally 'deathly', and argues instead for a more fluid concept of multiple, hetero-geneous *différance*, a *différance* which for her is the measure of genuine women's writing, a writing free from patriarchal hierarchies and oppositional constructions.[2]

Mary Jacobus develops this concept in her essay 'Reading Woman (Reading)' where she shows how the deconstruction of fixed gender oppositions in favour of 'the play of difference' will lead to the demolition of further oppositions:

it is in language – in reading and in writing woman – that femininity at once discloses and discomposes itself, endlessly displacing the fixity of gender identity by the play of difference and division which simultaneously creates and uncreates gender, identity and meaning.[3]

Hayton and McGregor both work within traditional genres, from which the reader would generally expect a reiteration of accepted meanings: conventional definitions of right as opposed to wrong, real as opposed to imaginary (or supernatural), masculine as opposed to feminine, for example. They work within a literary tradition where the plot of a detective fiction or a historical novel may be expected to uphold such definitions, and then they proceed to use the vehicle of the mystery plot to explore gender and sexuality in a manner which subverts traditional oppositions of masculine and feminine, and calls every other building block in the hierarchical structure into question as well.

Both use the traditional narrative method of a mystery, a tantalising question to which the reader can only find an answer by following the story that offers the solution, like Theseus following the thread through the labyrinth. Both writers present the reader with a *quest*ion, from which the *quest* develops. Both make use of the plot devices of suspense and mystification to ensnare the reader with the promise of a solution on the plot level to the problem of what is really happening. Both also allow these devices to raise deeper questions of identity and meaning, opening the way for the reader to demand answers not only to the plot mystery, but to the more mysterious question of what the events mean. In order to reach an answer on this level, both authors demand of their reader a psychic shift, an ability to read the conventions of the familiar genre in a different way. Hayton demands that we stop asking for historical narrative (which is what the narrators purport to give) and acclimatise ourselves to reading myth; McGregor demands that we stop insisting on 'facts' (which is what the genre suggests that we should do) and begin reading the psyche. In other words, both writers demand that their readers go beyond externals of genre, history, and fact, and start to read images, myths, the narratives inside people's heads.

Both Hayton and McGregor set their narratives in the past. Their choices of time and place are very different, but their shared use of a Scottish historical past suggests that both are borrowing and revising from the long tradition of the Scottish historical novel. It is worth considering what this implies. They are not only Scottish writers, but also women writers. Scott created the Scottish historical novel as we know it, and his influence on the genre has been examined by critics as diverse as Gregory Smith and Lukács, and many others.[4] His contemporaries, Susan Ferrier and Mary Brunton have received minimum critical attention until very recently, but perhaps they too are relevant forbears to the two writers I am considering now. Their use of the Gothic tradition, their ambivalent, often ironic relation to the area of Noble Savagery wherein the Highlands have so often been located in literature, above all, their insistence on woman as subject (deficient and ignorant though she may be), set a precedent for an alternative view of the Scottish past. That is to say, a view that by noticing the existence of gender makes woman subject rather than invisible.

Hayton and McGregor also share a subtle and skilful handling of narrative technique. Both make use of male subjects. In Hayton's trilogy, the story is told by one or two male narrators in the form of letters. McGregor's quest is undertaken by a male detective whose task is to solve the mystery. Some feminist criticism, notably the early work of Showalter, and that of Gilbert and Gubar, seems in its most simplistic interpretation to suggest that women's writing is (or should be) a direct reflection of women's experience. This seems to me to discount the possibilities of irony which are crucial to good fiction. Fiction is not autobiography; neither women nor men write their own experience, unfiltered and unformed. The nature of language and metaphor make such a feat impossible, since neither can simply reflect life in a mirror without a frame. So gender in writing is more fluid than some feminist criticism would suppose, and other critics, from Woolf to Jacobus, have focused on that fluidity as vital to the nature of writing itself.

The Scottish tradition has always been particularly subtle in its use of *personae*, of narrators or subjects who expose themselves and their limitations through ironic self-revelation and who tell a different story from the overt narrative they think that they are authoritatively presenting to the reader. Hayton and McGregor work very much within that tradition. McGregor, for example, does not follow the pattern of direct gender reversal which has been one method of feminist revision of the detective genre. Her detective remains as male as Sherlock Holmes, and offers about the same faint hint of heterosexual preference (although he is in other respects a very

different character). The women in McGregor's novels surround
McLevy just as shadowy female creatures surround Holmes, but
their role is utterly transformed, and so our view of McLevy is
transformed also. Thus McGregor subverts the traditional detective
novel, not by simply exchanging the gender of her detective, but by
building upon the long history of ambiguous relationships between
a woman writer and her male detective. Where, for example, Ngaio
Marsh and Margory Allingham show a thinly disguised sexual attraction between narrator and male detective, Josephine Tey, and later
P. D. James maintain a more subtle balance between identification
and ironic distance between author/narrator and detective, in which
gender becomes more flexible and ambiguous. McGregor develops
this revision of the genre in the hands of women writers.

Hayton too, takes an old bottle and fills it with new wine. The
epistolary narrative takes us back to Smollett in the Scottish literary
tradition, with all the contradictions and self-revelations that Smollett
so splendidly exploited. Carswell's use of the form in *The Camomile*
(1922) to strong ironic effect, has not yet been adequately analysed.[5]
Hayton's use of the form, like Carswell's, serves to reveal much
about gender assumptions, but her method is different. In Hayton's
trilogy we have two male, Christian narrators telling us about a
world they do not understand (although they learn a great deal as
they progress), a world that might be described as feminine in
more ways than one. But, as in McGregor's writing, there is no
simple reversal. The Celtic pagan world is full of supernatural events,
in which reality signifies something completely different from that
of either the tenth-century Christian narrator or the twentieth-century reader of a historical novel. But the inner world of the novels
is no simple matriarchal alternative; on the contrary, it is as patriarch-
ally oppressive as the Christian paradigm that seeks to replace it.
Indeed, the Christian monastic world becomes at times a place of
refuge from the enormity of the pagan patriarchy.

As I said at the beginning, neither writer offers us a manifesto,
and this means that neither offers a solution in terms of a simple
reversal of things as they are. They may each have set their narratives
in another time, but the distancing is in no way utopian. Savages
are not noble; a woman's world is not an alternative to a man's.
Gender, sexuality and morality are fluid and mixed. There are neither
heroes nor villains, no precise right or precise wrong. That is to
say, neither has set her narrative within a rigid moral framework
against which all things can be judged. There is no omniscient

narrator as we find, for example, in the novels of George Eliot, or indeed, in D. H. Lawrence, and it is significant that these two authors, in many ways so different, were both able, their texts suggest, to rest assured that distinctions of gender were absolute, and indeed cosmically significant in their undisputed separateness. In contrast, the questioning of gender and sexuality in Hayton and McGregor is directly linked to the refusal to erect a rigid moral framework. If one opposition is deconstructed, then others must crash to the ground in its wake.

The similarity, then, between these two authors, working superficially in very different genres, is the way they both use the quest motif, the necessity of solving a mystery, to go beyond plot level to examine the deeper questions of fixed roles, in terms of gender and sexuality. Their choice of genre is thus ironic, in so far as both the historical novel and detective fiction have on the whole worked within a convention of a determined structure of right and wrong, good action and bad, heroes and villains, males and females. By deconstructing these opposites within a genre that has traditionally relied upon their existence, these two writers have both produced highly ironic texts. This irony is also reflected in the subtle narrative technique, which again questions assumptions both about morality and about gender, showing the two constructs to be inextricably interwoven.

The connection between *Death Wore a Diadem* and *Alice in Shadowtime* is made through the detective McLevy. His part in the first novel is ambiguous; although he does act in solving the mystery, the actual mystery that he solves is not, as we have seen, the answer to the practical question raised by the plot. In the second novel, McLevy moves in closer to the psychic field of action. In both books, however, the focus of the mystery is in the minds of women, an ambiguous answer perhaps to Freud's notorious question. McLevy is no psychoanalyst; his job is to find a male murderer in both cases, and, aided by his female, canine *alter ego*, he is successful in both cases.

The critic Catherine Belsey has made a useful study of Conan Doyle's women characters and their relationship to Conan Doyle's central detective figure, Sherlock Holmes. In her study of the story 'Charles Augustus Milverton', she states:

The sexuality of these three shadowy women motivates the

narrative and yet is barely present in it. The disclosure which ends the story is thus scarcely a disclosure at all.

One of these women is the housemaid, to whom the disguised Holmes becomes engaged in order to gain information from her. Traumatic for her, perhaps, but as Belsey says:

> The housemaid is not further described in the story.[6]

Working-class female sexuality is of no consequence whatsoever; the sexuality of upper-class women or mysterious foreigners is vaguely menacing, but never specified: letters remain unread, allegations are never specifically substantiated. Belsey concludes:

> The truth the stories tell is the truth about ideology, the truth which ideology represses, its own existence as ideology itself.[7]

This analysis is highly pertinent to what we might regard as McGregor's revision of Conan Doyle and of the genre which he initiated. She works with the reactionary, repressive ideology that the detective novel traditionally upholds, but she does not work within it. As Colin Watson argues, in *Snobbery With Violence*,[8] the crime novel has developed as a precise reflection of an ideology which leaves no room for divergence from the assumed norm of male, white, upper-class heterosexuality. Maggie Humm, in her analysis of feminist detective fiction shows what it is that must be repressed in order to maintain a patriarchal ideology:

> The aim of traditional detective fiction is to dispel mystery and the deviant, and subject reality and mystery to scientific investigation. What so often escapes the formulae of science and necessitates a turn to narrative formulae is women's sexuality. The fiction of detective fiction is the 'enigma of women'.

The theme of Humm's book is crossing the border at which a patriarchal ideology demands that the text stop. In relating this theme to feminist detective fiction, she says:

> Crossing the border occurs when writers and their characters discover they need to stand outside the limits of the genre.[9]

So McGregor's treatment of McLevy can be seen as a subversive revision of the genre that Conan Doyle established, of a patriarchal ideology focused upon the figure of the detective/hero. McLevy is a detective in traditional style, a proper, sometimes even stolid, policeman, but the labyrinth he has to negotiate leads him off traditional ground into highly subversive territory, into the territory, in fact, of the repressed unconscious, the domain of female sexuality.

It is typical of McGregor's wry humour that McLevy's Watson is a female dog, named after 'his most audacious thief' (p. 3). Jeanie Brash is brighter than Watson, but unpredictable. She cannot be relied upon if let off her lead. She demands a good deal of care and attention; no doubt if left in the care of Holmes she would have become a neurotic half-starved canine wreck, but McLevy has all the domestic virtues, and Jeanie Brash flourishes. She also leads her detective to the truth. Her doggishness is reflected in the physicality of the characters, on which McGregor, in contravention of the genre convention, insists. The text is full of puns on doggishness, similes with dogs, equation of human and animal physicality. Death too, in the second novel, is a matter of basic butchery, whether human or animal.

McGregor's apparent levity and choice of a genre traditionally associated with light reading mask a considered exploration of self-deceit in character and society. Detective novels are necessarily about discovery of the truth. In this case the truth to be uncovered is not merely the discovery of a particular murderer, whose role as scapegoat exonerates everybody else, but the truth that each character has to confront in terms of their own implication in the murder, their own human condition. McGregor stretches the genre to its limit by finally refusing to present us with a murderer. The individual who pushes Peggy into the area is a mere cipher. We have to turn back to the society that produced him, that caused Peggy to be out in the street on a wet night, that gave rise to the whole web of petty misdemeanour and intrigue which leads to a pointless death. For just as there is no one murderer, there is no one motive. Instead we have a play of implication and motivation, which encourages the reader to re-examine the entire cast of characters.

McGregor's novel is set in 1860. Stevenson was at the time a sickly ten year old living in Heriot Row, five minutes walk from the Scottish Institute for the Education of the Daughters of Gentlefolk, which might so easily have existed in Moray Place. However, in considering McGregor as heir to a Scottish literary tradition, one is inevitably drawn to Stevenson. Like Stevenson, McGregor exposes the evil at the root of the mysteries of her fictional Victorian world. *The Strange Case of Dr Jekyll and Mr Hyde* (1886) is a study above all in hypocrisy, of a society that tells lies, to the extent that a man must literally divide himself into two in order to hide (or Hyde) the unacknowledgeable, brutal part of himself. Emma Tennant is another Scottish woman writer who has revised Stevenson in order to show how the divided self operates in the demands made on *women* by a society which requires for its myth of womanhood either angels or monsters.[10] McGregor's debt to Stevenson shows itself rather differently from Tennant's, but the focus on hypocrisy is similar.

Stevenson's *The Master of Ballantrae* (1888) demonstrates further that polar opposites like truth and lies, good and evil, are inadequate as a reflection of character. The narrators of the novel are unreliable, and just as McGregor offers us no one murderer, Stevenson offers us no one villain. There is something devilish at work, but in spite of Mackellar's partiality we cannot say it is the Master. The impossibility of the single narrative takes us back to Hogg and Burns, and forward to writers like Tennant and McGregor.

A consideration of McGregor's characters demonstrates her ironic refusal to deal in polarities, and her rejection of the single narrative. Her characters each have their own version, but in order to maintain it we see them struggling to establish identity within a web of lies and mistaken assumptions. Honesty and self-knowledge are the ultimate threat to a society based upon imposture, and so are rigorously punished. Ambiguity about identity is signalled clearly from the first pages of *Death Wore a Diadem*. The Empress Eugénie arrives in Edinburgh under a pseudonym, the assassin who turns out to be a young gentleman from the Military Academy is Christabel's cousin Ranald Mackenzie and also the Count Orsini; Peggy's mysterious lover is also Mr Cargill the singing master. Human beings are not the only subjects of misappelation. Christabel is seen reading:

> Mr Darwin's recently published *Origin of Species* hidden behind the covers of *The Churchman's Family Magazine*. (p. 29)

And of course the whole plot hinges upon a question of what is genuine and what is false, in the misunderstandings over the Princess Eugénie's diadem, which becomes a symbol of the harmful effects of mistaking identity and misreading human nature, as it careers through the plot, crashing through artifice, bringing first death and then truth in its wake. The diadem belongs to the Empress, and seems to represent her part as catalyst in the events, a *dea in machina*, perhaps. The Empress is in Edinburgh because she too has been the victim of lies for appearance's sake. The book begins and ends with her, and moves from 'A carefully suppressed scandal' (p. 1), to a final liberation from repression and deceit: 'The Empress laughed and laughed' (p. 219).

McGregor points out her main characters at the beginning, the ones who are to be affected by the plot that is about to be recounted:

> Christabel, her lover, two teachers at the Scottish Institute for the Education of the Daughters of Gentlefolk, and one dead servant maid. (p. 1)

The two teachers are ruled by their own overmastering need to conform to a pattern of gentility or morality too rigid to contain any whole human being. No one in McGregor's fictional world is quite what they seem, and Mrs Napier, the head teacher of the Institute, is the most alarming example. We have hints of her inability to reconcile various forms of untruth early on. Mrs Napier seems clear about her function:

> her young ladies must be trained as future wives and mothers of Christian men. (p. 23)

But a few paragraphs later we are told:

> Mrs Napier had hated her husband. (p. 25)

When she rebukes Miss Erroll for wishing to teach maths to the senior class, it is on the grounds that 'we are only women, gently nurtured' (p. 27). Mrs Napier is a model of falsity; every statement she makes is a lie, and her exposure at the end is a discovery besides which the identity of the literal murderers seems negligible. Mrs Napier may not have actually pushed a servant maid into an area, but in a sense she did murder a drapery shopgirl from the Gorbals, 'twenty years syne' (p. 215). The Victorian class system is demonstrated to rely upon the lie that some human beings are worth more than others. Mrs Napier counters this falsity with further lies. She defeats the system temporarily by using it, never by confronting or changing it. She becomes the worst liar in the book.

Miss Erroll has also forced herself into a false mould, but initially she appears to be victim rather than criminal. Forbidden on grounds of her gender to find fulfilment in the only place where she can see it, in mathematics, she conforms to the rigid role that her Calvinist background offers. She, like Peggy, is murdered by social attitudes, but she is also guilty of murder. It is her hate that lays the trail that leads to Peggy's death. Like Robert Wringhim in Hogg's *Private Memoirs and Confessions of A Justified Sinner* (1824), she is apparently unaware of her flagrant transgressions. She does not know she is the real thief of the diadem. Denying her physical self, she uses her own urine unconsciously to express her rage and hate, her outrage against the myth that genteel women have no bodies. She is destroyed by a misogynist religion to which she adheres, and incriminates herself in the process, just as another fictional Edinburgh schoolteacher was to do in the 1930s, the creation of McGregor's contemporary Muriel Spark in *The Prime of Miss Jean Brodie* (1961).

In contrast to the two teachers, Christabel and Eleanor are remarkable for their retention of integrity in the face of hypocrisy. Christabel is the subversive element in the establishment of lies, as she refuses to give into deceit at all, and insists on naming without compromise what she perceives to be the truth. The teachers of the Institute are incapable of responding to her frank answer to the essay on True Beauty:

> During the past week, I have seen nothing more beautiful than Miss Stephen's breasts. (p. 37)

Christabel is neither blinded by classism nor misled by appearances. She keeps a clear eye on Peggy, although she is a servant, and chooses for her lover a woman whom the other girls reject socially. Christabel confronts hypocrisy as though defending her castle of honesty against a siege, in terms of her own fantasy (p. 65). Eleanor complements her in so far as her challenge to the world is less overt, since she remains quietly steadfast to her own purpose. Eleanor's dilemma is the most overtly feminist in the novel, as she pursues her ambition to become a doctor against the same odds that defeated Miss Erroll. Neither Christabel nor Eleanor allow themselves to be misled, but ironically they have a relationship which in terms of the society around them literally cannot be named. The reader is bound to recollect Queen Victoria's famous dictum on lesbians, as the relationship between Eleanor and Christabel becomes the keystone of the novel. Eleanor and Christabel insist on the reality of Peggy's death and the events that surround it. Ironically, it is less easy for them to reveal the truth of their own relationship. The narrator can state it more directly, and in this we have a suggestion of hindsight, which comments ironically on the failure of language for her nineteenth-century lesbian lovers. Back in Edinburgh after an idyllic fortnight with Christabel at her uncle's house, it had dawned on [Eleanor] that the first laird's four-poster bed in Perthshire had been a private world in more senses than one. (p. 60)

Nor does the plot offer any conclusion about the relationship; Christabel hopes to keep Eleanor in Paris, while Eleanor intends to study medicine in the USA.

The title of *Alice in Shadowtime* draws attention to another candidate for McGregor's revisionary tactics. Alice Enderby's real wedding coincides with the publication date of Carroll's *Alice in Wonderland* (1865). Alice Enderby, we discover, in the first line of McGregor's novel 'broke the laws of time', just like her prototype. Like the first Alice, Alice Enderby runs into a labyrinth where surreal events and images reflect the workings of a suppressed unconscious. McGregor's novel demolishes the mythical opposition between innocent, asexual girlhood on the one hand, and precocious sexual knowledge on the other. The fusion of angelic and monstrous images which results is reminiscent of the film *Dreamtime*, which also re-examines Carroll's book in psychoanalytical terms, using the imagery of the childhood world of *Alice in Wonderland*.

McLevy the detective has to operate on two levels. On one, he is the stock detective using empirical evidence to consider and eliminate suspects for the murder. The external facts are vital, and are in no way neglected because attention is drawn to another kind of truth. McGregor's meticulous handling of detail is used in this novel to create a complex puzzle of dates, and the external plot hinges upon apparently slight inaccuracies in dating. But these inaccuracies are the result of the same hypocrisy in dealing with truth that we find in *Death Wore A Diadem*. What Henry Enderby calls 'A few fibs' (p. 36) result in three murders. There are lies told about the date of Alice's arrival in Scotland and the date of Miles's aunt's death, just as there are lies told about every human action and motivation. Nemesis arrives in the form of a solicitor in possession of a correct date. The 'few fibs' turn out to mean several atrocious crimes, the expression of a society based upon lies. Subconsciously, the characters are aware of the danger. They dream about murder, they anticipate it, they understand it. Only McLevy seems to be aware of the diabolical power of lies. When he lies about Jeanie Brash he has 'two fingers crossed behind his back' (pp. 56–7).

McLevy is intuitive enough to realise that the real enquiry is into the workings of Alice's mind. He shows startling insight into the meaning of Alice's recurring dream; unlike Freud, McLevy does not relegate the evidence from women's dreams to the realm of fantasy; on the contrary, he uses women's dreams as other detectives use the Holmesian clues of cigar butts and footprints, to formulate his case. But the creator of psychoanalysis was an eight year old in Moravia when McLevy was investigating his case in Perthshire; once again, the ironic effect is deliberately created by a narrator with hindsight. McLevy himself is not at all sure about his unorthodox line of enquiry:

> Yet wasn't it fanciful to probe the relationship between the Enderby women and the dead man when he had such a likely suspect in Hector McIver? (p. 110)

The first clue we are given to Alice's trouble is a revision of the first chapter of *Alice Through the Looking Glass* (1872). Alice Enderby has an independent self inside the looking glass, which is reminiscent of Carroll's Alice's words, and the Tenniel illustration that goes with them:

> Oh, Kitty, how nice it would be if we could only get through into Looking-glass House. I'm sure it's got, oh! such beautiful things in it! . . . Let's pretend the glass has got all soft like gauze, so that we can get through.[11]

Alice Enderby's Looking-glass House is far less innocent than this purports to be, but outwardly Alice Enderby does enact the myth of the innocent child, inappropriately, in a grown woman;

> McLevy was struck by the contrast between the face and the childlike gestures . . . The childish tone did not fit the maturity of her voice. (p. 6)

Even Jack, who loves her, is irritated by her 'cloying pettishness' (p. 140). Alice's malaise is revealed early on, when she sees her self in the mirror becoming independent, making gestures not initiated by the original, social Alice who stares at her. One is reminded of many other mirror images in nineteenth-century fiction, perhaps most notably Jane Eyre regarding her own reflection, the 'imp' staring back at her in the red room at Mrs Reed's. Jane Eyre's alter ego becomes embodied in Bertha Mason. Alice Enderby's also develops into a creature aligned with brutality and bloodshed. Both Jane and Alice have their childlike innocence corrupted by the atrocities that adults inflict upon them. We are given clues about Alice on this occasion:

The reflection had begun to misbehave on November 1st, 1860, which was Papa's birthday . . . she had forgotten almost everything between October 1860 and the end of the following March . . . Sometimes a shadow of recollection crept to the back of her mind; then her heart would begin to pound, and panic drove it away. (p. 22)

The effect of this forgotten period is a fragmentation of self:

Alice often thought that there were half a dozen Alice Enderbys inside her. (p. 22)

Loss of a whole self leads inevitably to pretence, a forced ability to play one role knowing it is not the whole truth. Loss of innocence is an education into dissembling, an initiation into the adult world of hypocrisy that we encountered in *Death Wore a Diadem*. Alice's contemplation of her other self in the mirror is followed instantly by a dialogue between Alice and her mother which shows that Alice has thoroughly learned her lesson. She gives her mother 'the special look that brought on Mama's warmest smile', she knows she must 'pretend to be surprised', she knows her mother will be relieved that 'she now sounded sincere' (p. 23). So she has been thoroughly inducted into a world of hypocritical self-consciousness.

But Alice is troubled by bad dreams. From the forgotten period in her seventeenth year, she has been subject to nightmares. Gradually the nature of the dream is revealed, and her father's implication is made explicit. In Chapter 9 Alice and her father are alone for the first time in four years. Before her father enters, Alice is aware of herself reflected in divided sections in the gilt mirror above the mantelpiece. Her father enters and addresses her:

My dear little love-bird. (p. 50)

after which she again sees her looking-glass self:

the right hand of her reflection rose into view and touched a side ringlet. (p. 52)

It begins to be clear why Alice dreads her wedding, although the accusation of her father is never explicit. But in the recurring dream her anger is clear, as we slowly discover that in the nightmare she kills him. When Henry Enderby is murdered, the dividing line between the mirror world and outward fact breaks down – the glass has 'gone all soft like gauze' – and:

Alice told Flora that she has [sic] killed her father. (p. 93)

From this point on McLevy makes Alice's dream world the subject of his criminal investigation. He is looking for a murderer, and a murderer of childhood innocence, of the whole self which was Alice, is what he finds. Dr Sandy gives evidence about the autumn of 1860, when Alice was found hysterical outside her bedroom, and blood was found on her sheets. Dr Sandy concludes:

Let us suppose your theory correct, and Alice repeatedly dreams that she has killed her father. Her mind must be inhabited by demons! (p. 106)

Jack Douglas later gives further evidence regarding the dream:

She said she was being hunted across a moor, and the heather flowers were the colour of blood. (p. 110)

and finally he tells McLevy:

Alice always woke up at the point where she lifted a knife and killed her father . . . (p. 141)

McLevy's final interview with Alice is more like a psychoanalytical session than a police enquiry. Alice's statement is brief and she herself is apparently unconscious of what she is saying; the scene is the denouement of the central mystery of the plot, and it is handled with subtle understatement. The dividing line between dream and fact is left misty, and indeed it no longer seems to be the point. What is quite clear is that there has been a violation against the wholeness of a child's mind.

The novel began, not with Alice Enderby, but with the horrific, entirely gratuitous murder of a girl child in Edinburgh's Royal Mile. The event bears a marked resemblance to Hyde's trampling over a young girl's body in similar circumstances.[12] It also coincides in date with the year that Alice Enderby was violated. The attack on a young girl is not crucial in Stevenson's story; here, it becomes pivotal to the plot. It acts as another reflection to the crime against Alice Enderby, and so extends the particular experience of one girl into something wider. The connection between the violation of women and the hunt serves the same purpose.

Alice Enderby's wedding is celebrated by a deer hunt on a massive scale. It is hardly even a hunt; the land has been fenced at vast expense, the deer are merely driven into the valley and slaughtered by the gentlemen. The sexual excitement which brought about the violation of Alice is precisely identified with the hunt and the kill. When Henry Enderby kills his first deer, they are pregnant hinds who are officially protected, but that does not deter him. He enjoys the butchery that follows:

> He felt a pungent thrill as he whetted his knife, which was increased by the odours that soon met his nose. (p. 65)

Henry Enderby's house is adorned with hunting and fishing trophies, but the antlered stag's heads are kept in his private study, of which we hear:

> Mr Enderby prefers ladies not to enter it. (p. 90)

His wedding gift to Alice is 'sacrificing his deer' (p. 66), which is revealed as entirely appropriate when it is revealed that the violation of Alice took place as the culmination of a deer hunt, under the same impulse, fouled by the same blood, and presided over by the dismembered stag's head.

The murders fall into the pattern. Mrs Vesey has been hung up in the larder as if her body were the carcase of a deer. As the antlered deer have their heads severed, so with Henry Enderby:

> After death his virile member was cut off. (p. 107)

The animality of humanity is as strong a theme as it was in *Death Wore A Diadem*. Miles Hatterton's self is reflected in the habits of the ferret which was his first victim. Jeanie Brash, unimpressed by outward appearances such as a minister's black side-buttoned waistcoat, acts as her master's instinct and knows a murderer when she smells one. Miles finally runs 'as fast as a deer', and is pursued appropriately by staghounds. The truth of the characters' physical, animal selves cannot be repressed, even by a hypocrisy so strong it leaves no words available to describe it. Social success, indeed, is signalled by becoming bereft of truthful language in which to describe things as they are. Rose Enderby used to:

> exchange cheerful smut with her fellow servants. The mistress of Kilcorrie House had no words to discuss an unconsummated marriage. (p. 147)

Both McGregor's detective novels are set in the Victorian era, when euphemism was at its height, and the animal aspects of humanity were at their most unmentionable. Her past is well chosen for her theme, but it is hardly unrelated to the narrator's present. The narrative technique shows a deliberate consciousness of its own hindsight. The narrator overtly draws upon a literary tradition which connects the Victorian past to her own present. Her use of the historical novel form acts as a looking glass; these are twentieth-century novels, with no hints of pastiche. The past she presents is equally satisfying in its scholarly accuracy. McGregor can be thoroughly trusted on questions of historical detail, language, and point of view. Fiction needs to be as accurate a narrative form as any other, and McGregor, like her detective, pursues her quest with integrity.

Hayton's trilogy also offers the reader a quest. The genre is different and yet there is a figure not altogether removed from the detective/hero. Where McGregor's McLevy has to go beyond the bounds of conventional criminal investigation, and consider the effects of sexuality on the psyche, the three monkish narrators of the trilogy have to go beyond the expected bounds of the Christian world, and investigate the pagan, supernatural, dangerous world that lies beyond the pale of Christian society. Where McLevy had to confront the psychological, Selyf, Hw and Josiah have to confront the supernatural. In the Scottish literary tradition, the two have never been very different. In the ballads the perilous world of *faerie* is often aligned with dangerous sexuality, and the Scottish poets and novelists of the eighteenth and nineteenth centuries frequently made use of the folk tradition of the supernatural or diabolic to reflect the inner workings of the psyche, even when embedded in the conventions of social realism.

At the beginning of *Cells of Knowledge* and *Hidden Daughters*, there are passages by an unspecified narrator, the first simply entitled 'Scene', the second with no title at all. This is in marked contrast to the careful introductions to the letters that make up the main text. The events in both scenes are the same. The first narrative is from the point of view of Kilidh, the second from that of Kigva. The reader has to wait for a whole volume before the woman Kigva is known and understood; in the first, male telling she is merely an object in the plot which centres around Kilidh. In the second telling woman has become subject, not object. Kigva is a girl who undergoes agony of mind, in trials which demand the reader's identification with her. This aspect of Kigva is crucial to understanding her part in the action, and yet neither Kilidh nor Kigva seem to be central to the mystery with which the plot is concerned. They are ordinary humans, and the quest is concerned with a giant and his immortal daughters and the battle between a Christian and a pagan world, involving all the spiritual forces of both. Why begin with two anonymous versions of Kilidh and Kigva's story? The anonymity, contrasted as it is with the epistolary form of the main text, gives the tales the authority of folk tradition. The man and woman become a type of Adam and Eve; they are the mortals around whom the Miltonic battle rages. Like Adam and Eve, they encounter a demon, the giant Usbathaden, who appears to be tempter and false friend to both. Also, like Adam and Eve, they are ancestors. Kilidh is the father of Kynan, who is in turn the father of Drust, and the child that Kigva bears after her brief union with Kilidh is Culhuch, the mortal man who is finally to destroy the giant Usbathaden. The question of ancestry and inheritance is crucial throughout the trilogy and so these archetypal human forbears become a key to the mystery. It is their dealings with the satanic figure of the giant, who appears on the edges of their human world, that set in train the events that are to follow. Kigva's part in the action acts out her primitive relationship to supernatural power. Like Eve, her actions find their source not in a moral conflict between good and evil, but in simple fascinated curiosity. She explains at the end of *Hidden Daughters*:

> But I wanted to see, just once, the power of the giant. I wanted to see it working. (p. 234)

The trilogy raises and examines questions about the nature of woman, and so, ironically, about the nature of men. In this narrative told by male narrators, men reveal themselves by ironic self-revelation, and by the assumptions they make about women. The final revelation is that the two polarities, man and woman, cannot actually be opposed. The answer to the riddle of the quest lies in the deconstruction of gender oppositions.

The two monks, Selyf and Hw, try to divine the nature of the immortal woman Marighal and her sisters, and in so doing unconsciously reveal a paradigm of gender and sexuality which is threatened by the very existence of the giants' daughters. Within their narratives are several first-person accounts, recorded by the monks. In *Cells of Knowledge*, Marighal tells her story in two parts, and her partial account is later complemented by Kynan's narrative, and at the end Evabyth tells the story of her father's death. So the monks, in spite of the boundaries laid down by the transcription of their manuscripts, make space for the oral narrative that transgresses the limitations of their order, and refuses to fit into the shape prescribed by the script with its marginal glosses. Hayton's method here bears comparison with Emily Brontë's use of Lockwood in *Wuthering Heights* (1847). He too attempts to impose an order and an ideology upon a world where he can only stand at the margins, so that the act of writing serves to reveal his own ineffectiveness, while it actually empowers the oral accounts he is trying to suppress. Like Lockwood, Selyf and Hw try to contain elemental forces within a construct of patriarchal rationality, and like him, their attempts only serve to demonstrate the inadequacy of their paradigm.

Both Selyf and Hw, however, become involved emotionally in the dangerous other world, and both learn from their experiences. In *Cells of Knowledge* Hw's marginal glosses seek to contain the subversive nature of Selyf's narrative, as Selyf has already become influenced by his experiences with Marighal. In *Hidden Daughters*, Hw becomes drawn into the other world in spite of himself, and Josiah's glosses give us a third, more empirical perspective on the whole quest. By the end of *Cells of Knowledge*, Hw's resistance too is crumbling, and Selyf's praise of Hw as his son 'unmans' him, to the extent that he too is caught up in the alternative reality. In *Hidden Daughters*, Hw goes on to learn for himself. Both monks are unable, in the end, to fit themselves into the rigid mould prescribed for them. They stray far from the boundaries of the Church into a symbolic wilderness, which some of their brother monks refuse even to contemplate or discuss. However, the later glosses show more sympathy for natural curiosity and scientific interest, giving a further dimension to the irony. It is a pity that in *Hidden Daughters* the glosses are no longer literally marginal (no doubt in order to save printing costs), containing the text on the page as they seek to contain its meaning. Towards the end of *Hidden Daughters* the glosses cease, as if containment were no longer possible. The narrative of *The Last Flight* takes the form of Josiah's enquiry, and the statements of the four witnesses that he cites.

The catalyst that causes the monks to transcend the boundaries of their world is an encounter with the essential nature of woman, and the implications of that for their constructions of gender and sexuality. At the beginning of his first letter, Selyf discusses the accusation that he has 'consorted with demons' (*Cells* p. 16). His answer presents a paradox between two versions of reality:

> When the woman came to us I saw neither demon nor succubus,
> but only a troubled soul thirsting for the truth it had glimpsed
> once in childhood. (p. 16)

The paradox is developed in the arrival of Marighal. She is certainly
a 'troubled woman', who needs help and succour, and yet when she
first knocks at the door she is mistaken for 'Leviathan' (p. 17), the
personification of chaos itself. Marighal comes from the wilderness
beyond the boundaries of the Christian order, and even as she
submits to Christian rule she shows her longing for what is beyond
the pale:

> sometimes she would look sadly back at the hills she had left.
> (p. 19)

This strange mixture of acceptable submission and dangerous wild-
ness sets the stage for the debate concerning Marighal's true nature
which is the central focus of the monks' quest. The similar arrival of
Barve in *Hidden Daughters* recalls the Leviathan image as she arrives
by sea. Her arrival also causes a controversy about womanly nature,
in which the new strain of empiricism and tolerance is first heard,
when Aelfrid the physician says:

> He has not enjoyed your rigorous training, Hw, and is disposed
> to see women as part of God's creation, not as demons waiting
> to drag his soul off to perdition. (p. 39)

It is made abundantly clear that although Marighal and Barve are
supernatural beings, the debate that rages over their nature is about
human woman. The supernatural elements of Marighal are in fact
part of womanly nature, expressed in the symbolism of magic and
uncanny power. This becomes evident when Marighal is driven
away because of her superhuman strength, and Selyf refuses to have
her exorcised on the grounds that she 'might not be a demon' (*Cells*
p. 73). The misogynist monk Cienach, who has cut off his manly
part in order to avoid sexual temptation, replies;

> Do you not know that all womankind, save only the virgin
> saints and sisters are inhabited by demons? You are foolish
> men and impure if you think otherwise. I can tell you what I
> know to be a fact, indisputable, for I have seen it in a vision.
> In the womb there sits a grinning devil, nor is a woman free of
> it unless she takes monastic vows. (p. 73)

He explains why this should be:

it is through woman that evil came into the world, and so it
will always be. (p. 74)

Cienach cannot distinguish between the essence of woman, and
man's reaction to her. It is part of the monastic narrative that
woman and the lust she engenders in men are one and the same
thing, and that woman, simply by existing, is responsible for male
lust. A telling marginal note by Hw shows how lust obsesses the
monks, so they deduce it from the most fragmentary evidence (p.
59). And yet Cienach is quite right: Marighal is indeed the daughter
of a demon, and inherits many of his qualities. The failure to distinguish between male lust and the wiles of woman recurs in *Hidden
Daughters*, in the debates between Hw and Barve. Hw tells Barve:

> The first cause is the perniciousness of women themselves . . . I
> have told you before of the tricks they play to drive men into
> frenzy . . . (p. 121)

He goes on to explain to Barve that for woman the road to sanctity
is to become as much like a man as possible, that is to say, there is
no feminine aspect of God. The final twist to the confusion between
the nature of women and lust in men comes in *The Last Flight*,
when one woman (Branwen) explains to another (Essullt) that she
must take full responsibility for men's lustful feelings towards her:

> You must remember men have their feelings. (p. 85)

Usbathaden is not only demonic, but incontrovertibly male. Marighal
is no representative of matriarchy. In some ways, she and her sisters
live in as profound a subjection in their father's stronghold as in the
cities of the Christian monks. One crucial element of their bondage
is identical: the emphasis on virginity in order to retain their power
and integrity. The giants' daughters must remain virgin, and in
Kynan's narrative, Marighal explains to him why:

> He knows that when you take my virginity he will die . . .
> Throughout the years many men have sought us women in
> marriage, for to wed a giant's daughter will give a man much
> power . . . (*Cells* p. 105)

When Culhuch abducts Olwen, Usbathaden does indeed die. But
before that, the effects of sexual union with a man are made clear
by Usbathaden himself, as he pictures them to his daughter:

> For a woman to be coupled to a man means only that she will

be his slave . . . What will you do then, clever Mari? . . . The freedom of the hills will be taken from you, and your lovely weaving will rot on the loom. All your talk will be on the health of your babes and children, or the state of the harvest. (ibid. p. 50)

The fall of woman through sexual union with a man is echoed by Hw, in his marginal note on Marighal's unconsummated marriage:

> *Rejoice, sister, that your state is untarnished. It would have been far worse to have been left without your innocence, and with a child on you, as too many have found.* (p. 53)

In fact, Usbathaden and the monks seem to be in agreement about the importance of virginity in woman. Ironically, Usbathaden's warning is repeated in almost identical terms at the beginning of *Hidden Daughters*, when the monk Selyf depicts the oppressed life of the married woman to the sisters, whereas the virgin is 'safe from the punishment of Eve'. 'Why', he asks:

> should a woman choose the fate of a clod of dung when she might be numbered among the angels? (p. 44)

Usbathaden's reason for decrying marriage is obvious: his life depends upon it. Perhaps, we are made to conclude, Christian life depends upon it too. Both the pagan giant and the Christian God require sexual containment in women. At this point we come to the central paradox of the novel, which consists in the demolition of constructed oppositions. A reading may begin with the expectation of polarities: good/evil, God/Satan, Christian/pagan, spirit/flesh, male/female. But in each of these oppositions we encounter only the mirror of the other. Marighal comes to the monks seeking grace. In their eyes she is both 'monstrous', and also 'kind and graceful' (*Cells* p. 142). This traditional division of the nature of woman recurs in *Hidden Daughters*, in Hw's extended meditation on the contrasting natures of Mary and Eve. The crucial difference between the two, in Hw's eyes, is Eve's lustful nature, and Mary's complete lack of sexuality (pp. 198–200). Ironically, it may seem that Marighal already possesses grace; certainly she possesses both the freedom from lust and the immortality that are the expected sign and reward of grace. The further irony is that on closer examination she seems already to be the daughter of a being not unlike the

Christian God, and that is precisely why she must protect her virginity as the key to her own identity.

Kynan discusses the nature of Usbathaden when he tells Selyf:

> All the heritage I got from him was a little part of his knowledge and one of his daughters. Terrible he was and ageless, and no one knew the place where he had been born. (*Cells* p. 88)

Usbathaden is creator and father, and also devil. His treatment of the young Kynan and his first playmates is diabolic, and yet to the growing boy he is also a kind of god. But Kynan is his catamite, and the women who mother his daughters die in childbirth. The giant is pitiless in his use of others to feed his own desires. He is also lonely; Kynan tells us that he is the only male person in the stronghold, and cannot create sons. Nor can he penetrate into the inner lives of his daughters. The weaving hall reflects the inner creativity and sexuality of the sisters, and Kynan, unlike their father, is able to penetrate it at last. Marighal tells Kynan:

> Time after time my father has sent his spies to seek a way into this room without success. At first he even made the attempt himself, but his eyes are too weak and his body too big to find the path through the mirror maze. (*Cells* p. 106)

The weakness of the giant's eyes is significant. Both Usbathaden and the Christian God are likened to Othin. Hw wrestles with the power of Othin in Orkney, and he mentions the correlation of Othin with Christ in a marginal note:

> *His followers blasphemously maintain that he was nailed to a tree and hung there for nine days to gain wisdom, and they say that Christ is no better!* (*Cells* p. 26)

Usbathaden is also associated with a sacrifice at a tree. When Kynan, assisted by Marighal, climbs Usbathaden's body in the likeness of a tree, he plucks out one of his eyes, in the form of a magpie's egg. Usbathaden has the wisdom and guile of Othin, and like Othin he loses an eye for such powers. As Othin reflects Usbathaden, so too he reflects the Christ of the monks. And, as we have seen, both the giant and the Christian god require the suppression of lust in men, and the virginity of women, to keep their power. The comparison between Christian and pagan gods does not stop there. In *The Last Flight* Essullt speaks of Mithras, yet another god who sacrifices himself, as kin to her family (p. 203). The presence of the Saracen (alias Merthun) in *The Last Flight* is more problematic, as his place in the plot remains peripheral, and his references to Allah obscure rather than resolve the riddle.

When Usbathaden takes on the likeness of a tree, Kynan takes one of his eyes, but the real sacrifice is not made by the father Usbathaden, but by his daughter Marighal. I have discussed the nature of Marighal's division of her self elsewhere.[13] In the present context, the division of Marighal, as the result of her death and resurrection, into the married woman and the virgin, demonstrates the truth of both Usbathaden's and the Christians' warnings: loss of virginity does indeed mean loss of integrity and immortality, within the confines of this patriarchal world. Thus Usbathaden designs the marriage bed of Kynan and Marighal as a deathbed. They make their escape, at the cost of an unconsummated marriage (*Cells* p. 128). The final consummation of Kynan's marriage with the real Marighal results in the death of Grig, who had held the secrets of the earth in safe, respectful hands.

Usbathaden, like Christ, has no mate. He had one once, but he tells Marighal:

> Many generations ago I left my immortal bride to seek dominion over mankind. (*Cells* p. 130)

Usbathaden now is damaged and divided against himself, and he longs for death (p. 157). The only hint we are given as to the identity of the 'immortal bride' is in the 'gigantic woman' who appears in Selyf's final dream, who weeps tears of blood, and begs her worshippers not to mutilate themselves in her name (p. 183). In *The Last Flight* the feminine aspect of god appears in Christian trappings, when St Brigid or the Virgin Mary appears to help Branwen in childbirth (pp. 68–9). Moreover, Branwen is unable to make clear in her account whether or not they are actually visionary aspects of the child/midwife Essullt, who has been skilled in midwifery for many lifetimes as Usbathaden's daughter. The only other feminine aspect of god is the earth mother worshipped and respectfully exploited by Grig and his brothers. Grig sees the earth and ore of his mine as the flesh and blood of his mother, and she also shows a godlike willingness to sacrifice an eye:

> This is one of my mother's eyes . . . Take it, and know she knows you, the first woman to see her secret self! (p. 67)

But Grig finally prophesies disaster as the result of his mother's willing sacrifice:

> Men, mighty only in their ignorance, rape her till she sighs and
> ceases from her generous fertility. (p. 166)

Otherwise the existence of the feminine principle of supernatural
power is only indicated by the lack caused by her absence. In her
place there is only a pernicious artefact that parodies womanhood,
the mechanical 'queen' hidden in the stronghold, whose very presence makes the sexually mature sisters fall sick. Instead of a supernatural mate, Usbathaden fathers his children on mortal women, in
a gross parody of the Christian Annunciation. He has, it seems,
sacrificed too much to gain dominion over mankind.

Where the gods fail, a mortal man may succeed. Kynan takes on
the role of Theseus and finally penetrates the maze. The distorting
mirrors that challenge his identity finally fail, because

> I looked down at my body, and behold, all was as it should be.
> (p. 103)

But the evidence of men's physical bodies negates the opposition of
man and woman, upon which the whole quest into the nature of
woman has been predicated. In the final pages of the book, Selyf
and Grig engage in a crucial dialogue on the nature of gender. Grig
tells Selyf:

> I saw that each gender, male and female, must carry the seed-
> substance of the other in it. (p. 179)

This threatens the whole structure of Selyf's world, and he replies:

> Male and female were created separately by the Almighty, nor
> should we confuse one with the other, for it is a blasphemy
> against the order He has created. (p. 179)

Hidden Daughters, as I have indicated, sets forth the same questions
as *Cells of Knowledge*, concerning the nature of women, and thereby
of men, and the meaning of gender and sexuality. Barve, like Marighal, arrives in a community of Christian monks, and this sets the
action in train. *Hidden Daughters* contains more debate than *Cells of
Knowledge*, but the action sustains it, as in this section of the trilogy
the quest alters focus. *Cells of Knowledge* is a quest beyond the
conscious, social world of men, into the magical, or indeed the
subconscious. *Hidden Daughters* takes the quest back into society.
Magical powers are carried into the arena of human history. This is

made clear by the sharpened focus on historical action. The Viking invasions come to the fore, in the attacks on the Christian cities; moreover, the Vikings themselves are named, and political relations between secular lords and monastic institutions are made clear. Olvir Brusasson and the monks at Rosnat have come to an agreement (p. 30), for example. The confrontation between the Roman and Celtic church is also specified. Not only history but also geography is more specific. The site of Usbathaden's stronghold is never stated, but the action of *Hidden Daughters* moves on to recognisable ground: Galloway, Strathclyde, the Solway. This is a recognisable tenth-century Britain.

However, the power of women, demonic or human, has not gone away, although it is deliberately subdued in the sisters themselves. The world they belong to still lies outside the bounds of external social realism, but in *Hidden Daughters* their task is to find a place in the human world. The adjustment makes this volume a kind of alternative New Testament, in which the debate (or word) must become manifest, and indeed in *Hidden Daughters* there are explicit New Testament parallels. The theme of sacrifice has already been well established, in the Christ/Othin correlation, and in Marighal's death and resurrection at the tree. In *Hidden Daughters* the nature of sacrifice becomes the central issue, precisely because the daughters of the giant must learn to be human. They deliberately put away their supernatural powers and submit themselves to Christian rule, but they only gradually learn what this requires of them.

When the sisters are leading a nun-like existence on the edges of Kynan's city, they endlessly debate the nature of virtue. The debate dissolves into mere words when they are forced to confront the state of humanity. The human society in which they find themselves is ravaged by pestilence and then by war. Suffering is new to the sisters, but in the plague they discover that there is a connection between love and death. When Derdriu finds a husband and wife clasped together in death, she asks, not without envy:

Is that how humans always die? (p. 50)

Derdriu wishes to experience humanity, while Gunnhild, at the other extreme, tries to retain her purity by keeping herself undefiled by everything human or physical. The sisters, in their long discussions, remain hidden at the edge of humanity; they do not yet belong. They are recognised by the townspeople as demons, when they set about burying the dead after the raid. The people are right, just as Cienach was right to call Marighal a demon. The sisters are demons or furies fulfilling their traditional role. Derdriu's wish to be part of human life transgresses both codes she has learned, both the magical powers of her father's house and the Christianity taught by Selyf. She defies both, in her enjoyment of the sun and the sea breeze on her face (p. 52) (an enjoyment echoed by Essullt in *The Last Flight* (p. 203)) and her curiosity about and appreciation of human life:

> 'It is very difficult to live as a human being,' said Derdriu. (p. 61)

In *The Last Flight*, Essullt echoes her words, seeing the human world as a state of punishment and exile:

> Is that my Penance? That I must go into the world of mankind? (p. 109)

It is a penance, and it also alters the nature of sacrifice. The Othin parallel is carried on into *Hidden Daughters*. When Hw describes his vision of the demon Othin to Barve, she says:

> I thought at first that you were describing my father. (p. 110)

Earlier, the corrupt bishop is hung on a tree with one eye gouged out. Othin's sacrifice was for wisdom: 'Myself for myself', but the real sacrifice required of those who choose humanity is different, as Hw explains to Barve:

> Your sisters died in an attempt to save others. This is sacrifice and as such is never in vain. (p. 125)

The hidden daughters carry their father's body with them into exile, like a macabre version of the ark of the covenant, as well as a travesty of the saintly relics that lie at the heart of a real nunnery. It is the father's foster-son Kynan who is found crucified when the city is destroyed. The sisters take down Kynan's body and wrap him in fine cloth, in a scene familiar from the traditional Christian *pietà*.

However, the major quest and final sacrifice made in the book are those of Barve. Barve and Hw venture all the way into the world of men, in the search for Olwen. Barve undergoes attempted rape, imprisonment, humiliation and finally death at the hands of Culhuch and his 'common kind' of men (p. 117). But Barve cannot die a sacrificial death until she has become fully human, a Kynan rather than an Usbathaden or an Othin. Hw explains unwittingly that it is a human, not a god-like prerogative, to die altruistically:

> That is a wonder of the human heart which I will never understand – they will die for a God. (p. 241)

Barve's death by drowning is reminiscent of pagan trials of the innocence of women, and of the trials by water of those accused of witchcraft. The breaking of her legs suggests her difference from the male Christ, whose body was deliberately left whole; the fact that it is Easter underlines the comparison (p. 247). But although Barve is a woman, Hw prays that her death may also be a baptism, and afterwards he has learned enough to stop Olwen from throwing Kigva on to the pyre with Barve's body:

> 'No,' I cried. 'Do not destroy another, when so many have been destroyed. Your sister died when she knew she could have taken her revenge and saved herself.' (p. 245)

The Last Flight is the final aspect of the quest, in which masculine and feminine finally come together, but in a flawed and terrible union which is to have repercussions through all time to come. The book ends with the sons of Grig, and their use of their mother earth. They are hopeful:

> Of one thing we can be sure, our students and successors will bring about changes on the face of our mother. We think they will give her pleasure. (p. 262)

The irony is obvious; with hindsight the reader realises that the exploitation of the earth is a horrible expression of an unhealed wound in the human psyche. The epilogue of *The Last Flight* forces a re-examination of the significance of the unnatural union between Drust and Essullt.

The weakness of the final part of the trilogy lies in Drust himself. The heir of Usbathaden, the hero of the quest who kills his (grand)father and goes on to an incestuous relationship with Usbathaden's daughter, is hardly short of ancestors. He is Oedipus; he is also Fafnir who tasted the dragon's blood and heard nature speak; he is Beowulf and St George and a hundred other dragon-slayers as well. He is Gunnar of Hliderend who wanted to be a hero without bloodshed; he is St Magnus of Orkney who had every characteristic of a warrior hero except that in the midst of the battle he refused to kill. He is explicitly Tristan, even before he meets

Essullt. It is a pity that with so many magnificent antecedents he should be such a bore, but perhaps it is inevitable, in so far as the novel form is not often kind to the archetypal hero.

Because Drust cannot quite carry the weight of symbolism demanded of him, there is a loss of impetus in *The Last Flight* which makes the conclusion of the quest anti-climactic. The initial shifting of territory to Iceland has a curious effect. The world of the sagas is cleverly evoked, and in particular the dialogue is a brilliant pastiche of the powerful understatement of saga language. But Iceland is not quite alive, as the Britain of the earlier volumes is alive. Like many Scottish historical novels, this one relies upon the evocation of Scotland the place, and the long tradition of invoking demons, devils and supernatural beings as aspects of the spirit of that place. The dragon/volcano in Iceland lacks substance, and as a result the synthesis of the dragon in mythological terms, the father, in psycho-analytical terms, and the volcano, in scientific terms, remains uneasy.

The final testimony of Essullt therefore does not quite resolve the riddle of gender, when she and Drust finally come together in incestuous union. The taboo on sexuality has been lifted at last. Drust is anything but virginal, and Essullt goes on to marriage and parenthood with March. Her submission to Drust when he defeats her in the forest demonstrates the power of lust and fulfils all the warnings of the earlier novels. Essullt does throw away her power and submit to men. She immediately loses stature as a result. Grig's epilogue shows the terrible consequences of her capitulation. In Drust and Essullt we have yet another Adam and Eve, as by their sin they seem to have brought everlasting evil into the world of men.

Perhaps it is asking too much that *The Last Flight* should provide a satisfactory resolution to the riddles propounded in the first two volumes. After all, no one has yet answered the riddle of the nature of gender and sexuality, and Hayton's trilogy is an extraordinary achievement, not because the quest is completed, but because of the enlightening and imaginative way it re-formulates the riddle.

The difference in genres used by McGregor and Hayton should not obscure the similarity of their explorations in fiction. Both writers push back the boundaries of their chosen genre, to make narratives about the external, social world encompass an unconscious, inner world, or, alternatively, in Hayton's case, a magical, supernatural world. The demolition of the boundary between what is within and what lies outside, a conventional fictional construct, is necessarily subversive of the form whose constrictions it calls into question.

The subversion of literary genre inevitably means subversion of the framework upon which that genre is structured. These novels refuse to allow a paradigm of simple oppositions, for example of truth and falsity, reality or imagination. The deconstruction of such polar oppositions is bound to call into question concepts of gender and sexuality based upon the polar opposition of masculine and feminine.

I have called both McGregor's and Hayton's narratives 'quests', because both approach issues of gender and sexuality as riddles, the resolution of which would have enormous implications for our conception of the nature of truth. In each case, the solution of the riddle is the task of a male hero, or heroes. The detective within his genre, and the tenth-century monk within his, are both descendants from the long line of literary heroes which arguably began when Theseus entered the labyrinth. Because the hero is male, the riddle of gender and sexuality becomes objectified in an image of woman. Hayton and McGregor do not reverse the tradition of male/subject trying to read woman/object. They treat their narratives more subtly, and so avoid the trap of merely replacing one hierarchy with its reverse. Instead, both writers use irony to reflect the question back on the one who asked it. If we are to read the hero correctly, we must read his attempt to distinguish between gender and woman. So both McLevy and the monks find in women's consciousness the reflected effects of male sexuality. The question about the nature of woman is a question about the nature of gender and sexuality because it is a man who asked it.

The quest in both cases takes place in a fictional past, but it is not over. Resolution is not possible because the heart of this particular labyrinth has never been reached. Perhaps McGregor reflects that most accurately. Hayton tries eventually to turn her quest into a myth of origin and fall that perhaps explains too much. Drust and Essullt finally seem to suffocate under a weight of meaning, whereas the monks who found riddle after riddle with no final answer kept the reader's attention throughout their inconclusive travels. The nature of detective fiction is that the neat closure offered by discovery of a murderer, and subsequent vindication of everyone else, is never final. We expect the quest to be repeated again and again. McGregor's choice of genre suggests that McLevy will appear satisfactorily in the same role until she is forced to throw him over the Reichenbach Falls. But then he too, like Usbathaden and his daughters, may legitimately hope for resurrection.

NOTES

1. Iona McGregor *Death Wore a Diadem* (London, The Women's Press 1989) and *Alice in Shadowtime* (Edinburgh, Polygon 1992); Sian Hayton *Cells of Knowledge*, *Hidden Daughters* and *The Last Ride* (Edinburgh, Polygon 1989, 1992, 1993 respectively). Subsequent page references are to these editions.
2. See the excerpt from 'Sorties' (originally in Hélène Cixous and Catherine Clément *La Jeune Née* [1975]) translated by Ann Liddle in Elaine Marks and Isabelle de Courtrivon eds *New French Feminisms* (Brighton, Harvester 1981) pp. 90–8.
3. Mary Jacobus 'Reading Woman (Reading)' in *Reading Women: Essays in Feminist Criticism* (London, Methuen 1986) pp. 3–24, here quoted from p. 24.
4. G. Gregory Smith *Scottish Literature: Character and Influence* (London, Macmillan 1919); George Lukács *The Historical Novel* (Harmondsworth, Penguin 1969).
5. But see Alison Smith's chapter in this volume, pp. 28–44.
6. Catherine Belsey 'Constructing the Subject: Deconstructing the Text' in Robyn Warhol and Diane Price Herndl eds *Feminisms: An Anthology of Literary Theory and Criticism* (New Brunswick, Rutgers University Press 1991) p. 605.
7. Ibid. p. 609.
8. Colin Watson *Snobbery with Violence: Crime Stories and Their Audience* (London, Eyre and Spottiswoode 1971).
9. Maggie Humm *Border Traffic: Strategies of Contemporary Women Writers* (Manchester, Manchester University Press 1991) p. 189.
10. Emma Tennant *Two Women of London: The Strange Case of Ms Jekyll and Mrs Hyde* (London and Boston, Faber and Faber 1989).
11. *The Complete Works of Lewis Carroll* (London, Penguin 1988) p. 134.
12. R. L. Stevenson *Dr Jekyll and Mr Hyde and Other Stories* (Everyman, London 1980) p. 5.
13. Margaret Elphinstone 'Contemporary Feminist Fantasy in the Scottish Literary Tradition' in Caroline Gonda ed. *Tea and Leg-Irons: New Feminist Readings from Scotland* (London, Open Letters 1992) pp. 45–59 and in particular pp. 52–3.

7

Barrie and the Extreme Heroine

R. D. S. JACK

'Barrie gives them far more honour than they deserve,
he forgets that women as a whole are far inferior to men.'[1]

James Barrie is not the most obvious writer to appear in a book on
gender. Is he not, after all, a backward-looking, sentimental writer
obsessed by mother figures? These claims can surely be confirmed
from *What Every Woman Knows* (1908), *Quality Street* (1902) and
Margaret Ogilvy (1896). Let us re-examine each of these claims in
relation to the texts cited.[2]

Maggie Shand, the heroine of *What Every Woman Knows,* chooses
to dedicate her life in motherly fashion to her less worthy and less
able husband. She does this at a time when the suffragettes are on
the march. Her choice led a well known anti-suffragette – Mrs
Parker Smith of Glasgow – to use Barrie's title as the heading for a
pamphlet claiming that 'childbearing, menstruation and the meno-
pause ensured that women could never play an equal part in life
with men'.[3] Need any more be said?

How, first of all, does this evidence square with Barrie's vehement
support for the women's movement during his time as leader writer
for the *Nottingham Journal* in 1883 and 1884? He used that column
consistently to champion women's rights generally (for example, 14
December 1883, p. 5); as 'rights' opposed to 'privileges' (for example,
31 January 1883, p. 5); the democratic education of women at
elementary and university levels (for example, 26 June 1883, p. 5
and 26 April 1884, p. 5); the Married Women's Property Act (for
example, 21 June 1883, p. 5); women as political orators (for

example, 2 February 1884, p. 5); women's mental health rights (for example, 4 August 1884, p. 5); women entering the professions on the American model (for example, 27 June 1893, p. 5) and so on.

In the *Nottingham Journal* one may also find the key to this conundrum. Almost as persistent as Barrie's support for the women's movement is his pride in his own education. For men at least, schools and universities in Scotland were open to the lower classes and so gave them greater social mobility than in England. In any battle between his mother's apron strings and his own training, the latter won hands down. Margaret Ogilvy and Kirriemuir seldom saw their most talented son as he went for his early schooling to Glasgow, then did his senior secondary work in Dumfries. University studies in Edinburgh followed and then, immediately, the pursuit of his writing ambitions in Nottingham and London.

In *An Edinburgh Eleven*[4] (1889) the playwright pays tribute to the broad Scottish Ordinary degree and the wide range of erudition it provided. His scientific and anthropological studies encouraged him to apply 'the Darwinean method' to the study of mankind's past and future (*Nottingham Journal* 8 April 1883, p. 5). That is, he viewed the gender question as a Darwinian battle within which the naturally superior sex (woman) was gradually freeing herself from the delimiting restraints imposed upon her by a patriarchal society and male-dominated institutions. As times change, so the opportunities open to women expand. This implies viewing woman's role dynamically in relation to changing political and social realities. 'Now that the ladies of England have clearly seen the folly of hiding their lights under a bushel, mankind will have a lively time of it until they give the so-called weaker sex everything they wish' (*Nottingham Journal* 7 August 1883, p. 5).

How does this evidence apply to *What Every Woman Knows*? Clearly Maggie belongs to an earlier age, to the lower classes and has taught herself everything she knows – including French. The supporters of women's rights as they file into her husband's room at the start of Act 2, have more education, are from the upper class and belong to the new age. Maggie's subverting and manipulative powers are consequently more circumscribed than those ladies whose *actual* names were read aloud in the 1904 acting text as a role of honour (Beinecke W43: III, 1: 'As they enter, the names of Lady Sybil Lazenby, Mrs Rupert Roy etc. are read aloud.').[5] In that text, Maggie also enthuses about their cause to the Comtesse:

COMTESSE: Tell me, who are these women?
MAGGIE: Suffragettes – they are noble ladies who have sworn to get votes for women. (W43, III, 1 p. 1)

Maggie, in her chosen, secondary role makes a more positive practical contribution to the cause than she could have from her position as an open supporter. She dramatically moves Parliament to support a Women's Rights' Bill by having her words read aloud by her husband. Woman, for Barrie, was not only cleverer than man by nature but also more practical in defining where best she could manipulate his simplicity. That, and not the retreat to servility supposed by Mrs Parker Smith, is what Barrie's women 'know'.

Barrie's curt reaction to the proposal that *all* references to the suffragettes be dropped from the 1923 revival of *What Every Woman Knows* corroborates this evidence. To Bright, he replies, 'Your suggestions could not be followed without making it a different play. I want you to understand clearly that it must remain as it is.' (A3; 9 April 1923). This is unsurprising. The first planning Notes for *What Every Woman Knows* define it as concerned with women's 'equal rights with men to earn bread' (A2: 5, f17 Note 12) and the myth that man is stronger or more able than woman (A2: 5, f19 Note 25 and f25 Note 42).

If this suggests that Barrie is forward-looking on women's issues, surely he also wants to get the best of both worlds? Indeed, does he not (in his sentimental, popular dramas such as *Quality Street*) retreat from his political position to placate a popular and conservative audience? There are two separate questions here. The first concerns his view of woman's nature and may conveniently be introduced by quoting from *Quality Street* itself. When Phoebe Throssel finally overthrows all the pent-up frustrations she had endured within the impotent gentility of the Street, she does so to play a role (her own niece) and to fulfil the myriad-mindedness, which – Barrie believes – characterises the female nature:

PHOEBE: Susan, I am tired of being ladylike. I am a young woman still, and to be ladylike is not enough. I wish to be bright thoughtless and merry.[6]

Barrie's earliest autobiographical recollections and first prose works obsessively record his own, male inability to hold to any one personality for any time. Later, this will translate itself into his various alteregos – McConnachie, Anon, etc. It accounts for his tormented student interest in Berkeley's theories on the fragmentation of essence through perception as espoused in the Edinburgh class of metaphysics by Campbell Fraser and recorded in *An Edinburgh Eleven*.[7] If the continuous process of thought is, indeed, the mode of perception and the imaginative man only perceives irregularly and inconstantly through images of things, then the fate of Sentimental Tommy – psychologically fragmented, distanced from life and passion – is already formulated in the mid-1880s. His view of his own impotence stems from these beliefs and is fully explained in both *Sentimental Tommy* (1896) and *Tommy and Grizel* (1900).[8] For the role-player artist, analysing each self-contradictory perception and each enacted feeling as it comes, before passing on to another briefly held role, neither the spontaneity of passion nor the depth of love is possible.

Woman, on the other hand, has *naturally* a complex mind which she controls and uses to manipulate the simple male. Barrie, in *Peter and Wendy*,[9] imagines that mind as a Russian box, holding ever smaller compartments within a controlling ego. As he adds to this the tenet that woman's under-privileged social position has forced her into additional manipulative roles, his 'feminist' position bears comparison with Judith Butler's arguments on gender as performance in *Gender Trouble*.[10]

The second question impinges on Barrie's literary theory. It is seldom adequately emphasised that this was quite complex, as befits Britain's first, fully qualified dramatist-cum-English Literature graduate. Barrie was a product of the first English Literature department in the world – Edinburgh's Department of Rhetoric and Belles Lettres, led by Professor David Masson. Indeed, for a while he hankered after academe. To that end, he wrote long critical articles on Skelton (Beinecke S354) and Nash (Beinecke T63) in which Masson's preferences for artifice over naturalism, poetry over prose, allegory over simple narrative, the conceptual over the actual are all supported by his student.

This is all relevant to the question of how – or indeed whether – Barrie, as working playwright, dependent on the box office to keep him alive, tried to make the notoriously conservative London West End listen to serious radical messages of this sort. Did he not, finally, sacrifice his ideals to sentiment? The *Nottingham Journal* provides a third helpful obsession in the form of 'letters' addressed by its young leader writer to the greatest popular dramatist of all, Shakespeare. Barrie over and over again laments that William was comparatively lucky to be writing in the Renaissance when drama was the main popular mode and not trying to influence the 'frivolitie' in an age of naturalism. More directly, in the *Nottingham Journal* of 24 April 1883, he reminds his readers how low theatrical tastes have sunk. Shakespeare, like himself, was a writer 'from necessity' but 'had he lived to-day he would probably never have written more than one drama. It would have been returned by some Manager as "Not quite up to the mark of the Frivolity"' (p. 5).

His solution, encouraged by Masson's priorities and the Renaissance-based curriculum favoured in his classes, was to profit from Skelton's light handling of allegoric duality, Nash's wit in seriousness and Shakespeare's romance structures. The narrative line might provide sentiment but dislocations in the story-line would signal the serious message to the *cognoscenti*, while imagery subliminally moved the less intelligent to tears as well as laughter. In *Quality Street*, Phoebe may escape the man-made prison of ignorant gentility which is the blue room. But to do so, she has to marry an unworthy man through acting out the role of her own non-existent niece within a fiction. Even then, she is the only one of the entrapped spinsters to escape the street and the genteel innocence in ignorance which defines it. If that is the message of fictive fantasy, how dire the state of the real Miss Phoebes in the real Edwardian world, and little wonder that so many leave the play wondering why they are crying rather than rejoicing.

It will be clear from this that I have reservations about the Oedipal Barrie and the psychological bias of Barrie criticism. None the less, the same author did write a novel purporting to celebrate his mother. Moreover, in *Margaret Ogilvy*, he calls her his only heroine and the source of all his fiction. If this can be taken at face value, then all Barrie's heroines stem from the middle of the nineteenth century and are 'mothers only'. This is certainly the view held by those who derive Barrie's supposed Oedipal complex from the one presumed traumatic moment which constitutes the dramatic opening of *Margaret Ogilvy*.

I do not think Barrie's written evidence *can* be taken at face value as most of his heroines in fact only contain motherliness as one box among the many. Nor is there any reason for us to suppose that the story-line, the biographical method or a personal psychological message are appropriate for an academic author whose extensive critical writings have carefully asked us to substitute polysemy for the first, artifice in fantasy for the second and the five levels of allegory (potentially) for the third. *Margaret Ogilvy* will of course be amenable to sensible psychological analysis as Birkin's work in particular has demonstrated.[11] But it needs to be carefully approached via an awareness of its author's own imposed conventions in artifice.

The more basic question I am posing comes at the psychological level, thus refined. Did Barrie worship his mother as *mother*? Indeed, did he worship her at all? This second question may seem churlish after Birkin's expert biographical account of the playwright's childhood, centring on the death of his elder brother David and the young Barrie's childhood sense of maternal rejection at that time as he tries in vain to substitute himself for that lost, beloved son.

While there is no doubt that his mother exerted a strong and damaging influence over him, the line of argument: Barrie wrote a book (*Margaret Ogilvy*) about his mother in which he says all his characters derive from her; Barrie was incapable of sustaining a sexual relationship; ergo he had a massive Oedipus complex; deserves to be tested against the precise evidence of the text. I believe such a procedure, while not negating the Oedipal interpretation, does provide a different angle on the problem.

Margaret Ogilvy was written and published after Barrie's marriage to Maude Adams in 1894. *Sentimental Tommy* and *Tommy and Grizel* belong to the same period prior to the divorce. As lightly disguised autobiographies of 'the artist as young man' they provide more direct sexual confessions than the book about his mother. But its date suggests that *Margaret Ogilvy* also was motivated by a need to work out the problems of his marriage and the part his mother's influence had played in them. As he explains to Burlingame in a letter composed at the time of its publication, it should be seen not just as 'a little book about my mother' but 'still more about her and me' as 'it is my biography as well' (Barrie/Beinecke, A2: 5 April 1896).

Tommy and Grizel deals most directly with the artist facing and failing the challenge of adult sexuality. It continues the emphasis in *Sentimental Tommy* on the 'many minds' of the dramatic artist. In the later novel, Tommy's inability to love is viewed as a necessary concomitant of the flawed, egotistical personality which has given him literary success. The artist is accustomed to analysing his emotions the moment he feels them, so that they may later serve his writing. Therefore, the concept of an act which defies rational control terrifies him. The narrator comments:

> Ah, if only Tommy could have loved in this way! He would have done it if he could. If we could love by trying no one would ever have been more loved than Grizel. (p. 168)

If analysis stands in the way of spontaneity, role-playing prevents depth. Barrie dramatises Tommy honestly giving way to passion but only briefly. He is unable to sustain mature emotions because he is soon tempted by another sentimental part. Passions, like personalities, he wears and casts off like clothes, knowing that any true feelings are momentary suspensions of disbelief in the game of art rather than signs of enduring love:

> There were times in her company when he forgot that he was wearing borrowed garments, when he went on flame, but he always knew, as now, upon reflection. (p. 340)

The dramatic genius is great because he 'contains multitudes'; Sentimental Tommy in both volumes of his history probes the possibility that multitudes of assumed feelings may be gained by sacrificing spontaneity and depth of passion. 'I cannot speak for myself an hour in advance; I make a vow, as I have done so often before, but it does not help me to know what I may be at before the night is out' (p. 340).

Later in the novel, both aspects of one artist's tragic dilemma are fully explained by Tommy in his confession to Gemmell:

> You know I am a man of sentiment only . . . It has its good points. We are a kindly people. I was perhaps pluming myself on having made a heroic proposal, and though you have made me see it just now as you see it, I shall probably soon be putting on the same grand airs again. Lately I discovered that the children who see me with Grizel call me 'The Man with the Greetin Eyes'! If I have greetin eyes it was real grief that gave them to me, but when I heard what I was called it made me self-conscious, and I have tried to look still more lugubrious ever since. (p. 380)

True feelings exist but they are cut short by analysis and deprived of depth-in-continuity by role-playing.

How does this evidence relate to *Margaret Ogilvy*? First, the fact that Barrie chose to 'sell' such a sentimentalised account of his mother's influence on him is more remarkable than the account of it *per se*. In itself that decision seems to fulfil Barrie's guilty sense of worshipping art more than his mother. This line was anticipated in the *Nottingham Journal* where he laments his *lack* of mother love as evidenced by his flight from Kirriemuir at the first opportunity.

Viewed as metafiction, as Barrie the critic clearly asks us to, the first chapter of *Margaret Ogilvy*, through its very overstatement of 'Look, here's an Oedipal complex!', is itself suspect. (This is a distinction which Jacqueline Rose also makes with regard to *Peter Pan*.[12]) The sentimental topic ('the first great victory in a woman's long campaign') sustained by a melodramatic series of parallel clauses ('how . . . what . . . when . . .') parodies those 'grand airs' of art, which its author so consistently describes as the literary symptom of his own major psychological flaw. Barrie expects us to understand this. His exaggerated rhetoric parodies his own sentimentality in art, valuing strong effects above accuracy. He is not only or primarily saying 'I idolised my mother', but 'Look how I can sentimentalise that love to move you more powerfully!' Sentimental Tommy believed what he wrote only until he had finished writing it and valued the power of melodramatic manipulation above all else. Barrie was, in his own eyes, an ambitious artist first and a mother-worshipper only second.

I think the young artist came to recognise in Margaret Barrie the same egotistical self-dramatising traits which he sadly accepted as the basis for his own genius and that it was in this sense he saw her as the genetic source of all his heroines and the psychological model for their resourcefulness. The focus of the opening chapter in *Margaret Ogilvy* is not on the death of David but on the battle in self-interested, upstaging strategies between Margaret and the young James Matthew. His mother wins hands down. Like the Tommy of the confession scene in *Tommy and Grizel*, she has a real grief, but it becomes a determined and continued illness, supported by the 'prop' of 'the christening robe with its pathetic frills'. This is used to represent the dead child; 'petted' and 'smiled to'. 'She had not made it herself', we are told (pp. 6–9). This is a cynical detail, dissociating it from maternal love and contextualising it as a borrowed garment used by an actress to dramatise her own grief. In the face of this, young James's two 'crafty ways of playing', as physician and clown, are doomed from the outset.[13] What chance has either of these for top-billing in the face of Margaret Barrie re-playing the virgin Mary at the cross? Even in the scene where James enters and merits the spotlight of attention, he sees how a quick change from laughter to tears 'deprived [me] of some of my glory' (p. 11). On this reading, the frequent Biblical images and echoes[14] employed by Barrie in the chapter are not just excesses caused by idolisation of his mother. They also mark a frustrated acceptance that she defeated him in determining the script and seizing the best part. With David dead, Margaret (Mary) of the Sorrows moves to a bed of pain from which she dominated the Kirriemuir play until her death.

Aware that he could not compete, Barrie left, not without guilt, to serve his own sentimental egotisms and practise his mother's manipulative strategies on others. It is surely significant that, both in fiction (*Tommy and Grizel*) and fact (his letters), he reserved his deepest love and respect for his sister, who suffered quietly, naturally and deeply as neither James nor Margaret could. The first chapter of *Margaret Ogilvy* may foreground the actions of son and mother but the narrative voice regularly directs us to find the true Christ parallel in Jane's loving, silent sacrifice.

A thorough study of Barrie's lecture notes, journalism, letters and play drafts is necessary to get a full picture of the man and the writer. Only once they have all been interrelated can the triumphant procession of his 'Russian doll' heroines and their Darwinian battle against patriarchal institutions for the benefit of the species be fully appreciated. In an earlier article, I showed how Barrie systematically re-defined Carlyle's practical definition of the warring political hero and replaced it with a series of dramatic heroines – particularly Becky Sharp (*Becky Sharp* [1893]), Phoebe Throssel (*Quality Street*) and Wendy (*Peter Pan* [1904]).[15] That Barrie should take this view is unsurprising. He willingly accepted Carlyle's ground rules for defining heroism. In the practical battle of life, however, he believed and had consistently argued that woman possessed these powers much more fully.

The crucial criteria presented by the Sage of Ecclefechan in this area of heroism are: (i) dynamism, (ii) the ability to assess oneself honestly and (iii) the power of persuasion. That these are all 'male' character-istics, he does not question. 'The History of the World, I said already, was the Biography of Great Men'.[16] He then produces an all-male line of heroes led by Napoleon to 'confirm' his unexamined premise. Barrie's dramas enact the counter-thesis. For him history is what women have accomplished by letting men believe Carlyle's view. In the Dedication to *Peter Pan*, he defines Wendy as the 'disturbing element',[17] the catalyst of the entire action. She has 'bored her way' into the comfortable all-male games statically presented in the photo-graph collection of *The Boy Castaways of Black Lake Island*[18] and turned them into *her* drama. Phoebe Throssel wins her way out of Quality Street's claustrophobia by understanding in equal measure her own nature and the range of masculine delusion. Becky Sharp is the arch-persuader, routing good, bad, stupid and clever men with equal ease.

But Carlyle has six categories of heroism only one of which, the king, is defined at the level of political action. It is not my claim that the other classifications of divinity, prophet, poet, priest and man of letters are specifically differentiated by Barrie and then claimed for women. But I do assert that he knew Carlyle's work and shared his view that the metaphysical, ethical and artistic dimensions of heroism had to be examined as well as the practical. Barrie, no less than Carlyle, accepted 'this mysterious Universe' and the need to study all aspects of human 'duty and destiny' in relation to that mystery.[19] Like Carlyle, therefore, he saw the Napoleonic combative hero/heroine as only part of the intellectual problem posed. Using three of his plays – *The Ladies' Shakespeare* (1913), *Little Mary* (1903), and *The Adored One* (1913) – I shall show how he tried to present to the popular theatre in London and America a radical vision of the heroine in relation to art, theology and morals.

The Ladies' Shakespeare is a feminist reworking of Shakespeare's *Taming of the Shrew* and so permits a 'simple' beginning in metadrama. It is seldom discussed when the playwright's views on women are being critically considered as it is, to all intents and purposes, un-known. Composed for Maude Adams's 1914 tour of the United States and Canada, it has never been printed. It was given a short matinée run by Beerbohm Tree at Her Majesty's shortly afterwards.[20] Labelled 'A Parody', the Beinecke texts advertise musical settings by Edward German.[21]

It is a model of subtlety and economy within its chosen mode. To adapt another work in order to reverse its apparent moral usually involves awkward transitions and a good deal of re-writing cum explication. Barrie's claim to have turned a Renaissance celebration of male dominance into an exemplary feminist tale suitable for the age of the new woman by changing only three words in Shakespeare's original proves somewhat exaggerated. But it is not far from the truth.

His major strategy is to feign a naturalist interpretation of the front-of-curtain scenes involving Sly the tailor. The 'play' which suffers only three word changes therefore effectively means the 'play within the play'. Sly disappears, and with him any associated sugges-tion that Shakespeare wished to present a play teaching women to endure male subjugation. That was Sly's perverted vision at work. Kate and her father take Sly's place in the front-of-curtain scenes, which precede each of the play's three acts. Prior to Act I, they reveal that 'this play was first performed before one Sly, a tinker, who being drunk entirely mistook its purport, the which did so amuse Will that he proclaimed "Let it ever be presented as thro' the eyes of Sly, until women come to their own and do me the honour of reading my tale aright"'.

Kate assumes the roles of explicator, producer and stage manager rolled into one. Her father plays a quietly supportive part. In particular, they discuss how easy it is to manipulate a braggart in the Petruchio[22] mould. The key is, simply, to demand of him what you do not want him to do. Kate comments, 'So thick his skull that I have but to say "I will not wed thee, I will not be tamed", when at once he'll roar, "Thou shalt!"' In short, a comic humour is defined in Bergsonian terms. As foreseeable puppet, Petruchio is easily manipulated and so becomes the butt of all laughter in Barrie's version. Later front-of-curtain scenes add brief details to keep the audience in touch with developments in planning but in essence the change from Sly to Kate as commentator gives to woman those heroic qualities of understanding and control over the action which Carlyle's *On Heroes, Hero-Worship and the Heroic in History* had reserved for men.

Barrie's acting text for the 'play within the play' consists of a cut-up version of the Temple Classics *Taming of the Shrew* pasted to the page. The ordering of scenes is sometimes changed; lines are excised; individual exchanges from one scene may be transferred to another. But the text as spoken follows Shakespeare's lines exactly.

The second re-definition of what constituted Shakespeare's play comes with the omission of the entire Bianca sub-plot. ('Baptista: The love-sick tale of Bianca, we shall not perform, for Will did not write it and it is intolerably dull.') Only where her presence impinges on Kate is her dialogue retained. The front-of-curtain scene re-defines her role. She is her sister's ally throughout rather than her rival. When, in Shakespeare's Act II Scene 1 for example, Bianca is seen fleeing in terror from Kate, Barrie's stage directions advise the actresses to reveal 'from their manner [that] the two sisters are very fond of each other'. Bianca lends Kate the handkerchief with which to tie her wrists and they play out a conscious act for Petruchio, who is eavesdropping.

This drastic reduction of the sub-plot shortens the playing time and so permits Barrie to introduce some extended miming sequences as well as the longer, explicatory front-of-curtain-scene discussions. The mimes are designed to re-contextualise events, giving superiority in power to Kate. When Shakespeare has Petruchio imprison his wife without food, for example, Barrie's stage direction reads:

> After the bed has been made etc, he locks door from outside, she from inside and then produces from her luggage little packages containing a choice meal and cutlery. Back to luggage and out with cushion. Thus propped comfortably she continues in matter of fact manner to eat meal. He makes his noises. He opens door from outside and so cannot get in. She continues to eat.

Another mime reveals her taking the clothes, which he will later maliciously destroy, out of the case. Kate is to try them on in a manner indicating how much she hates them. She then puts them back 'and the scene goes on as in play without alteration to the end of the scene, but of course Kate is now pretending she likes things in order to turn him against them, and she is secretly delighted when he destroys them'. In this way silences hilariously conspire with Kate and Baptista to turn the dramatic tables on Petruchio.

The infamous Act V Scene 2, where Shakespeare makes woman parade her obedience to man, becomes Act 3 of *The Ladies' Shakespeare*. Barrie advocates that the opening be played with the company sitting backstage at a raised table. The stage directions confess that three words in the original have been altered. They then direct the company's attention to the lines which have been deleted from the text and tell the actresses to leave the table and descend to the front-stage area, 'quite in manner of moderns going from dining to drawing-room and leaving the gentlemen – a sort of burlesque of the procedure'. This of course additionally implies that Barrie has permitted himself one further dramatic licence – giving the men's speeches to the women and vice versa. The effect is to make the bet a female one and docile obedience a male characteristic.

The three word changes promised are, more accurately, three word-substitutions with one word added. 'Wife' and 'husband', 'master and mistress', 'he/him and she/her' are consistently interchanged. Kate orders Petruchio *not* to appear when it is her turn to demonstrate male servility.[23] This last change from 'Go to your mistress, Say I command her come to me' to 'Go to your master, Say I command him NOT to come to me' subtly underlines just how completely the gender tables have been turned. The erstwhile infallible method of controlling male chauvinism by demanding of it what you do not want, finally becomes the most complete proof of Petruchio's new servility. Offered the opportunity to avoid making his humility public, he chooses to advertise it.

If Barrie rather overstates his case in suggesting complete fidelity to *The Taming of the Shrew*, the original text is closely followed and the additions become part of the comedy rather than standing awkwardly outside it as explications. Only one further cut need be noted. It is only advisory, but of some interest in showing with what care Barrie was following through imaginatively the logic of his own world upside down. 'Probably the last ten lines will be omitted.' This would end *The Ladies' Shakespeare* with Petruchio for once saying one of his own Shakespearian speeches ('Come Kate we'll to bed . . .'). Even here, however, Barrie suggests this last dramatic focus may be taken from him. Instead, the last laugh could literally go to Kate's co-conspirator, Baptista. 'He (Petruchio) exits with her triumphant, the others follow amazed. Baptista is left alone, his eyes on the ground. He slowly raises his head and grins at the audience.'

Minimal the textual alterations may be, but the tables have been turned so that a play putting woman in her hierarchical Renaissance place becomes a prophecy that, in Barrie's own day, this hierarchy will be inverted. In the comparative safeness of Renaissance artifice, he demonstrates the power of the woman actress creating her own text to stage-manage men in accordance with her greater capacities in imagination and intellect. His own views on this subject are clear – only social structures have so far constrained woman from exercising a power in domination much greater than any conceived by the simple mind of men. Once women get their rights 'mankind will have a lively time of it until they give the so-called weaker sex everything they want' (*Nottingham Journal* 7 July 1883, p. 5). The artistic, theological and ethical implications of this changing situation he had already dramatised from the viewpoints of conventional virtue and Darwinian competitiveness in *Little Mary* and *The Adored One* respectively.

Actresses have a special place in Barrie's theories on woman's 'Russian box' mind. As early as the mid 1880s he had written a quasi-sociological treatise entitled 'Women Who Work' (Beinecke W67). In it he breaks down current payment for actresses in the West End, proving that only 3 out of every 200 earn a living wage. He suggests the idea of house-husbands to make the peculiar lot of the actress better. 'It is perhaps fitting that on stage the natural order of things should be reversed, and that the wife should support the husband instead of the husband the wife.'

In this article, there also appears for the first time his concern over the psychological health of actresses. The acting profession involves the unnatural addition of assumed roles to those already contained in woman's 'Russian box' mind. There is a danger that these may destroy the usual female control of their variety, bursting the outermost box. This is precisely the sad theme of Barrie's memoir, 'The Hunt for Mrs Lapraik' composed about 1913.[24] Haunted by her natural self but unable to sacrifice the glory of her professional roles, an actress vividly describes her own mental breakdown. The one act play, *Rosalind* (1912), had presented a happier alternative. The leading lady when 'resting' adopts the old, comfortable personality she might have become. Refreshed, she can then return to the unconnected roles and perpetual youth demanded of a leading lady. Whatever the outcome suggested, the theme shared by all these works depends upon the dual premise that Barrie saw heroism as primarily a female domain and founded her superiority over the male on a greater capacity to contain and assume, 'in *her* time . . . many parts'.

At first sight, the only obvious similarity between *The Ladies' Shakespeare* and Barrie's riddle-play, *Little Mary*, would seem to be their very brief period in the theatrical spotlight. A brief résumé of the latter's plot is unlikely to change that initial view. Its overtly bizarre story opens in a chemist's shop. The old chemist, also associated with magic and alchemy, is an Irishman (Terence Reilly). In the opening scene, an English peer (Lord Carlton) meets his granddaughter, a twelve-year-old girl (Moira Loney). She divides her time between mothering a crèche and studying her grandfather's three-volume thesis on how to cure the English upper classes of their unspecified 'illness'. When next we meet Moira and Carlton, six years have elapsed and the grandfather has died. Moira, with the thesis as her medium, is trying to cure Lady Millicent Carlton, who has gone into a decline, following an unhappy romance. She succeeds in bringing the entire family into a healthier way of life but, at the height of her triumph and against her grandfather's advice, she reveals the root of their problem – the stomach. Hearing this, the aristocrats deny her. Only Lord Carlton remains an ally. He proposes marriage, so diverting potential tragedy at the last moment.

While most of Barrie's plays work on different sentential levels, *Little Mary* is the only one which follows Dante's fully allegorised structure.[25] As a student, its author had become an enthusiast for

Renaissance drama – Shakespeare primarily, but also Skelton. In a lengthy article on the latter (Beinecke, S354) he discussed allegorical techniques and in this, his only 'Divine' Comedy until *The Boy David*, he adopts a five-level allegoric structure centred on Reilly's claim to have discovered the *Quint*essence. Translated into Carlyle's terms, this implies that 'Moira Loney' must represent A L L the heroic categories, from divine to martial.

Moira's *name* is defined on five distinguished, if overlapping, referential levels: those of theology, ethics, politics, aesthetics and romance. She is called Moira *Loney* (alone; the loner) to associate her nominally, at the personal romantic level, with the problems of solitude in sacrifice of the missionary heroine. As *Maire* (the Irish Gaelic form of Mary) she involves herself in the politics of the Irish Question, and the ethical questions arising from it. (This topic had formed the substance of many of Barrie's leader columns in the *Nottingham Journal*.) Specifically, the play questions whether an effete, gluttonous, lethargic English upper class has the moral right or the political understanding to legislate successfully for hard working starving Ireland. (Another favoured *Nottingham Journal* topic.) Aesthetically, *little* Mary obeys an alchemist-grandfather created by Barrie and modelled on Ibsen; ontologically, little *Mary* serves a mystic figure with a long beard who is defined through three books – a trinity of the word.

This fivefold interpretation is founded securely on Barrie's own words as set out in his planning Notebooks and followed, as this ambitious aim evolves, into the early drafts of the play. At both stages (Notebooks and drafts), names are introduced, cancelled out, re-introduced, changed again, as Barrie seeks to find the one with the widest referential resonance.

To match the quintuple allegorical references of the heroine's name, her role as a 'Medium' is also defined in five senses. *The Medium* is the title of Reilly's three-volume thesis and the sub-title of Barrie's play. The play strongly argues the impossibility of fulfilling that ideal in practical living. As servant of the mystic word, Moira Loney cannot also fulfil the romantic and maternal instincts of a loving personality. She must devote herself entirely to teaching that word and curing mankind of its ills. In the workaday world, she may be a new woman with a full-time job as teacher-physician explaining political and ethical truths to her ignorant patients. But she does so as servant of a man's will, at the expense of her own womanly needs. The inadequacy of words as an artist's medium has also been examined, particularly in the sub-plot, with its continual references to Shakespeare's 'all interpretation is misinterpretation' play, *Much Ado About Nothing*. In the final act of *Little Mary*, this line is highlighted and adds a further tragic dimension to the virgin-heroine's dilemma. There, the cure as 'stomach', is furiously rejected by those who do not wish to hear 'the bitter unpalatable truth'.

> ELEANOR: Really, I never heard of such a thing.
> LADY MILLICENT: Disgusting! Preposterous![26]

A proselytiser's sacrifice may not only be destructive and servile; it may also be pointless.

The definitive text clearly enacts the quintuple sense of Moira's nature and role but, significantly, does not explain her cure, the stomach, in five senses. An incomplete pattern of quintuply defined character preaching quintessentially defined text with only one message emerges from the only available printed version.

In the late Medieval and early Renaissance texts which formed the majority of the syllabus at Edinburgh University, clues to the riddles of allegory were usually signed by oddities of this sort on the surface narrative level. The first such oddity in *Little Mary*, advertised as a dramatic riddle, might be posed as follows: 'If the answer's so simple, why is grandfather's three-volume thesis so long?' The version heard by the first-night audience provides a less covert answer to both problems.[27] It has Lord Carlton secretly reading parts of Reilly's work. He is then caught consulting a Greek dictionary, where he finds 'phrenos', the Greek word for stomach, signifying the seat of the emotions (romance), the will (political, ethical) and the spirit (theological). As this leads to a realisation that he has been working on a false understanding of language (aesthetic), all five levels 'meet' in the cure as well. Moira as type of the Virgin is also more explicitly seen as ushering in the Word as Trinity. The conceptual quintessential pattern for a Divine Comedy is complete and a linguistic side to Reilly's research-in-depth uncovered.

Unsurprisingly, all this was too much and too subtle for West End audiences. Shaw was one of the very few who saw the play's complexity, at least at the political, sociological, and literary/linguistic levels of interpretation. He hailed *Little Mary* as proof that Barrie was a serious, adventurously radical writer. For Shaw, it is 'a didactic lark compared to which my most wayward exploits are conventional, stagey and old-fashioned'.[28] Less than a year after *Little Mary*, he composed his own 'Irish Question' play, *John Bull's Little Island*, to compete with the political line in Barrie's earlier drama.

But Shaw knew from experience that philosophy and the popular stage did not mix easily: 'it is not too much to say that it is only by a capacity for succeeding in spite of its philosophy that a dramatic work of serious import can become popular'.[29] Barrie's 'heaviest' play failed to carry its fivefold message across the footlights, ironically becoming a proof of its own central tenet, that those who cannot understand reject the complex out of misunderstanding or self-protection. The helpful narrative oddities were in particular condemned by critics, so he literally deconstructed the play, removing those aids. In his own lifetime, he refused to allow *Little Mary* to be published, preferring that it enact its own message by disappearing.

In this chapter, my concern is with the theological, Marian line of enquiry. Moira does wear a Napoleonic hat as visual sign that she represents the active heroine-ism of Carlyle's martial heroes. Along with the working actress of the sub-plot (Moira Gray), she enacts the contrasts between new working woman and the old decorative one, politically and artistically. But the new argument in *Little Mary* concerns the heroine as woman-priest, woman-prophet and woman-divinity; on that I shall concentrate.

In *Alone of All Her Kind*, Marina Warner perceptively distinguishes between God and Mary at the anagogical level. Each is a mystery of reconciliation beyond reasoning. 'But unlike the myth of the incarnate God, the myth of the Virgin Mother is translated into moral exhortation'.[30] Moira Loney is frequently compared imagistically and via Biblical references to the Virgin. Barrie's allegoric-fantastic structure permits him to make the same careful distinctions between Mary as icon and Mary as political counter. On one level, Moira is unique and valuable, the perfect realisation of the Christian ideal of minister-servant. She herself enjoys that role and never doubts her value within that definition. Equally, however, she becomes more and more conscious as she grows older of something which is clearly spelt out in the first scene. The Word is male. It is composed by and defines her grandfather and she must preach it so that he may be confirmed in immortality (divinity).

> REILLY: This (*the Book*) is what I have grown into – in this I
> shall pass young and hale down the ages.

Barrie's choice of the fantastic mode permits him to move beyond actuality. He can invent extreme situations to test his chosen 'case' thoroughly and absolutely. Not only does Reilly ask for sacrifice in service from his granddaughter; he has already killed her mother and alienated her grandmother:

> REILLY: They tired of it – they hated the book. It was because I experimented upon them. They didn't like that. Women are strange.[31]

The twelve-year-old Moira is thrilled by the Joan of Arc model he holds out. She cannot, at this stage, relate his warning that 'Self must be sacrificed and all your aspirations turned into the path of duty', to anything other than love and motherhood as games. Her ultimately insoluble problem comes with adulthood.

This approach explains why *Little Mary*, like *Peter Pan* a year later, opens with childhood games prefiguring birth, love and death. Barrie's theme demands that first we see young Moira *playing* at being a mother in her crèche and flirting passionately with Lord Carlton. Once she grows up and is committed to Reilly's word, the sexual tragedy defined by her prototype, the Virgin Mother, will relentlessly be pursued. A series of dialogues show games becoming life, words becoming experience:

> MOIRA (*woefully*): I can do – almost anything. I suppose I am the most remarkable woman alive. (*Smiling*) But – I don't want to be. (*Passionately*) I should so love to be an ordinary woman.
>
> LORD CARLTON: You'll never be that.
>
> MOIRA (*crushed*): Oh! Oh! (*Weeps*)
>
> LADY GEORGY: David – (*to Moira*) My dear, how can you cry in the moment of your triumph?
>
> MOIRA: I don't want to triumph, I want to be loved. I can't do without everybody loving me.[32]

This is a precise, dramatic evocation of Warner's argument that men 'use' the passive, proselytising Marian idea, to locate women as servants within a hierarchical model of society, created by a Man-God. In his conclusion, as so often, Barrie allows us to see a new dream. Carlton, having understood her problem and the complexity of her psyche's demands for a servant, father, husband, child offers to be all these things to her. He will become her medium as romantically fulfilled new working woman-priest -- a comic end dramatically presented as one possibility. The tragic truth is enacted in the huge gap between joyous, imagined hope on stage and our knowledge of the impossibility of realising it in life.

Naturalist critics see this as sentimental escapism and, on the narrative level, this is true. But to define the dramatic experience, without allowing for the audience's role and reading only the bottom line of the text, is akin to assessing a symphony on its 'tune'. First, marriage between Lord Carlton's text and Moira's text has never been claimed, by their creator, to be anything other than that – a verbal solution to a 'case' tragically imagined in art. This particular, happy outcome is validated by the conventions of 'Let us suppose' and not of 'I believe this to be'.

Secondly, the mythic mode permits antithetical extremes of absolute misery and joy to be posited and counterpointed. This is because Barrie (following Masson's Aristotelianism) sees art as quidditatively concerned with using one case in its fullest probable range, in order to move his audience. Emotively, the more the sympathetic viewer-listener rejoices at the chosen conclusion to *Little Mary*, the more he is likely to understand the bleakness of its author's perspective. As Sheila Kaye-Smith shrewdly put it:

> [Barrie] has been inspired to see that the greatest tragedy of human life to-day is that its tragedy cannot be faced, that it can only be shown to us by a trick.[33]

When one further considers that, even within this trick, both Barrie and Moira have their messages cruelly rejected by their chosen audiences, the common 'escapist' view of the playwright threatens to return with doubled force on the heads of its perpetrators. Whose is the comfort in myth? Barrie's in escapism or theirs in wishing so to believe?

As a man who believed his own myriad-mindedness had more in common with the female than the male perspective and as an artist working within a comprehensive, questioning mode, Barrie starts from the position that all human personality is a mixture of male and female. As mirroring, questioning, Edwardian playwright, it is inevitable that at times his methods of presentation will differ from even those twentieth-century feminists with whom he is in broad agreement and it is no part of my purpose to exaggerate the parallels. Broadly, he sees the issues of the Marian dilemma in the same way as Marina Warner, but his dramatic position and Russian box model for the female psyche lead to his comprehending potentially where she sets up polarities sociologically. Warner comments, 'The Virgin

Mary is not the innate archetype of female nature, the dream incarnate; she is the instrument of a dynamic argument from the Catholic
Church about the structure of society, presented as God-given code'
(p. 338). Barrie's reaction would have at least three constituent
parts. He would accept the distinction and the need to make it.
Indeed, *Little Mary* starts from an awareness of the conflicting
demands made on the servant-heroine as that model is tested in
action. Next, he would distinguish the sociological, evaluative mode
espoused by Warner, from his own questioning, exploratory one.
He is concerned with 'both . . . and . . . maybe' rather than 'either
. . . or . . . actually'. Shaw's dramas in conception and methodology
are closer to Warner's methods here. Finally, there is the conceptual
difference. Barrie believed that woman could achieve in potential
any one archetype, Dante's included. It was only the limited human
state in individuality within time which forced different women at
different times to choose which they could most effectively realise
amongst them.

What is equally clear is his belief that only patriarchal social
structures have so far controlled woman's potential in power. Having
deeper understanding in multiple self-definition, woman finds man
simple-minded in two senses (single and gullible). So far, however,
she has had to work within the constraints of male dominance.
Now, he foresees, the social game must change: 'The one excellent
reason why women should continue calling for their rights is that
they are sure in the long run to get them' (*Nottingham Journal* 14
December 1883, p. 5). But this poses a different ethical problem.
As woman's multiple personality with its greater manipulative powers
is, progressively, allowed to participate in political areas from which,
previously, it had been excluded, what will happen when women
with a will to power rather than service are so released?

Dramatically, Barrie had already explored the question of the egotistical, manipulative heroine constrained by social structures. In the
Notebook for 1892, he called Thackeray's Becky Sharp 'the Napoleon
of fiction'.[34] He did so because Napoleon is, for Barrie, the type of
the diminutive, socially disadvantaged, self-interested hero. He became Britain's 'Ogre' and Emperor of France from lower-class origins
on the Corsican fringe of that Empire. Barrie wrote *Nottingham
Journal* leaders on Napoleon with suspicious frequency, because he
saw in the Little Corporal his own stature, birth and nature writ
large. And the parallel, as the evidence of the autobiographical

novels confirms, was not an uncritical one. If Barrie came from Celtic lower-class origins and enjoyed comparing the obstacles they had both overcome, he knew also their shared egoism in ruthless ambition.

Barrie's one act drama. *Becky Sharp* (Beinecke B42) pre-dates *The Adored One* (1913) by twenty years. His other study of the Napoleonic literary heroine, Lady de Winter in *Pages from Dumas* (Beinecke P34) does not appear until 1917. Barrie's admiration for woman's capacity to subvert society through myriad-mindedness and role-playing is no passing fancy but a deeply held belief, which influenced his prose and drama from youth until death. Lady de Winter has greater freedom than Becky due to her higher rank and is, in Barrie's version, defeated only by greater physical male power. These are, however, one act plays with stories controlled by the texts of Thackeray and Dumas. Only in the full-length, original tale of *The Adored One* does he offer an extended study of the egotistical heroine conceived at the limits of imaginative possibility.

In it, a more equal society has not yet arrived but its imminence and desirability is accepted by men and women alike. Its heroine, Leonora, is as relentless a representative of the 'will to dominate' as Moira Loney is of the 'will to serve'. The conventions of fantasy permit polarities of character in potential to represent the logical extremes of theory. In Moira or Leonora we watch specific dramatic embodiments of the dialectical strategy, 'Suppose the case were carried to its furthest extreme'. Suppose social equality does arrive, Barrie asks, what chance does the weaker male of the species have against a Darwinian rather than a Christian heroine? If he is no match for the power-in-submission of Moira Loney, Phoebe Throssel or Maggie Wylie, there can be no contest when he faces for the first time a woman who wills her own success in the battle for supremacy. As with his feminist reworking of *The Taming of the Shrew*, Barrie's daring Edwardian dramatic fancying has become an actual political concern in the later twentieth century.

Barrie knew that he could not raise such radical issues directly within the popular theatre. His audience still lived under the delusion that no new age was coming. How could he confront them with a study of the female will to domination, when they had already rejected in misunderstanding the benevolent version of his premise in *Little Mary*? The answer, on the evidence of *The Adored One*, is that he could not. Usually he started with an overtly radical text and then accommodated it to the limitations of his audience. Here he lost the battle before he began, trying to appease through farce while addressing no less serious a topic than the capacity of a clever murderess to subvert the law.

Four different versions of the plot survive, each evidence of Barrie's own artistic Never Land at its bleakest. To accommodate radical thought and complex literary theory to the needs of the West End box office involves more concessions the more complex and more radical your thought becomes. In one sense Barrie's road to his own Never Land of artistic failure ends most disastrously with this text in its various forms.

The four texts in question (with audience reactions appended) are: (1) *The Adored One: A Legend of the Old Bailey* (Barrie/BL: LCP1913/28) played on the first night, 4 September at the Duke of York's – disaster, actors booed at final curtain call; (2) a speedily revised version, under the same title (Barrie/BL: LCP1913/28a) which went into performance on 28 September – less disastrous, but only sustaining its run until 24 November; (3) the American version entitled *The Legend of Leonora* (Barrie/Beinecke 144) which ran for 136 performances at the Empire Theatre, New York, opening on 5 January 1914 – a limited success and (4) the revised version of Act One alone, *Seven Women: or Leonora*,[35] which opened at the New Theatre on 7 April 1917 – another success.

What, then, was this Legend, or holy story, all about? It is easiest to begin by comparing (1) with (4). The first Act, in both its 1913 and 1917 forms, is Barrie's most explicit dramatic transformation of his Russian doll model for woman's psyche. Captain Rattray, recently returned from abroad and so a socially innocent *persona*, is warned that his friend Tovey has invited seven women to meet him. Their varied characters are listed, first in the dialogue of the two friends and then in the Captain's attempt to memorise them. Leonora enters and, in turn, makes Rattray believe she is the clinging woman of earlier days, the new educated suffragette (who has emerged during his absence), the mother, the coquette, the humourless woman, the humourful woman and the murderess. Finally, it is revealed, that she is the *only* female guest, containing all the other roles within her multiple personality. The novelty here is the directness with which the female psyche's complexity is translated into the conventions of the theatre. Practically all Barrie's earlier heroines in prose and drama have this capacity for role-playing. Why was this old ground so precisely re-traced?

Because the extreme case from the dominant perspective was to be dramatically examined to 'balance' *Little Mary*. Democratic America understood this; class-ridden England did not. As *The New York Times* of 16 August anticipated, Barrie's heroine would be 'a suffragist . . . and the clash of her will against a man's is understood to have provided him with his theme' (p. 1). Discussion of the three major differences between the Act as written for Version 1 as against Version 4 will help to explain Barrie's thinking and account for the same journalist wondering, on 5 September, how someone as 'wayward, inconsequential and feeble-minded' as Leonora could possibly 'show that a new spirit had grown up among women' (p. 4). Barrie was about to overestimate the subtlety of critics and audience once more.

As a first step in the presentation of so daring a study, the Mr and Mrs Tovey of the 1913 version were firmly established as literary types of the gender war by linking them clearly with their dramatic originals, Punch and Judy. In the Lord Chamberlain's text, for example, the stage directions instruct Tovey to make 'Punch-like dabs' at his wife with a 'rolled-up paper like *The Sketch*' (BM28: I.2). As in the first version of *Peter Pan*, this was consciously done to represent the Darwinian battle between the genders. It also signed allegory and artifice rather than naturalism. As with *Peter Pan*, only a few critics understood the code and approved. The rest applied naturalist criteria anyway and were furious in their wrong-headed bafflement.

Specific references to the suffragette movement abound in Version 1. There are fewer in Version 2 in deference to the London audience's desire to remain undisturbed; even fewer for Version 3 as the work became Americanised and practically none for Version 4, which gives up the extreme case of the wilful, unapologetic murderess and only re-states woman's psychic complexity.

The opening scene in *The Adored One* asks particular questions about a particular political movement, whose ultimate success, the playwright believed, was merited and guaranteed but whose militant tendencies worried him.[36] Leonora reveals that she has thrown a man out of a railway carriage to his death because he would not put up the window. As her daughter had a cold, she felt quite justified in murdering him despite his polite remonstration that he had a headache. The slightest opposition to her will has met with the most extreme punishment. Barrie is therefore following his, by now normal, dramatic procedure of using an extreme, imagined 'case' to warn polite society that it is about to face a social revolution. The men in his audience, in particular, are being warned that there will be wilful heroines let loose by this new regime with greater potential psychic power than Napoleon.

The plot of Acts Two and Three as presented on that first night had much in common with Gilbert's *Trial by Jury*. A male judge, male lawyers and male jury face an open and shut case. Leonora is clearly guilty, but, in a series of farcical scenes, they fall victim to her manipulative charms, deny the law and acquit her. Barrie's analytic mind, however, relates the general farce to the seven roles in which, successively, Laura has manipulated Rattray in Act One. Now she has a greater challenge. As the most evil, a murderess, she uses each and all of the other roles to turn an entire court of law into puppets of her will.

To gain her freedom, she usually poses as the helpless, clinging woman because that is the role which most appeals to the male ego. It is also the role which Barrie in his planning Notes for *What Every Woman Knows* specifically isolated as assumed rather than natural, 'Note 13: There are all kinds of women *except* adoring ones' (A2, 5: f15). Leonora, we are told, is a Girton graduate and a new woman. Effortlessly, she turns the male models and the laws of a past age to her own advantage. Whenever a change in tactics is needed or knowledge of the law serves her purpose, she reveals her university training. She uses humourlessness in apparent misunderstanding to trap the prosecuting lawyer, only a moment later to charm him with sycophantic laughter at his weakest jokes. She imitates Margaret Barrie's self-dramatising strategies in having pathetic props (for example, a child's sock) when the role of the mother needs pathetic underlining. As a beautiful woman with all the arts of the coquette, she seduces Rattray, the judge and the entire jury.

The subtlest irony, however, is reserved for the summing up. The judge accurately defines the moment of social change within which the events have taken place but he remains completely oblivious to Leonora's devious nature.

> You are not of to-day, foolish, wayward, unselfconscious, communicative Leonora. The ladies of to-day are different, and the future lies with them – not with you. (B128: III.28)

In fact, she has shown how woman may conquer male society while still entrapped by its institutions. As the conclusion to a torrent of sophistry, ending in a blatantly illegal judgment, his opinions have already been subverted.

Only women in the play see Leonora in her true colours. Mrs Tovey, in particular, is the voice of understanding, pointing out to those who wish to hear just how far the mask of open innocence in ignorance conceals a very different, manipulative nature. She it is who comments: 'Though she (Leonora) has a gracious manner which makes one think her peculiarly open – almost a bewildering childishness . . . despite all that, I believe we confide in her more than she does in us' (B128: II.14). To the idea that Leonora can be summed up as a childish innocent, Mrs Tovey provides the crucial anecdotal counterpoint. 'We were at Girton together' (B128:II.11).

The planning of Version 1 and its place in Barrie's evolving examination of woman's heroism in superiority is quite clear. Within the battle of the species, Judy is capable of thrashing Punch. This is now possible because society is changing. In most cases this advance is something to be welcomed without question; woman's greater abilities will accelerate the evolutionary process. *The Adored One*, by way of dialectical counterpoint, shows how a resourceful, amoral heroine can turn the most conservative and supposedly rational of all social institutions, the law, upside down before that new system has come into being. Leonora kills a man for a supposed slight, seduces an entire courtroom to pervert the course of justice and is applauded for the very characteristics she least possesses.

Some critics did see this. On 10 September 1913, the reviewer in *Era* linked Barrie with Shaw. They had both demonstrated that women with the acting ability and physical charms of Leonora, 'rule the world. For her, man will put aside all laws, will perjure himself, will count himself blessed to be allowed to die for her' (p. 19). But the sanguine prophecy of *The Atheneum* on 13 September that 'only the very stupid will succeed in missing the underlying satire of our ways of regarding women and usage' (p. 262) overrated not only the intellectual curiosity of West End audiences but the acuity of most of his colleagues.

Barrie had become used to his more radical ideas being misunderstood by that group. With *Little Mary* he had satisfied his bruised ego by deconstructing the original text and replacing it with the one the 'frivolitie' deserved. The re-writing of *The Adored One* carries this process a stage further. His revision after the first-night booing was so speedily put into production that it may well have been composed in advance. In Version 2, not only is the entire trial scene turned into a dream by Rattray, it parodically confirms every one of the romantic motifs Version 1 had hilariously satirised.

Leonora is now *not* a Girton graduate. (Mrs Tovey's reference is excised along with those lines which revealed her academic training) and the whole court scene becomes Rattray's dream. After a shortened version of the trial scene, she emerges in real life shelling peas in an idyllic garden outside a rustic cottage. Here, she is reconstituted as the clinging woman the audience wanted and would now pay in larger numbers to see. She sings pastoral verses of excruciating winsomeness. ('A garden is a lonesome thing, God wot,/Rose plot,/Fringed pool,/Fern's grot-/The veriest school /Of Peace . . .' B128a: III.12). Wooed rapturously by Rattray, now consumed with guilt for having (literally) dreamt her capable of murder, she first of all refuses. However limited her experience of life, she does not want to extend its limits, having already 'reaped . . . her little field' of experience. Finally, however, she agrees to marry him in a spirit of unworthiness in sacrifice. A final cameo enacts Rattray's last words: 'Sit down, my Leonora, and let me watch you shelling peas' (B128a: III.15).

Barrie has also changed his focus of satire in Version 2. If he is testing any thesis now, it is not how far the new woman might go in manipulating men, but how many sentimental *non sequiturs* a popular theatrical audience would take in the interests of only hearing comfortable lies about their current situation. He has sadly accepted that the West End cannot free itself from the self-protective delusions of the judge because it is, if anything, even more impervious to uncomfortable evidence than his Lordship.

I have much more sympathy with that audience's earlier confusion when faced with Version 1, than I have with their comparatively enthusiastic acceptance-in-smugness of Version 2. The earlier text does contain many textual and visual signs, which Barrie clearly hoped would define adequately the direction of his satire and the literary conventions within which the first night audience was to 'read' it. The fact remains that *The Adored One* offers very serious social comment through the most trivial of farce. The temptation to identify the medium with the message rather than to see the medium as a palliative to the severity of that message would have been strong even if Barrie had matched thesis and farce as closely as thesis and structure. He did not. It asks a lot of any audience, popular or otherwise, to relate jokes and slapstick to a serious overall artistic intention when so often their laughter has been elicited as an end in itself. The satirically irrelevant golfing jokes in the trial scenes are intended as sugar on a pill which, Barrie knew, would be particularly bitter for an upper-class, business-class audience. But, dramatically, they have no relevance to that message. It is in this context that I understand the concern noted in *The Stage* of 11 September 1913. The reviewer accepts that there is a serious question being raised about women and power but doubts 'whether playgoers other than the severely analytical' are likely to 'discover it among all the froth and extravagant farce which are the main characteristics of the play' (p. 22).

The real (and ironic) tragedy concerns the preference shown by the same London audiences for the revised version. Soon advanced bookings for Version 2 surpassed those for its major London competitor, a revival of *The Admirable Crichton*. It was never a hit[37] but it did run for 89 further performances, the boos now transformed to applause. Few were those who saw that they were now the major focus of its satire. Fewer were those who saw how Barrie had wilfully destroyed his own theme. The only critic who links the two sides of the question from a non-English perspective is, again, the *New York Times* reviewer. In his 7 September report on the London first night, he recorded Barrie's belief that Scots would see the play as supporting the woman's movement but questioning its new militancy, precisely the view taken a year later in his one act play *Fantasy* (1914). The London audience, however, did not see it that way. Astutely he now switches to accusation of Barrie: 'The author had so wrapped up his point in allegory that those who suspected what he was at were afraid to commit themselves' (p. 3).

Four years later George Sampson would link cause and effect more precisely. Identifying *The Adored One* as 'the one instance [where] Barrie forsakes not merely his world but his thesis', he blames the audience:

> The public in front, which likes its caricatures to be coarse, rather missed the point; so the obliging author re-wrote the play with most of the jokes left out, and has since, I believe, made even a third attempt to catch the ear of the groundlings. A too delicate fable ought not to be retracted because the public taste is dull. What fault there was in [it] was not in its purpose, proportions or invention, but in its texture, which was too fragile for stage use.[38]

'Texture' is right: farce and regular doses of Barrie's own brand of sickly sentiment, intended to palliate, effectively obscured. This judgement is in accordance with the variant texts, English and American, their disillusioned author's continual revisions and his major artistic weakness.[39]

Sampson's reference to a 'third' attempt implies an understanding of the ways in which Version 3, *The Legend of Leonora*, differs from *The Adored One* in its original (Version 1) and revised (Version 2) forms. For America, Barrie returned to Version 1 as his copy text with Leonora as murderess and university graduate. He also made the conclusion open-ended, suggesting that the judge's summing-up might be part of a dream rather than cold reality:

> JUDGE: I think you said not guilty. Leonora stand up, are you there? Has everybody, melted away? Am I alone in Court? Am I melting away too? Help – help! (L44: III.33)

This is sensible – it retains the original force of satire without prejudging the reaction of one audience by forcing them to sit through a sentimental parody occasioned by the fatuity of another. Unwilling to overplay his dramatic hand, Barrie does not excise the final subtlety of the judge satirising himself but offers an escape route in stage effects and mystery to those unwilling or unable to understand the re-instated message.

American audiences and critics did not go overboard about *The Legend of Leonora* but they did identify without much trouble the satiric focus of the play. Most were willing to accept the new ending as posing questions with regard to what was happening in England. Indeed, the actor, William Gillette, as reported in *The New York Times* on 22 February 1914, identified *The Legend of Leonora* as an exciting return to 'the comedy of ideas or the comedy that springs from socially illuminating ideas' (p. 7).

Barrie, in his journalism and biographical writing, admits to sharing Leonora's academic hubris, her role-playing powers and her ambitious egoism. It is tempting, therefore, to wonder with what mixed feelings he deconstructed her for London audiences. As reclusive inheritor of David Masson's wisdom or as his own anarchic alter-ego (McConnachie), he must surely have found it hilarious that a play written to warn Edwardian society of its deafness to the radical changes surrounding them had enacted its own message through being booed off the stage in incomprehension. Once it had been re-written, making male illusions seem the truth and the truth the dream, only then did it gain applause. But if the anarchic McConnachie may have laughed, the crusading, earnest James Barrie was left with his own version of unpalatable truth. The comfort of the prophet, that he is unheard because he is ahead of his time, or the genius, that he is writing ultimately for himself, is a cold one.

When I called my own book *The Road to the Never Land* I was signing, in the last two words, the impossible literary task Barrie set himself. He is an English Literature graduate and, as such, a highly sophisticated literary theorist, who anticipates many post-modernist views. His thinking is academic, sophisticated and eccentric. Yet lack of money drove him to write for the popular stage. He composes best in comic or farcical mode; cannot convey passion convincingly and often lurches from acceptable sentimentality into what, even in his own day, was seen as honeyed sickliness. I have tried to call attention to his own consciousness of that dilemma and the skill with which he used his dramatic craft and layered plotting to delimit the problem.

His view of women, while necessarily partaking of Edwardian values, is especially forward looking and it is no coincidence that *Little Mary* and *The Adored One* met with puzzlement and misinterpretation from their intended audiences and deconstruction in frustration from their creator. On the question of women's rights, Barrie's views were at their most radical and, in the case of the extreme heroine, advanced thought drew him so far from his popular medium that even the Kirriemuir writer with all his theatrical skills could not bridge the gap. Failure to achieve, however, should not disguise his intentions, crystallised in *The Ladies' Shakespeare*, nor the sincerity of his endeavours.

NOTES

The research for this chapter was carried out during a fellowship at the Beinecke Library, Yale University in spring 1992.

1. Patrick Braybrooke *J. M. Barrie: A Study in Fairies and Mortals* (London, Drane's 1924) p. 149.
2. For *What Every Woman Knows* and *Quality Street* see *The Plays of J. M. Barrie* ed. A. E. Wilson (Definitive Edition London, Hodder and Stoughton 1942); J. M. Barrie *Margaret Ogilvy* (London, Hodder and Stoughton 1896). Subsequent references are paged for these editions.
3. Leah Leneman *A Guid Cause: The Women's Suffrage Movement in Scotland* (Aberdeen, Aberdeen University Press 1991) p. 70.
4. J. M. Barrie *An Edinburgh Eleven* (London, Office of the *British Weekly* 1889).
5. Manuscript material by J. M. Barrie is cited from the following sources:

Beinecke Research Library, Yale University: Barrie/Beinecke A2 *Note-books*, A3 *Letters*, L33 *The Ladies' Shakespeare*, L44 *The Adored One*, P45/1903 *Peter Pan* 'Fairy Notes', S354 'The Satirical Rector of Diss' (Skelton), T63 'Tom Nash', W43 acting text of *What Every Woman Knows*, W67 'Women Who Work'.

British Library, Lord Chamberlain's Papers: Barrie/BL LCP1913/28 *The Adored One*, LCP1913/28a *The Adored One* Act 3 revised.

Humanities Research Center, Austin, Texas: Barrie/Austin Hanley B III.28 *Little Mary*.

6. *The Plays of J. M. Barrie* p. 299.
7. *An Edinburgh Eleven* pp. 67–8.
8. J. M. Barrie *Sentimental Tommy* (London, Cassell 1896); *Tommy and Grizel* (London, Cassell 1900).
9. J. M. Barrie *Peter and Wendy* (London, Hodder and Stoughton 1911).
10. Judith Butler *Gender Trouble* (London and New York, Routledge 1990) pp. 134–41.
11. Andrew Birkin *J. M. Barrie and the Lost Boys* (London, Constable 1979).
12. 'In point of fact it is too easy to give an Oedipal reading of Peter Pan', Jacqueline Rose *The Case of Peter Pan* (London, Macmillan 1984) p. 35.
13. The image of donning personalities like clothes, which dominates *Sentimental Tommy* and *Tommy and Grizel*, is thus given a literal source in his mother's behaviour.
14. 'The daughter my mother loved the best'; 'that daughter she loved the best' (Margaret to Jane Ann as Christ to John); 'the soft face was wet again' (Margaret's lamentations for David as Mary's for Christ).
15. R. D. S. Jack 'James Barrie and the Napoleonic Heroine' *Carlyle Annual* 1993 pp. 1–16.
16. Thomas Carlyle *On Heroes, Hero-Worship and the Heroic in History* (London 1897 [reprint of the 1841 edition]) p. 13.
17. *The Plays of J. M. Barrie* p. 499.
18. J. M. Barrie *The Boy Castaways of Black Lake Island* (London, privately printed 1901).
19. *On Heroes, Hero-Worship and the Heroic in History* p. 186.
20. J. A. Hammerton *J. M. Barrie: The Story of a Genius* (London, Sampson Low, Marston 1929) p. 282.
21. My references are to L33/2, the text used by Beerbohm Tree.
22. Barrie associates Petruchio with Peter (Pan) in some versions of the text. A proposed ending has him crowing like Peter. Male childishness in egotistic simplicity links the two.
23. Compare Shakespeare II v. 96: 'Say I command her come to me'.
24. R. D. S. Jack 'The Hunt for Mrs Lapraik' *Yale Library Gazette* 1992 pp. 1–12.
25. R. D. S. Jack *The Road to the Never Land* (Aberdeen, Aberdeen University Press 1991) pp. 130–54.
26. *The Plays of J. M. Barrie* p. 484.
27. This version is held in the Humanities Research Center at Austin, Texas, Hanley B III.28.

28. George Bernard Shaw *Collected Letters 1898–1910* ed. Dan H. Laurence (London, Reinhardt 1972) p. 383.
29. Bernard Shaw *Plays Unpleasant* (Penguin, Harmondsworth 1981) p. 20.
30. Marina Warner *Alone of All Her Sex* (London, Weidenfeld and Nicolson 1976) p. 336.
31. *The Plays of J. M. Barrie* p. 435.
32. Ibid. p. 480.
33. Sheila Kaye-Smith 'Barrie the Tragedian' *The Bookman* 1920 pp.107–8.
34. Dennis Mackail *The Story of JMB* (London, Peter Davies 1941) p. 205.
35. *The Plays of J. M. Barrie* Definitive Edition pp. 945–61.
36. See Beinecke F25. This unpublished one act play was written in 1912 as *The Little Policemen*, then revised and produced as *Fantasy* in 1914 (Beinecke F25). It directly depicts the overthrow of male institutions by the suffragettes. In a letter to Frohmann in 1912, Barrie regrets that excessive militancy may have dimmed sympathy for the movement and so obscure his own purpose of presenting dramatically what they (the suffragettes) 'had talked so grandly of doing this year'.
37. *The Story of JMB* p. 459.
38. George Sampson 'Barrie as Playwright' *The Bookman* 1918 pp. 103–6.
39. That Barrie was aware even of this is suggested by him parodying, for the Cinema Supper at the Savoy in 1915, his own revision failures with yet another ending (this time outrageously ridiculous) to *The Adored One*.

8

Feminine Pleasures and Masculine Indignities

Gender and Community in Scottish Drama

ADRIENNE SCULLION

The bridge leading from male to female communities lies in the differing connotations of the word 'code'. All true communities are knit together by their codes, but a code can range from dogma to a flexible, private, and often semi-conscious set of beliefs. In literature at least, male communities tend to live by a code in its most explicit, formulated, and inspirational sense; while in female communities, the code seems a whispered and fleeting thing, more a buried language than a rallying cry, whose invocations, like Cranford's reiterated 'elegant economy' or the ostensible etiquette of Jean Brodie's 'la crème de la crème', have more than a touch of the impalpable and devious.[1]

Plays written for the Scottish stage tend towards a drama of groups and of communities: indeed, one of the characteristic features of Scottish drama is a tendency towards narratives, not of heroic individuals, but of anti-heroic groups. With writing as diverse as Roddy McMillan's *The Bevellers* (1973), John Byrne's *The Slab Boys Trilogy* (1978, 1979, 1982) and Sue Glover's *Bondagers* (1991) the drama evokes a sense of community that militates against characters being read solely as individuals.[2]

It is, of course, the aim of writers of even the most literally-minded fiction that characters, while operating on a simple, commonplace level, may also function on another, more complex, sophisticated and metaphorical front. This parallels an idea which, for Scottish drama, has broader application: that the individual is most meaningful, most powerful, within a group, in social communion and as metaphor. As a consequence of this, in a significant proportion of Scottish plays the narrative core is unsettled, the focus of interest being shared amongst a group. This may be suggested structurally, with narrative attention shifting amongst a group of characters, the plot itself becoming diffuse or fragmented. More crudely, one central character may function metaphorically, as an abstraction, a personification of, for example, the nation, the working class, masculinity, or motherhood. Alternatively, the whole play, the theatrical event itself, may be directed towards establishing a moment of unity, a recognition of community, in the audience. At these instances culturally prejudiced codes of gender and community interact, 'knitting together' to offer particular points of access and interpretation, preferred readings of the characters and the environments presented.

It is the distinctive, and perhaps defining, emphasis on groups and communities that this chapter will highlight, suggesting that within this abstraction gender representations may be analysed within the broader perspectives of cultural poetics and interdisciplinary discourses. Using three quite simple principles – one, that different communities may be defined through different sets of codes; two, that these codes produce, or at least display, particular defining and emblematic characteristics; and, three, that Scottish drama is marked by a series of distinctive and more or less fixed codes which limit and enable its literary and cultural agenda – one might suggest a major subset of plays in which the sense of community is constructed in exclusively gendered groupings, paralleling in interesting ways the mythology of community as socio-cultural ideal and countering the easy categorisation and stereotyping of gender in Scottish drama.

Whilst acknowledging the prevalence and the importance of a Marxist reading of gender-based analyses of culture (women being used and exploited as a symptom of and/or metaphor for colonial exploitation), one might be able to move beyond these models and counter with a reading constructed by and through textual analyses and cultural heritage. Insisting on characters as even loosely represent-ative of gender, class and nationhood has led Scottish culture to a myopic nexus of overly simplistic, endlessly transferable meanings. From Flora MacIvor to Mrs Mack, Ma Broon to Rab C. Nesbitt, Dr Finlay to Taggart, Scottish culture has been seen to be obsessively attracted to a core of easily transferable character stereotypes, ubiquit-ous images and predictable politics: together they constitute debilitating and constraining versions of national and gender identities. However, these easy assumptions do not go unopposed. Increasingly, one might point to a group of writers and practitioners who, while using and referring to the defining myths and recognisable semiotics of Scottishness, aim to produce a revisionist account of ourselves and our culture. It may be possible for the audience, and the critic, to engage with Scottish drama in an analogous spirit of cultural awareness and revisionist enthusiasm, adapting the critical framework within a praxis that remains distinctively our own.

> It's no exactly going to be your sex n' drags n' rock n' roll tour. More like your family outing.[3]

The family is the paradigmatic community described by Scottish culture: from the Darlings to the MacFlannels, the Broons to the Nesbitts, the family has been a repeated source of narrative, the domestic a customary setting, the familial a recurrent model of social organisation. The family has proved useful in that its organisation may be read as replaying society's preferred and ideological relationships and structures in microcosm, offering a reduced version of society's hegemonic power relations. Problematically, the family is often set as an ideal, with disfunctionality manifest as a denial or disavowal of the familial, and, by extension, a violation of general order, to be depicted as socially uncontainable transgression.

The imaginary of the family is worked out in opposition, in play and escapism, in relief and with heightened realism, each manifestation of the familial functioning within a wider analysis of the community, the family offering itself as easily symbolic of broader cultural concerns and issues.

Although the family is a potent symbol in rural dramas like J. A. Ferguson's *Campbell of Kilmohr* (1914) and Neil Gunn's *The Ancient Fire* (1929), it is perhaps with urban drama, a tradition developing through Robins Millar's *The Shawlie* (1922), Paul Vincent Carroll's *Green Cars Go East* (1941), Robert MacLeish's *The Gorbals Story* (1946) and Ena Lamont Stewart's *Men Should Weep* (1947 and 1982) that community and family, and by extension community and identity, are most clearly enmeshed.[4]

Since its 1982 revival *Men Should Weep* has been acknowledged as one of Scottish drama's seminal texts. Ena Lamont Stewart's radical rewriting of her 1947 Glasgow Unity play *Poor Men's Riches* works within the conventions of the domestic melodrama and knowingly activates that tradition. *Men Should Weep* presents a hegemonic and simplistic view of the working-class community suffering under economic and political pressure and simultaneously offers a revisionist reading of this mythology. The clear-sighted depiction of the public hardships of the social environment is typical of Unity's incisive and ongoing analysis of slum dwelling. Stewart's drama of family life within a Glasgow tenement flat refers to but transcends the easy stereotypes of earlier working-class dramas. Maggie, her complex and challenging heroine, is on one level the archetypal mother of Scottish drama – suffering real hardships, publicly and psychologically forceful, deeply nurturing of her charges. However, on another level, she transgresses the roles normally ascribed to women through her culpability and her distinctive and defining self-awareness (including the acknowledgement of her own sexual and emotional needs). At the climax of the play, she attacks her husband, John, with a withering account of his sexual inadequacy, forever resetting the gender relations possible on the Scottish stage:

> Aye, I wis your whore. An I'd nae winnins that I can mind o. Is that the way it goes, John? (p. 95)

Stewart depicts Maggie as a deeply flawed, wholly human character: she is morally feeble in her relationship with her son, Alec, jealous and distrustful of his wife, Isa, obsessive in her concern for her younger children. The power of her characterisation is in her identification with an extended set of social conditions, issues and characters. Throughout she is within and part of a wider community, whose identity is founded on poverty and unemployment. More particularly in her relations with Lizzie, Lily, Granny and the neighbours she is to be understood as part of a group of women finding communion in their shared need to survive under severe economic pressures and determined to maintain the structure of the family despite social crisis. Thus, the play's climax is all the more shocking because the characters maintain a strong connection with familial roles established as both archetypal and illusive: Jenny returns, one might argue regresses, to the role of daughter, demanding that John maintain his familial and social role as 'father', not his personal and individual role as 'lover'. She kneels at her father's feet:

> Daddy . . . Daddy . . . forget it. It doesnae matter. Daddy? (*She tries to draw his hands from his face*) When I wis wee, you loved me, an I loved you. Why can we no go back? (p. 96)

The play acknowledges the latent but, in practice, diffuse potential of gender roles within the family. Socially and culturally Maggie is empowered in her role as 'mother'; individually she is constructed as impotent. However, her final outburst counters and explodes the myth of the mother as Madonna while reclaiming her identity as a fully drawn, independent person. Alasdair Cameron can, therefore, argue with some conviction that Maggie is 'no indomitable Working-Class woman of spurious and patronising socialist mythology',[5] because her identity is rooted firmly in its moment, its own community, its own morality. Indeed Stewart insists upon a set of principles and responsibilities that are uniquely relevant to the environment she has depicted. The moral order she describes in her community eschews the fallacious middle-class morality imposed upon characters in contemporary plays like *Green Cars Go East* and *The Shawlie*. Stewart's familial drama gains wider potency because of the specificity of her imaginative world, its unsentimental climax and its defining motif of the family infrastructure imploding under socio-economic pressure.

Men Should Weep reinvents a set of national and gender identities whilst remaining part of a tradition of urban melodrama. Despite the fact that the conventions of the genre remain pervasive and ubiquitous, Stewart's reassessment assures that the images of the indomitable mother, the hard-drinking hardman and the egalitarian spirit of the tenement community face increasingly concentrated critical interrogation.

Within the grammar of Scottish writing such images and ideas maintain their potency to the extent that writers can refer with confidence to a set of shorthand indicators and familiar images in order to reassess the mythology. The most sustained example of this tendency is Chris Hannan's 1985 radical deconstruction of the urban myth, *Elizabeth Gordon Quinn*.[6] This play, or at least a partially contextualised reading of this play, is only possible given the permanence of the source legend of the strong and suffering mother, the mythology of the community spirit of the tenement, the tradition of the uniquely brave Scottish soldier and the half-truth of the socialist cast of the Scottish urban identity.

Hannan depicts a whirl of social activity and organisation bubbling around the aloof and solitary Elizabeth. Denying heroics and sentimentalism Hannan creates a character at odds with her environment and our received images of that environment. Living in a tenement, Elizabeth rejects the mythology that insists on the ethos of collectivism and togetherness described by, for example, MacLeish's *The Gorbals Story*. Hannan describes a flat, a room and a character surrounded by life but determinedly separate from it. Elizabeth's front door may be open but the egalitarian ideology that might suggest is rejected:

> Please come in, Mrs Shaw. This is a tenement after all. We have no alternative but to enter into the spirit of it. (p. 114)

But Hannan's heroine does disown the 'spirit' associated with the tenement. She consistently denies the existence of community in two directions: she defies the community of the working-class environment around her (the close, the street); and she repudiates the ideal of the nurturing, mutually supportive community of family.

Around Elizabeth movements of collective activity (primarily a rent-strike organised by the women of the district) and national military mobilisation threaten the ideal of splendid isolation she has constructed. These two points of collective responsibility are symbolised in her relations with her children. Aidan and Maura attempt to embrace community, primarily to spite and to escape their mother: Maura works with her neighbours in what develops as a highly politicised rent-strike, while Aidan has first joined and then deserted from an Irish regiment.

Analysing the tradition of working-class drama as contributing to and supporting social protest, Hannan offers a character who transgresses not just gender roles but refuses the identity imposed by politics, economics and convention: 'I refuse to learn how to be poor' declares the defiant Elizabeth at the end of the play (p. 146) countering a version of Scottish drama which, if it does not celebrate, at least sustains the dominant mythology of staunch working-class identity within an aggressive and ignoble capitalist hierarchy. Hannan's play is a complex psychological minefield in which his central character steadfastly refuses the myth of collective and social responsibility.

> I am not the working class! I am Elizabeth Gordon Quinn. I'm an individual – although that is becoming increasingly difficult to believe. It seems there's no room for the individual in this world. (p. 122)

The play, while concentrating on the individual at odds with her family and society, still offers the ideal of the group as a valid and effective force for social organisation and political change. While Elizabeth denies her commonality with the striking women, their joint action is successful: rents *do* fall. *Elizabeth Gordon Quinn* is radical in the emotional and intellectual complexities it unearths within the myth of the family and the tenement community. However, it still acknowledges and allows for characters finding strength and power in the celebration and mobilisation of their commonalities.

The antithesis of this urban, working-class realism and its remarkable and consistent view of a supportive local community would seem to be the London milieu of J. M. Barrie's social comedy. His plays are set against the backdrop of Bloomsbury, Mayfair and Kensington Gardens, and yet many of his themes parallel and repeat the key familial debates and imaginative motifs of other Scottish dramas: the family and the complications of familial relations are of repeated concern, as is an interest in the fey, the fantastical and the supernatural.

The reputation of this most successful of Scottish playwrights has suffered to a degree matched only by the parallel decline of James Bridie. However, the combination of Andrew Birkin's *J. M. Barrie and the Lost Boys* (1979), the R.S.C.'s 1982 revival of *Peter Pan* and increasing interest from academics shows that his long-overdue rehabilitation is well under way. R. D. S. Jack's *The Road to the Never Land* (1991) is perhaps the critical high point of this reassessment which insists that Scottish cultural studies return to Barrie's writing and reconsider his distinctive and imaginative world.

Barrie develops a surprisingly sustained critique of the construction of gender played out within the conventions of family. The traditional narrative structure of his plays effaces his active engagement with the ideological meanings of the family as distillation of a society's gendered hegemony. In *The Admirable Crichton* (1902), *Peter Pan* (1904) and *What Every Woman Knows* (1908), for example, he examines with determined accuracy the predictable gender images assured within the idea of the family and the hedonistic and, potentially, liberating disorder that comes of violating such codings. The metaphor of the familial as social ideal, with the threat of disorder as penalty for transgression, is most clearly debated in *Peter Pan*.

In a world marked by a lack of hierarchical structures Peter's identity is that of a misrule character: he is both endlessly childish and fundamentally devilish, the manifestation of society's fears of the unrestrained id. The dichotomy of the unconscious and the socially restrained conscious self is dramatised in the narrative of Wendy's seduction. Within such a reading, Peter offers the temptation of transgression to the Darling children who are initially introduced as fully subject to conventional family roles in the safe, nurturing environment of their nursery. In their games and play-acting the Darlings explicitly rehearse the gender roles preferred by Edwardian society:

> JOHN (*histrionically*): We are doing an act; we are playing at being you and father. (*He imitates the only father who has come under his special notice.*) A little less noise there.
>
> WENDY: Now let us pretend we have a baby.
>
> JOHN (*good naturedly*): I am happy to inform you, Mrs. Darling, that you are now a mother. (*Wendy gives way to ecstasy*) You have missed the chief thing; you haven't asked 'boy or girl?'
>
> WENDY: I am so glad to have one at all, I don't care which it is.
>
> JOHN (*crushingly*): That is just the difference between gentlemen and ladies. Now you tell me.
>
> WENDY: I am happy to acquaint you, Mr. Darling, you are now a father.
>
> JOHN: Boy or girl?
>
> WENDY (*presenting herself*): Girl.
>
> JOHN: Tuts.
>
> WENDY: You horrid.
>
> JOHN: Go on.
>
> WENDY: I am happy to acquaint you, Mr. Darling, you are again a father.
>
> JOHN: Boy or girl?
>
> WENDY: Boy. (*John beams*) Mummy, it's hateful of him.[7]

Wendy is the character most wholly in thrall to socially constructed gender roles, giving full expression to the explicit codes around the hegemonic identity of the nurturing 'mother'. No sooner is she transported to the idyll of Neverland, a world without the cultural and economic structures which shape the limits of the conscious world available to her in Bloomsbury, than she is spring cleaning, cooking meals and reading bedtime stories to the boys. Wendy misreads the potential liberation of Neverland and attempts to impose the structures of social organisation she has rehearsed in the nursery on the disorder she perceives around her: the Boys, including her brothers, John and Michael, enact their fantasies as sprites, hunters and buccaneers, while the limit of Wendy's imaginative engagement is to be a mother.

Wendy's cultural inhibitions are further revealed in comparison with the other feminine characters in Neverland. On one level Wendy, Tinker Bell and Tiger Lily function as three separate characters competing in different ways for the attentions of Peter. However, they are more completely understood as distinct aspects of the one female identity. In fact, it might be better argued that Tinker Bell and Tiger Lily represent different manifestations of the unconscious of unrestrained femininity (or 'female-ness'), while Wendy is contained as idealised Edwardian womanhood: so, the ideal of the nurturing mother, enacted by Wendy, is countered by Tiger Lily as the wild, sexually aggressive, untamed savage and Tinker Bell as the sensuous, free spirit liberated from all moral responsibility. Together they may reveal the prejudices and fears of Edwardian society in relation to the sexuality of women.

With Peter as troll and cultural *Doppelgänger*, Barrie tempts Edwardian femininity to transgress society's rules and conventions. But, despite her dalliance with the fantastic, Wendy's seduction, her fall, is incomplete. Although she hints at her desire to be transformed into lover, her determined and sustained appropriation of the role of mother precludes the overt declaration, or even acknowledgement, of her own sexuality. In her criticisms of Tiger Lily and Tinker Bell she censures herself and limits her potential for expression:

> WENDY (*knowing she ought not to probe but driven to it by something within*): What are your exact feelings for me, Peter?
> PETER (*in the class-room*): Those of a devoted son, Wendy.
> WENDY (*turning away*): I thought so.
> PETER: You are so puzzling. Tiger Lily is just the same; there is something or other she wants me to be, but she says it is not my mother.
> WENDY (*with spirit*): No, indeed it isn't.
> PETER: Then what is it?
> WENDY: It isn't for a lady to tell. (p. 550)

Using the motif of a fantastic and alternative universe, Barrie holds a mirror up to his own community. The escape from everyday reality to an antic, ethereal and analogous world – Neverland in *Peter Pan*, the wood in *Dear Brutus* (1917), the desert island in *The Admirable Crichton* – is both temporally limited and psychologically constrained. The transient emancipation effected by Barrie's imagined communities is away from a problematic view of the contemporary community towards a fantastic, though not necessarily idealised, version of its supernatural parallel where characters may still assume their traditional roles.

The use of a comparative community, an alternative world, is a common feature in fables, stories, legends and non-Christian and pantheistic religions and it functions to mythologise and, like metaphor, re-interpret events in the 'real' and tangible world. Barrie's Neverland resets our understanding of Bloomsbury because it distils particular aspects of its social organisation. In *Peter Pan* gender relations within the structure of the family are highlighted with humour, sympathy and accuracy: the central role is that of mother. Wendy's fantasy of being mother to the Lost Boys is motivated by her imaginary life in Bloomsbury and the intervention of Peter to reclaim his familial role as son. However, just as Wendy's assimilation into the role of mother is incomplete (because of her unspoken and unspeakable desire for Peter), so he too is ultimately disillusioned in his desire to return to innocence:

> Wendy, you are wrong about mothers. I thought like you about the window, so I stayed away for moons and moons, and then I flew back, but the window was barred, for my mother had forgotten all about me and there was another little boy sleeping in my bed. (p. 552)

Peter's articulation of the loss of childish innocence, played out as the loss of the mother, resonates through Scottish drama.

> Ah tellt ye. You're no in the school noo. You're with the big men ootside. Yur faither cannae come divin up tae see the heid-maister an' tell him somebody's been unkind tae his wee boy. That's in the past. Make up yer mind tae it, you'll get a lot o knocks afore you're done . . . if you want tae chuck it on the first day, that's up tae you, but ye havenae made much o a stab at it, hav ye? So either feed up, or take aff yur apron an' pit yur jaicket on . . .[8]

If Barrie's middle-class drawing room has been an infrequent locus of attention for Scottish drama, the workplace has proved to be a more constant and ubiquitous vehicle for Scotland's stories. Workplace dramas, however, rarely depict a bourgeois environment – Scottish drama seems remarkably uncertain as to what the middle classes do or talk about – and instead often echo the social issues raised by domestic dramas like *Men Should Weep* and *Elizabeth Gordon Quinn*.

Workplace dramas tend to replay and rework narrative strategies, codes and conventions familiar from a range of representations. One can point to a number of repeated structural conventions and narratives: an examination of the processes of production, on occasion a vaguely lyrical and celebratory form, as with Bill Bryden's *The Ship* (1990); an account of economic crisis (immanent closure or strike) as in Bryden's *Willie Rough* (1972); the revelation of a dark underside to an overtly respectable situation, as with Iain Heggie's *Clyde Nouveau* (1990) or Chris Hannan's *The Evil-Doers* (1990); and, with remarkable frequency, the arrival of a new worker to disrupt the established *status quo* or be integrated and reaffirm the workplace (*read* social) hierarchy.[9]

Plays that revolve around the 'new boy' and, more particularly, the 'new boy's first day' include McMillan's *The Bevellers*, Heggie's *A Wholly Healthy Glasgow* (1987) and Byrne's *The Slab Boys*. Generally these dramas are about rites of passage or turn on a series of ceremonies or rituals of initiation. Such plays are often exceedingly formal, even classical, in construction with a clear semiotics of gender being referenced and repeated: a 'new boy' enters a pre-established community of adult men, his 'masculinity' is tested, and he is either accepted by or expelled from the group. Acceptance can result in moments of celebration, expulsion in moments of extreme violence. It is these dramas which most clearly highlight the phenomenon of 'gender-specific' communities, a convention which appears repeatedly and influentially within Scottish drama.

Workplace dramas have traditionally emphasised communities of men – groups of male workers wherein women are totally absent or, at best, marginal players – and tend, therefore, to concentrate on the prevalent Scottish myth of an aggressively dominant masculinity, played out against an industrial backdrop. Such dramas concentrate on communities of urban men, where the mythology of the 'hardman' is never far distant and the cult of the mother a defining phenomenon – although occasionally both conventions are ready for ironic deconstruction or satirical implosion. Despite the prevalence of wholly or predominantly male communities, the dynamic of the family is a frequent structural paradigm, with characters assuming various levels of familial identification and the community maintaining a political vision of the family as an ideal social structure.

In McMillan's *The Bevellers* the generic conventions of workplace drama come so sharply into focus that the play may be viewed as a useful benchmark for subsequent texts. The action is limited to the single location of the basement bevelling shop of a Glasgow glass firm; the story unfolds in the space of just one working day; the characters on stage represent a strong, aggressively coherent community of men; the one woman who appears is reduced to a totemic sexual prize for the dominant male; and the new boy's first day ends with violence, humiliation, and a reaffirmation of the phallocentric *status quo*.

The society, the community, of this workplace is highly organised, emotionally and physically brutal, its corporeal and verbal aggression heightened through its containment within the crucible of the workshop. The language passes from terse, staccato, angry exchanges, pitting character against character in a scarcely-contained battle for dominance to long, poignant reflections on the art of the beveller and the passing of the craft. Within this boisterous, even barbarous, hierarchical environment there is communion: typical of the workplace drama is a fellowship based on the trade and a mutual respect for skill and craftsmanship. The play allows an explicit brotherhood of bevellers – with the drama turning on one character's entrance into this community.

Norrie's initiation into this adult association is highly structured and remarkably formulaic, paralleling general rites of social initiation. He is introduced by an elder, Leslie, the manager; he is (re)named by the new community ('Boys call ye Norrie?' (p. 9));entrusted to the care of a guide, the foreman Bob; and through and with him is introduced to new sign systems ('Dae ye know whit bevellin' is, young Norrie? . . . It's a' ower the bliddy place, though no wan in a million wid recognise it' (p. 9)), with new and specialised vocabularies ('silvered', 'chamfer', 'feedin-up', 'rouge', 'slurry'). Norrie's access to these new ways of seeing, this new identity, is carefully divided into a series of lessons. Each beveller introduces Norrie to some different aspect of their world, a skill (how to feed up), a task (when to make the tea), a word ('Ye know whit culet is?' (p. 42)), a shared joke ('Teuchter, teuchter. You no know whit "teuchter" is?' (p. 10)) so that they are seen to be *both* empowered with knowledge *and* able and willing to extend the community by passing on this knowledge, often symbolised in language, to the new boy.

The community of men takes the young boy and educates him into the systems and structures of the group: they invite him to take on a new and adult character. The process of education, the tutelage, creates a new set of responsibilities for the initiate within a mutually dependent group, each member of which must, to some degree, compromise his individuality to the group or at least work within and for that group for the collective, greater good. So Joe, at first kind, supportive and seemingly caring of Norrie, must later align himself with the Rouger when burning the old newspaper, and deny Norrie until he too has proved himself part of the group or failed in the attempt:

> NORRIE: Ah thought you wur goan tae be ma mate in here, Joe.
> JOE: No chance, Mac. (p. 37)

The celebration of the craft and the craftsman is the explicit coding which gives coherence, structure and meaning to this group. So Peter, a character who suffers a form of epilepsy, is accepted, cared for and even celebrated by his colleagues because of his skill as a craftsman: he is, quite simply, 'The best' (p. 12). The name Peter, of course, connotes solidity, reliability, a role as the very keystone of the community. The potential fragility of this communion of bevellers, the parallel fragility of the glass and the glass-worker, is suggested, in metaphor, by questioning Peter's dependability – his illness, the fits he suffers from, endangers them all.

The beveller's identity has a more imaginative dimension, however. Bob's reminiscences, his taking on of the role of storyteller, are part of Norrie's initiation. The bevellers are clearly identified though their skills and their craft, but this is heightened and celebrated in their imaginative life, their distinctive and defining history and mythology. Bob introduces Norrie to the trade by showing him skills, teaching him words *and* telling him stories and legends. He shares memories of ancient bevellers, 'Hard men, but good bliddy men, some o them' (p. 35). He tells of past accidents, perhaps exaggerating for effect when he tells of one when a shard of glass

> planed right across the shop and caught this other fulla on the thigh. It went right through aprons, troosers, the lot. Severed his hamstring, an' though they got him tae hospital in time, he never walked right again. (p. 24)

He recalls times past when apprentices, trying 'tae get wur hauns lookin like bevellers'', would rub pieces of glass into their hands, so keen were they to win an outward sign of identity and belonging (p. 24). Finally, he conjures up the phantasmic presence of Alex Freer, once skilled beveller, now dying drunk, surviving on the very fringes of the community but unable to exist completely away from it:

> Ah try tae stey away, no bother anybody, but then the time comes when ah miss the smell . . . The burning at the polisher, an' that peculiar smell fae the edgers. It's no like anythin' else ah can think o . . . I noticed it the first time ah ever went intae a bevellin shop, an' ah can smell it noo. (p. 42)

Freer's appearance, at the very centre of the play, is as a spirit of the past. And it is he, the oldest and most impotent of the ages of man represented by McMillan, who is most acutely aware of bevelling as a passing, even doomed, craft. His description of the smell of the workshop may hint at post-industrial lyricism, but his vision is clear and rapier-sharp. He knows that there is no future for these men as bevellers, and if there is no future for them as bevellers there is no future for them as men, for their understanding of masculinity is measured within a community of like-minded fellow workers united as a protective shell against uncertainty and doubt. He tells Norrie to escape the bevelling shop:

> Get away fae it. Ye spend yur days grindin gless, an' at the finish yur life's like slurry at the bottom o the wheel. Yur back's like the bent bit o an oul' tree an' yur hauns are like the jaurries aboot the knuckles. Ye never get away fae the sound o watter drippin in yur ears. The damp gets in at the soles o yur feet an' creeps right up tae yur neck. Yur face turns tae the colour o pomas an' ye cannae stop it. That Rouger, he tries tae keep the shine on his face by gallopin like a bliddy eediot oot on that bike o his, an' Charlie thinks he can pit aff the evil day liftin that stupit weight o his ower his heid, but they cannae stop it. Somethin' breks doon in the chest, an' the sound o yur voice gets thin, an' wan day you're an oul' man like me, bent and brittle. Don't stey at it, Norrie. Get somethin' else – anythin'. Get intae the sun an' the fresh air. Get a job on a motor, a van, anythin', but don't stey at this trade. Fur if ye dae, it'll bend ye. (p. 43–4)

Alex Freer's caustic condemnation of the posturings of Charlie and the Rouger criticises the version of masculinity legitimised in the workplace drama and by the masculine community. He condemns an understanding of masculinity as an externalised set of signs that are about strength of body not self-awareness, competitiveness not fraternity, whereby masculinity is revealed as a more or less aggressive display of physical skill, and potency distinguished as acts of violence.

Throughout the play, the community of men described functions in a way that is not simply hierarchical (manager, foreman, workers, apprentice, novitiate) but replays the more complex though equally commonplace structures and relationships of the family. Identifying different versions, different ages of masculinity, and isolating them in the bevelling shop, McMillan describes the classic archetypes of Scottish drama, without reducing his characters to one-dimensional stereotypes. From Norrie, childish, 'innocent' and 'doe-eyed' (p. 10) through the enthusiastic apprentice, Joe (just one step ahead of Norrie in learning the trade but respectful of his teachers and their craft), to the sexually combative Charlie and the Rouger, the master craftsman Peter and the pseudo-paternal figure of Bob, the economically powerful, if practically impotent, Leslie, and the 'ghost' (p. 29) of Alex Freer, McMillan's community personifies society's myths of masculinity and by replaying a series of bankrupt and sterile father/son and sibling relationships sets the family as product of economic, not emotional demands.

In the isolated and subterranean world of the workshop, the group is removed from the real world, isolated to the extent that it functions outwith society's morality, humanity, kindness and instead operates with its own codes and values. Throughout the play Charlie and the Rouger bait and test each other, their potential for violence displaced into enactments of physical prowess, the bicycle and the weights overloaded with the symbolism of sexual competition. In the hierarchy of the workshop they are in the ascendant, but they are also in direct competition to be the dominant, sexually fulfilled male in the group. Although they miss no opportunity to humiliate each other, finally they belong to the group of bevellers, and ultimately they must rely on and trust each other above the naïve Norrie:

> NORRIE: Hey, Charlie, Nancy wis here at dinner-time. The Rouger tried tae shag her.
> *All stop. There is a long silence . . . Charlie considers his hand but advances slightly on the Rouger.*
> CHARLIE: Ah'm wan-handed, Rouger, but if whit that boy says is true, ah'll take you, an' ah'll mash ye intae the slurry.
> ROUGER: He's a liar, Charlie. Honest tae God on the old-lady's grave, ah'll give ye ma genuine Bible oath, he's a liar.
>
> . . .

CHARLIE: Ah believe ye. Now, you listen, boy, that's the
second time you've raised Nancy's name the day, an' each
time ye soiled it.
Charlie punches Norrie in the stomach, and Norrie folds up. (pp.
69–70)

Anthropologically, rites of initiation take the adolescent boy away
from a community of women, away from his mother, into an age of
sexual potency and the society of men. *The Bevellers* parallels this
structure depicting an extended and ritualised trial that even extends
to the rousing of the spirit world. At the end of the play Norrie's
failure, which is essentially his emasculation, returns him to a childish
community. His ejection from the community of adult men is signalled physically, by the mock-baptism effected by Joe and the
Rouger, and linguistically, with Leslie's soft, caring tone, as if tending
a crying child, set in stark opposition to the verbal assaults of the
rest of the play. Where baptism is a rite of initiation, the public
recognition and acknowledgement of the birth of a child, its acceptance into the community, the Rouger's sham baptism is an act of
exclusion and expulsion. Throughout the play Norrie (itself the
diminutive of Norman) has been called 'son', 'boy', 'young boy',
'young-yin'. If baptism connotes naming then Norrie's exclusion
from the world of adult men is complete with the final confirmation
of the appellation 'sonny':

> What's the matter with you, sonny, have they been giving you
> a rough time? It sometimes happens with new boys. They
> haven't really hurt you, have they? That's all right, then. I
> think you better get up the stair. Where's your jacket? I'll get it
> for you. This bag belong to you, too? All right, come on then,
> up you go. Your stomach sore, eh? Ah, you'll be all right.
> Away home to your mother, and you'll be all right. (p. 70)

Norrie is ejected from this masculine community and from its symbolic location, the workplace, and the play ends with this calling on
the nurturing, healing power of the mother. The irony is, of course,
that Norrie's mock-baptism not only excludes him from the male
community but returns him to a state of doubtful childishness, an
incomplete family, for his mother is dead.

Narrative and structural orthodoxies, as well as gender codings,
have proved to be formative in the development of Scottish drama.
Referencing a series of images and characteristic motifs playwrights

have used comparison and opposition to tell their stories. Where Chris Hannan referred with distinguished success to the conventions of working-class urban realism and the idea of the family, a similar project has been undertaken by Iain Heggie in relation to the work-place drama. Heggie's *A Wholly Healthy Glasgow* uses the conventions of the workplace drama and its analysis of community but fails to complete the implicit reassessment of the source-genre achieved by Hannan.[10]

An easy way to read Heggie's play is as an immoral tale of seedy characters and lowlife happenings in a grim and debilitating environ-ment. But this sets the play in a world of virtue and moral judgement, allowing the framework of responsibility and humanity it consistently refuses. However, this social contextualisation is not really on the agenda of the workplace drama, where convention isolates the charac-ters in something of a moral vacuum, so that the consequences of choices and action made in the workplace have little or no ramifica-tions in the 'real' world. In practice the world the play offers has no conscientious benchmark legitimising 'right' and 'wrong': Heggie's imaginative community is not immoral but determinedly amoral.

This workplace is a rather tawdry Glasgow health club. The 'com-munity' is a bitter alliance of convenience between Charley Hood, smooth, unprincipled health instructor and hard-sell salesman, and Donald Dick, determinedly politically-incorrect gay, preying and ageing masseur. The new boy is Murdo Caldwell, at first convention-ally sympathetic, a seeming innocent abroad, who is ultimately re-vealed as unscrupulous and morally rootless. It's not that he's näive, nor that he's ruthless, ambitious and scheming, its not even that he goes with the dominant flow of events, looking out for the best chance for himself all along the way, although all these are true. He is simply without conscience, obdurate, unpredictable and con-sequently uncontainable. Heggie resets the impotence of the conven-tional 'new boy', instilling Murdo with a dogmatic and purposeful agenda that goes beyond acceptance into the community and the empowerment of group membership. His vision surpasses the locus of the workplace for he has a mission to create 'a wholly healthy Glasgow':

> a city of perfectly proportioned, sinuous but not over-developed physiques . . . a city of non-smoking, non-drinking joggers . . . a city of reposeful but alert minds. (p. 23)

Familiar devices are repeated. The action is contained within a single location; the story unfolds in the space of just one working day; the characters on stage represent an aggressive, if essentially fragile, masculine community; the men perceive the woman as something of a prize for the dominant male; the new boy's first day of misunderstandings and humiliations ends with reproaches and a re-establishment of the amoral order. No character is actually ejected, indeed one might argue that Murdo's initiation is complete in that he is exactly incorporated into the atmosphere, structures and dubious virtues of the pre-existing community.

The process of initiation into the community of the Spartan Health Club is no simple, formulaic rite of passage, however. The existing community is no educative and socialising force for change. Charley and Donald are actively defending their authority against disruption and interlopers. The newcomer is never conceived of as a potential member of the community, instead he is 'A bastarding, *interfering* new boy' (p. 5) subject to plottings and schemings designed to expel not include. Donald's project is clear: 'All I'm wanting's *decapitation plans for the new boy*' he insists at the opening of the play (p. 5). However, the characters' structural roles remain remarkable consistent with those identified around *The Bevellers*: Charley, the guide, introduces the *actual* conventions and practices of the Spartan regime as opposed to the official version intoned by Murdo; Donald exaggerates, tells stories, mythologises his past, and is depicted as an absurd caricature of the paternalistic senior partner who, for different reasons, offers the 'new boy' the same advice as Alex Freer offers Norrie: 'So my advice to you is get to hell out of it.' (p. 17); Murdo experiences the same disillusionment as Norrie in his dealings with those in seeming authority. Indeed, there is an ironic variation on the handing on of skills and experience, a clear awareness of a workplace hierarchy and an understanding that the established community is in possession of a set of knowledges to which the new boy might aspire and gain access:

> MURDO: I wasn't to know Donald can't be trusted . . . Mr Bybugger didn't warn me.
> CHARLEY: Because he's got none of our *talent*.
> *Pause.*
> MURDO: So why did Mr Bybugger *employ* Mr Dick? . . .
> CHARLEY: Oh ho now, Murdo son gorgeous: because talent does not grow on pavements. And. You go out to work every day/ If you *choose* to go out to work every day you are

surrounded by a total dearth of talent. *Oh* aye: a plethora of wankers: this world, this city. (I try to act normal.) (p. 24)

The play demonstrates Heggie's characteristic linguistic sophistry, a heightened language, a poetic dirty-realism influenced by David Mamet and activating the parallel mythic environment of his *noir* cityscape, so clearly part of the 'no mean city' version of urban Glasgow, connoting a set of images wholly in keeping with the myth of industrial, male-dominated culture, social disintegration and moral displacement.

Workplace dramas isolate their subjects, corner them in single rooms, enforce intimacy, apply deadlines, exert pressure to a point where they must explode and burn with life, energy and passion. And yet their engagement with classicism, in some respects such a strength, limits their scope and their ambition. There is the implicit and unspoken understanding in such communities that beyond the tangible structures and repeated patterns of the workplace there is disorder, displacement and confusion. Few of the playwrights who use the powerful symbol of the workplace will follow their characters into the world outside. John Byrne is, perhaps, the one writer who consistently completes this logical progression from order into chaos, assured community into uncertain society. Byrne's work offers a sustained examination of group relations and gendered communities. His plays and television dramas describe groups and communities as their members engage and interact with the world beyond the confines of the workplace.

Byrne's best-known workplace drama, *The Slab Boys*, parallels in important ways the narrative, structure and themes of *The Bevellers* in particular and the workplace drama in general. Byrne, however, rewrites the conventions of time, locus and representation: the 'wrong' subject is expelled and his female characters are given an energetic and provocative voice.

On a *prima-facie* reading Byrne's plays concentrate on male com-munities and male characters (the slab boys, the male-dominated design department at Caledonian Television in *Normal Service* (1979),[11] The Majestics in *Tutti Frutti*). while marginalising female characters into bit-part players and off-stage mothers. Byrne's female characters, however, have a shrewd, not to say jaundiced, understand-ing of the myth and reality of gender roles prescribed by family and workplace hierarchies. The masculinity deconstructed by Byrne's

communities of men is described by his female characters with
ironic detachment and scorn. These women are no mere sexual
accessories and narrative functionaries, they can deflate the collective
male ego with a single glance or barbed aside. Lucille, 'every slab
boy's dream', is quite capable of turning into their worst nightmare:
faced with the prospect of an evening with the wretched Hector
she dismisses him declaring 'I've seen better hanging from a Christmas
tree!'[12]

Byrne's female characters come into their own when poised to
discuss ideas around gender representations and, in particular, the
worth of men. Sadie, Lucille and Bernadette variously come together
in captivating displays of verbal dexterity and sustained characterisation. In *The Slab Boys* Sadie, the cantankerous tea-lady, and Lucille
discuss their plans for 'the Annual Staff Dance of A. F. Stobo &
Co., Carpet Manufacturers':

> SADIE: . . . I'll not be seeing any Town Hall the night, sweet-
> heart. If I thought these had to burl me round a dance floor
> . . . (*Cradles feet*)
>
> LUCILLE: Are you not going? Aw, Sadie, it was a right scream
> last year.
>
> SADIE: I know, flower . . .
>
> LUCILLE: That man of yours was a howl.
>
> SADIE: Aye . . . hysterical. Who else would sprint the length of
> the hall with a pint of Younger's in their fist and try leap-
> frogging over the top of Miss Walkinshaw with that bee-
> hive hairdo of hers . . . eh? Only that stupid scunner I've
> got . . .
>
> LUCILLE: How long was he off his work with the leg?
>
> SADIE: Too long, sweetheart. He had my heart roasted, so he
> did. Sitting there with his bloody leg up on the fender
> shouting at me to put his line on at the bookie's for him.
> 'See that?' I says. 'If you're not up and back at your work
> tomorrow I'll draw this across your back!' I had the poker
> in my hand . . . and I would've done it and all. Had me up
> to high doh. Couldn't get the stookie down the dun-
> garees quick enough. Men? I wouldn't waste my time hen.
>
> LUCILLE: Come off it, Sadie . . .
>
> SADIE: I'd to take the first one that came along. I'd've been
> better off with a lucky bag.
>
> LUCILLE: They're not all like that, for God's sake.

SADIE: You'll learn, flower . . . you're young yet. You can afford to shift through the dross . . . till you come to the real rubbish at the bottom.

LUCILLE: Not this cookie. Lucille Bentley . . . Woman of the World . . . Fling Out Your Men!

SADIE: Wait till you get to my age and all you've got to show's bad feet and a display cabinet . . . (pp. 36–7)

Byrne's conversation is both an artful exchange of ideas and information and an incisive display of refined social analysis.

As McMillan uses Bob's reminiscences in *The Bevellers*, so Byrne uses the idea of shared memory and common histories to construct the easy intimacy of familiarity, belonging and community. Although Byrne is skilled in the witty art of the one-line put down, it is his extended dialogues and conversations which create the feeling of community so marked in his writing. Humour is used to weave together the narrative and illuminate characters and their relationships, with particular jokes and word-plays threading through the entire play. So, the strength of the relationship between Phil and Spanky is revealed as they adopt the register and repartee of a comedy double-act, their conversation spiralling into impenetrability as each responds to and exceeds the other's wit. Their ingenious prattle is, however, less a means of communication than an evasive tactic. Together they construct an ever-more intricate wall of sound as a barrier against the invasive demands of the workplace and beyond. Their dialogue is about creating a community in opposition to the economic hierarchy of the workplace. In terms of the managerial organisation of the slab room Phil and Spanky are relatively powerless. Through their conversational adroitness, however, they create an exclusive space wherein they control meaning. They *use* language aggressively, understanding that rhetorical power determines psychological territories and establishes alternative relationships. To outsiders their conversation might appear to work at a very superficial level, but really a strategy of displacement is at work, setting up different social structures and counter-communities. Ultimately, however, Byrne is concerned to reveal the mendacity of this use of language: Phil and Spanky hide in banter and comic routines. They cannot talk of their real feelings because the locus of the workplace refuses such honesty. Instead, jokes become overloaded with a series of internalised emotions, and even violence is barely concealed by the humour.

Byrne is remarkably aware of and engaged with the history and mythology of Scottish popular culture as it shapes and defines images and representations. Generically *The Slab Boys* is a workplace drama, about the creation and identity of a community of men, focusing on points of inclusion and exclusion. Using comedy, Byrne explodes its essential myth of the strong and suffering male worker and its implicit agenda of fearfulness and misogyny. As in *The Bevellers*, the slab boys constitute a community of knowledge, constructed in relation to a trade and a craft. In *The Slab Boys* the new boy is Alan Downie. Like McMillan's Norrie, Alan's initiation to this adult community is symbolised in language and the introduction of, more or less, new sign systems. In a parody of naming, Alan is variously referred to as Archie, Andy, Eamonn, Alec, Albert, Alfie, Alma and Agnes:

> PHIL: . . . let's show you some of the mysteries of the Slab Room. Mr Farrell . . .
>
> SPANKY: Mr Mac?
>
> PHIL: I'm just showing young Dowdalls here some of the intricacies of our work. If you and the boy would care to stand to one side . . . Many thanks. Right Alec . . . this here is what we call a sink . . . s—i—n—k. Now I don't expect you to pick up all these terms immediately but you'll soon get the hang of it. And this (*grabs Hector*) is what we cry a Slab Boy. (p. 6)

It would be wrong, however, to limit one's understanding of Byrne's writing to trifling and inconsequential parody and pantomime. Byrne does not write mere cartoon characters equipped only for facetiousness and jest. His creations are complex, humane characterisations, demanding our critical respect for their vivacity and their integrity. The plays are sustained and extravagant engagements with some of the themes and myths which constrain the Scottish imagination and veer headily from sparkling, vibrant wit to earnest and deeply affecting tragedy. Unlike the workplace dramas of McMillan and Heggie, Byrne's communities are hopefully and imaginatively contextualised, insisting upon an environment distinguished by its humanity and morality.

Such compassion is at the root of Byrne's television drama series *Tutti Frutti*, itself a bravura variation on the theme of the new boy and rites of initiation. Danny McGlone returns to Glasgow for his brother's funeral but finds himself at variance with a series of distinctive definitions of community and family. After the funeral he is offered a lift by the band's roadie, Dennis:

DENNIS: Where do you want me to drop you?

DANNY: I thought we were going to Theresa's.

DENNIS: No. *They* are going to Theresa's.

DANNY: Good God! He was my brother, I can surely go back tae his hoose fur a few drinks after his funeral.

DENNIS: There are three outfits where blood ties don't count *that* much, Danny Boy – the Magic Circle, the Mafia and The Majestics. Now, where did you say you wanted me to drop you?

The series, then, is about the realignment and reinterpretation of such codes of belonging and a precise response to the dominant themes and images suggested by and discussed within contemporary Scottish drama: ideas of belonging, a series of shared histories, revisions of the idea of family, masculinity in various degrees of crisis, the definitive role of women as mothers.

The exclusivity and the psychological importance of the existing community is stressed repeatedly in *Tutti Frutti* where the prestige of being a Majestic is both celebrated and satirised. Danny is tested as the 'new boy' – 'You're still on probation, watch it' says Fud, quite clearly establishing thematic links with the hierarchical exclusivity of the workplace drama. As with Norrie, in *The Bevellers*, and Alan, in *The Slab Boys*, initiation is signalled by rites of naming, so Danny is referred to as 'Danny Boy' and 'the boy McGlone' until he has 'proved' himself worthy of membership to the Majestics. The narrative and structural role of the novitiate is later assigned to Suzi Kettles, who is employed to replace first Vincent and then Danny, although her role is further complicated because of her gender. Suzi articulates the overt sexism of masculine communities when, with heavy irony, she declares:

> I'd just like to say what an honour and privilege it is to be the first genetically unsound person to join the fabulous (*feigns laughter*) . . . sorry . . . Majestics.

Workplace dramas seem, almost by definition, to deal with masculine communities, groups of men, not groups of women, 'new boys' not 'new girls'. However, Scottish drama has come to reset the conventions of the workplace drama and to encompass the patterns of women's lives and work routines. A lively alternative has emerged which deals with communities of women, constituted not just within a discourse of family (although this is still a strong element) but within different types of community, different conventions of belonging, reset with different visual, linguistic and dramatic codes.

In *Communities of Women*, Nina Auerbach's project is to reset the literary phenomenon of the specifically female community within the revisionist framework of feminism, so reinstating sororial strength in moments of shared recognition:

> Initiation into a band of brothers is a traditional privilege symbolized by uniforms, rituals, and fiercely shared loyalties; but sisterhood . . . looks often like a blank exclusion. A community of women may suggest less the honor of fellowship than an antisociety, an austere banishment from both social power and biological rewards. (p. 3)

Contemporary Scottish drama's marked interest in the depiction of communities of women has indeed found moments of exclusion, disillusionment and disenfranchisement. However, and perhaps in reaction to the determinedly formulaic drama around communities of men, and developing from the drama's engagement with the idea of family, Scottish playwrights have found and described moments of celebration and release in their engagement with female communities. Whilst it is true that female communities may be subject to socio-economic austerity and marginalisation, within that locus Scottish writers have found cause for pleasure in the recognition of shared identities and common interest. In plays ranging in tone and style from Tony Roper's *The Steamie* (1987) to Donna Franceschild's *And the Cow Jumped Over the Moon* (1990), Sue Glover's *Bondagers* and *Sacred Hearts* (1994) to Rona Munro's *Bold Girls* (1991), unity is affirmed in song, in dance and in play.[13] Although the moments of release may be fleeting – as transitory as the escape to Barrie's faerie land – such experiences are dramatically poignant, transcending the individual and insisting upon group participation and collective action. Within communities of women belonging is assumed and implicit in the simple acknowledgement of sisterhood, not constructed and restricted within the exclusive cabals of masculine structures. Indeed, within the female community the pleasures of sharing are potentially more egalitarian than are the hierarchical structures which connote masculinity. In such a context it is perhaps easily apparent why female communities will so explicitly celebrate friendship:

> When you've got pals
> You've got something so rerr

> Tell me what could be as fine as
> Passin' time with all your chinas.
>
> When you've got pals
> Makes it easy to bear
> All the pain and all the pressure
> Bless your pals.[14]

Although masculine communities replay similarly strong relationships, there seems to be a common resistance to the outspoken avowal of such sentiments. (It is, indeed, inaccurately stereotypical, if not prosaically untrue, to allow that women will share and discuss their feelings while men refuse such openness. It is nevertheless a societal norm advanced with surprising regularity.)

> I want a place on a big farm. Plenty lassies for the crack. Plenty plooman [sic] for the dancing![15]

Accurately or not, the dominant image within Scottish drama is of women offering a consistently more supportive and emotionally open community than is available within masculine communities. There is little evidence of language being used aggressively or as avoidance technique and women are depicted as being more willing to accept and to share their emotions, to be mutually respectful in rather different ways to the support offered to members of masculine communities. For example, Mrs Culfeathers in *The Steamie* is as powerless as McMillan's Alex Freer and yet her position within the community of women is affirmed by Magrit, who assures the oldest member of the group that 'you deserve respect Mrs Culfeathers. Yer a fine old woman' (p. 255). Age is no guarantee of respect or indicator of unanimity either in the bevelling shop, where Alex Freer is to be dismissed out of hand, or in the slab room, where Curry and Miss Walkinshaw are teased and hectored.

And yet with these positive depictions of sharing and open communities of women the range of character-types is limited and there remains a traditionalist tendency to value the stoical woman, the indomitable mother, the woman defined within the exclusive structure of the family. Following this axiomatic premise, the family remains under less threat within Scottish theatre culture than within post-industrial society generally. In Scottish texts the family has maintained its ubiquity as structural motif. As such the literal, 'real' family group is both common in itself and frequently reworked to structure other versions of community, so that communities of all descriptions replicate the internal relations of the family. However, the family, despite its seeming ubiquity, is never unproblematic – it is clear that the social and gender roles available within this totemic structure are often described as limited, prescriptive and constrained.

What is important about the conventions and the model of the family is the consistent set of structural roles it replays. Despite, or because of, the fundamental phallocentricity of the myths of Scottishness, the depiction of women functions comparatively to illustrate a wider set of gender representations. In this the role of 'mother' is most revealing of the scope of gender images and familial structures described. It is the mother who habitually takes on the dominant or idealised position within the family and it is the mother who, through a series of parallel representations and received images, is formed into something of an idealised and mythic figure. Thus, Maggie in *Men Should Weep* is archetypally a strong influence on the make-up of her family. She, like Dolly, Magrit and Mrs Culfeathers in *The Steamie*, like Elizabeth Gordon Quinn, like Maggie in *Bondagers*, functions knowingly as the public representative of her family, whose moral worth will be judged through her ability to hold the family together and take full part in the general community around her:

> God knows there's none of us got money
> Still and all the things we do have
> They were bought and paid for, working
> With the fruits of honest labour.
>
> And there's none of us would covet
> Any special things that you have
> Cos there's none of us are better
> Than a good and decent neighbour.[16]

This is, of course, the mythology of the tenement refused by Elizabeth Gordon Quinn but by which she is judged by her neighbours, who significantly find common ground only in terms of gender:

> You're a woman! Your house might not be as clean or as well-kept as most, but you're still a woman. (p. 118)

Despite the currency of mothers as defining presence, it would be wrong to suggest that they are mere ciphers. The point about mothers in Scottish drama is that as characters they are diverse and unexpected, yet structurally they remain familiar: Phil explains this point to Spanky in Byrne's *Still Life* by arguing that, 'One guy's maw is another guy's gonk'[17] (p. 116). Alasdair Cameron is more re-strained, advancing the analysis by arguing that:

> In recent Scottish drama mothers seldom make an appearance, but still contrive to become the centre of attention in many plays.[18]

Even in *The Bevellers*, an archetypal workplace drama about men and relationships within a community of men, the idea and the ideal of the mother is woven into the drama. Norrie is questioned about his mother, eliciting, albeit briefly, a degree of sympathy from all the characters:.

NORRIE: . . . Ma mother's deid. Died when ah wis thirteen. Two years ago.

. . .

BOB: . . . Must've been sudden, eh?

NORRIE: Aye, it wis during the school holidays it wis. I wakened up wan mornin an' there wis this noise in the kitchen. A lot o voices. I went through an' they widnae let me in. I jist saw her lyin in a chair. That wis it.

BOB: Ah didnae mean tae make ye greet noo.

NORRIE: Ah'm no greetin. It's a long time. Two year.

BOB: Aye, a long time fur a boy tae be withoot his old-lady. Hear that, youz fullas. This boy here's been tellin me aboot his oul'-wife dyin, and he's no greetin. No much wrang wi a boy that can dae that, eh?

. . .

ROUGER: Whit wis wrang wi her? (*Norrie doesn't answer*) . . . It's a'right, young-yin, we're no trying tae extract ye. Jist askin whit happened tae her. (pp. 14–15)

It is significant that this hint at kindness is elicited around the idea of the dead mother and the child, specifically the male child, without a mother. It is typical of this myth that the death of a mother is permanently debilitating, arresting emotional development and test-ing independence and maturity.

John Byrne is most consistently interested in this theme of the 'off-stage presence' of the mother. Throughout *The Slab Boys Trilogy* characters talk about and around the role of the mother: Phil's highly destructive, mentally ill mother is a source of poignant drama and psychological tension and Miss Walkinshaw's repressed rage towards her aged mother is released in an extraordinary moment of material violence in *Cuttin' a Rug*, with Lucille as expectant mother in *Still Life*, itself the starkest example of Byrne's fascination with the absent mother -- the drama being set at Phil's mother's grave. This image is a starting point for the subsequent *Tutti Frutti* where the idea and mythology of the mother is a central theme of the drama, established at the very start of the series with Danny and Dennis's first conversation:

> DENNIS: So, how you been since we last seen ye? Be your auld-dear's funeral, wasn't it? Better watch it doesn't become a habit, eh? When was that again? . . . '77?
>
> DANNY (*tight-lipped*): '78.
>
> DENNIS: That's right. Ah remember Eddie breaking the news tae the Big Fella. Cowdenbeath, it was – right in the middle of 'Alright Mama'. No kiddin'. Straight up. Strolled on stage, right in the middle of the boys' big number. Never even took his hat off.

The image of the mother becomes something of a structuring absence in the series. The mother is continually celebrated as metaphor for childhood simplicity and lost innocence, a totemic embodiment of virtue and rectitude, so that when Suzi scolds the somewhat inebriated Danny, he responds with predictable self-pity:

> SUZI: If your mother could only see you now. (*Exit*)
>
> DANNY (*drunk and morose*): Somebody mention my mother? Did ah tell you she was dead? Where ur ye? Likewise ma brother and ma father . . . all dead. You are lookin' at . . . where you got tae? . . . you are lookin' at . . . you are lookin' at an orphan, Kettles.

Whilst masculinity is often tempered with this fantasy of lost simplicity and an idealised memory of the mother, most of the women in the community which orbits around the central core of the Majestics are to be understood in more substantive relation to motherhood. In the course of the series it is revealed that Suzi is pregnant by her estranged and violent husband and Noreen is unhappily childless, adopting something of a maternal role towards her husband. Vincent, whose masculinity is at the root of the series' narrative complexity, is central to this analysis. The self-styled 'Iron Man of Scottish rock', he is the most stridently masculine of the group, wearing leathers, striking an aggressive pose of seemingly assured virility and power – a rock and roll version of the urban hardman, he maintains a disintegrating and barren relationship with his wife, Noreen, and an unequal sexual relationship with the infatuated Glenna. Her phantom pregnancy (combined with the fact that her name has connotative associations with natural Scotland) transforms her into something of a mythic figure. From this, then, the depiction of her suicide (ritualised through the use of music) shifts her role further into the metaphoric. Ultimately, however, Noreen's angry revelations of Vincent's impotency expose the delusive nature of the myth and iconography of the hardman within Scottish culture, and affirm the structural role of woman in the translation and deconstruction of the signs of masculinity (a definitive role throughout the twentieth century). Classically Barrie allows Maggie Shand, in *What Every Women Knows*, a similarly mordant insight into the mythology of Scottish masculinity and the correlative role of women:

> Every man who is high up loves to think that he has done it all himself; and the wife smiles, and lets it go at that. It's our only joke. Every woman knows that.[19]

Far from this being the 'only joke' available to women, contemporary Scottish drama is full of an eclectic mix of female figures who are perceptive and incisive in their analysis of the myths of masculinity. Indeed, new Scottish drama is notable for its dynamic use of comedy and verbal sparring between the sexes, both the stuff of inconsequential banter and a blacker comedy of recognition. Sadie, in *The Slab Boys* and *Cuttin' a Rug*, is a delightfully acid observer of human foibles, always ready with a misanthropic jibe:

> You not with an escort this year, Miss Walkinshaw? They're not worth it, are they? By the time you're halfway through a St Bernard's their tongues is hanging out looking for a barrel of drink.[20]

But it should not be assumed that women only find humour at the expense of men and moments of celebration in sybaritic release. Scottish drama proffers groups of women who counter Auerbach's gloomy diagnosis and find the recognition of themselves as a group reason enough for stepping outwith the limits of their usual identities. Such empowerment of community, while spontaneous and animated, may have a more serious purpose, for the dynamic which brings together a group of women is likely to be motivated by more than revelry. Women are only occasionally fully empowered and independent of a phallocentric economic order, more often being on the edges of or dependent upon groups of men and patriarchal communities. The conceits used to bring women together – washing in the steamie, being treated in a cancer ward, agricultural labourers working on a Borders farm, prostitutes being threatened by a serial killer taking refuge in a church – are reflections of this marginalisation. Their togetherness may be politically motivated (as in *Sacred Hearts*), socially and economically imposed (as in *The Steamie* and *Bondagers*) in ways that seem not to be the case in connection with communities of men, where there is a dominant ethos around the dignity of labour. Women's work patterns seem to efface such discourses, and while one might find these representations of the exploited and disenfranchised limited and limiting, their communion is manifest with a democratic egalitarianism that celebrates and empowers where masculine communities exclude and humiliate.

Scottish drama is habitually concerned with the nature and politics of the community, with the moment of inclusion or exclusion from that community as recurrent narrative spine. The community as structuring principle is complicated in the drama by a tendency to focus on gender-specific communities. Such exclusive groupings may find definition in an unsettled negotiation between the 'explicit' and 'formulated' codes of certainty and the 'whispered' and 'impalpable' structures of the disenfranchised. Ideological codes, identified by Auerbach's study of the literary novel, define communities and social groupings ranging in scale from the family to the nation. The vocabulary she uses to describe belonging to communities of women and communities of men is very similar to the vocabulary used by many commentators to describe belonging to nations. It seems possible to suggest that the understanding of identity in Scottish culture is in a similar negotiation between the explicit codes of the legitimate and the whispered codes of the illegitimate.

The gendered communities of Scottish drama, following Auerbach's categorisation, seem to function in predictable directions: male communities tending towards a prescriptive set of codes may produce a drama typified by its engagement with rites of passage and initiation, describing a community that is defensive and near impervious to attack by outsiders. In comparison, drama centring on groups of women, where the gendered codings of communion may be less dogmatic, may show a tendency for community and gender to be constructed less as an exclusive club and more as a social idea, a sense of kinship and belonging, offering rewards of marked intangibility, mere moments of escape and delight. Internally, the community of women may be more egalitarian than equivalent communities of men. New and different members of feminine communities are not subject to any particular tests of constituency: Doreen, the new comer in *The Steamie*, and Tottie, the 'daftie' in *Bondagers*, are easily accepted into the pre-existing community of older women without the formulaic rituals of initiation indulged in by communities of men. A fundamental difference is that the male group is isolated, if not isolationist, whilst the female group is almost always defined through its relationship to others, and in particular though its subjection to men and to male power. This is clearly articulated in Glover's *Bondagers*, an extended account of women finding communion within a context of economic subjugation:

> 'Don't be ridiculous, Ellen,' says the maister. 'We can't do away with the bondage. I can't employ a man who hasn't a woman to work with him. One pair of horses to every 50 acre, one hind for every pair of horses, one bondager for every hind. That's the way its done,' he says. 'I'm all for progress,' he says, 'but I won't do away with the bondage,' he says. 'We need the women. Who else would do the work? . . . Women's work, for women's pay.' (p. 36)

Sociologist David McCrone is one of the many commentators who identify and describe the essential phallocentricity of Scottish culture. He suggests a limited palette of identities available within Scottish culture, constraining the roles available to characters into gendered archetypes and consequently '. . . relegating women to walk-on parts, and to their role as keepers of the moral and family values of the nation.'[21] Such prescriptive tendencies thread through the whole range of texts and representations and are manifest in the recurrence of distinctive character types, quintessentially in the image of the mother. It seems possible to suggest, therefore, that debates around nationhood (as it concerns commonality and the expression of distinction *and* as it restricts access to the community) parallel representations of gender-specific communities and the limited set of identities legitimised within the culture's collective imagination.

In his influential study of *Imagined Communities: Reflections on the Origin and Rise of Nationalism* (1983) – the one canonical theoretical volume within contemporary Scottish studies – Benedict Anderson is much preoccupied with the definition, delineation, and experience of

the 'nation' in a way that may parallel structures of gender organisation. Anderson's liberal and aphoristic definition of the nation as
'an imagined political community'[22] may be interpreted as rather
similar to the illusive nature of feminine communities. In arguing
for the efficacy of the imaginary, Anderson allows for a version of
belonging which is eclectic, multifarious and resists closure. He
allows for a version of the nation, a version of community, which is
open, egalitarian and pacific. In opposition, and in practice, the
application of the idea of the nation may be less tolerant, for nations
also define themselves as exclusive and 'sovereign',[23] building barriers
(both literal and metaphoric) to limit access and regulate membership, determinedly separating the elect from the ostracised. It follows
that nationalism will prefer, prioritise, value and reward one grouping
over another. The point in the establishment of society, of community, at which one group, one identity, is legitimised and the other
disenfranchised, marginalised, cast, however crudely, as 'other', is a
result of the socio-cultural development of the community, a conjunc-
tion of historical, economic, social and political factors but defined
in the nation's traditions, myths and collective imagination, replayed
in cultural texts. One might suggest that whilst nations emerge as a
geo-political phenomenon, developing through an interaction of
socio-economic, cultural and political factors, gender is a similar
construction, a bio-political system whose meaning is as dependent
on shared moments of recognition and rites of passage as is that of
national identity and nationalism.

Debates around identity, and particularly a concern around
national identity, have been of continuing currency for Scottish
criticism: but are the issues around political and cultural nationalism,
political and cultural history, debated by McCrone, Tom Nairn,
Colin McArthur, Craig Beveridge and Ronald Turnbull and others
of any real use for the literary critic, the arts practitioner or indeed
the audience?[24] Although Nairn has been criticised by subsequent
commentators such as Beveridge and Turnbull and McCrone, his
formulation around national identity, cultural heritage and political
process is of enduring interest. Nairn is only one of the critics who
have, in the context of historiographical analysis, characterised Scottish culture as divided – often irreconcilably so:

> 'Identity' tends . . . to be a term of approval. In the psychologistic
> terms which inform so much discussion of nationalism, 'identity'
> is what frustrated nationalities want and nation-states possess

. . . Scotland appears as a highly-developed society (as distinct from simply being part of a larger development area, the United Kingdom), which, nevertheless, does not possess all the standard fitments of development. It is hard to avoid metaphor in describing the situation – 'decapitation', 'neurosis', or even 'schizophrenia', and so on.[25]

Nairn's description of Scotland as a schizoid nation – a culture of madness, or at least of mental and emotional instability – has a degree of relevance to aspects of Scottish cultural criticism, but seems less than definitive for cultural praxis, where engagements with the 'impalpable', the 'devious', the 'imagined' and the 'other' are remarkably common and easily confinable within structural and historical analyses. The role of mythology, legend and fable, the Gothic, the supernatural and the unconscious within the development of the Scottish imagination is not a symptom of psychosis but a sophisticated engagement with the fantastic that other cultures might celebrate as magic realism.

However, it is pertinent to bear in mind that the state of psychic disorder examined by Nairn is a recognisable metaphor used to describe the woman who, in transgressing social and sexual convention, is labelled lunatic and hidden away from corruptible eyes. This discourse of psychological derangement may parallel Auerbach's analysis of female communities as suggesting 'the impalpable and the devious'. It is, then, but a short step to recognising the female community and its potential for excess and indulgence as an uncovering of society's fears of the *unheimlich* aspects of the feminine, an uncanny display of female communion against the hegemonic male hierarchy.

Rather paradoxically (and despite the various representations and thematic concerns developed within Scottish culture as being dominated by a mythology of masculinity) there is another tendency, prevalent particularly within film, for 'Scotland' (physical Scotland as opposed to cultural Scotland) not to engender a negative psychosis but to be magically transformative and psychologically healing: in *Brigadoon* (Vincente Minelli, 1954), *The Maggie* (Alexander Mackendrick, 1954) and *Local Hero* (Bill Forsyth, 1983) the physical experience of being in Scotland, and, of course, being connected with a woman who functions as the personification of Scotland, returns urban man to his contented, complete and natural self.

In an unexpected, and certainly positive, way it is *not* Scottish culture as subject that is psychotic – Scottish myths and stories are rich as any in terms of psychological scope, crossing and recrossing between different states of being, interacting with the shady, the hidden, the unknown and the fantastic, playing out epic and formative dramas. It is their limited, one-dimensional interpretation which has compromised contemporary culture to the point of psychosis. Debate around the semiotics of Scotland, laid bare in engagements with popular culture, has failed to advance beyond a tendency to categorise texts and images into a series of more or less predictable classifications. It is almost redundant to name them; but they are, of course, variations on the themes of tartanry, kailyard and latterly Clydeside-ism.[26] The continued currency of these discourses reveals a crisis not of the culture *per se* but of the critical agenda. It is a restrictive and destructive cult which has allowed Barrie to be, at best, ignored, at worst, blamed for traitorous excesses of couthy parochialism, Byrne to be dismissed as kitsch purveyor of irrelevant and apolitical escapism and Scotland's stories to be reduced to Glasgow's stories, narrated by a hard-bitten male detective. This obsessive pursuit of critical neatness may indeed be a psychic disorder, a neurosis based on the immaturity of a critical programme and agenda which seeks to limit the meanings of a culture debased as obscure, inferiorist and parochial by the imposition of one, all-encompassing and hermetically ubiquitous identity which, it is claimed, is fully representative of a set of multifaceted images, movements, characters and politics.

It need not be so. It is evocative of the emphasis placed on the role of 'emotion' and 'sentiment' within the Scottish world view that one can so easily parallel and compare Anderson's distillation of 'imagined communities' with Nairn's formulation of the nation, based as it is on medical and psychoanalytic discourses. 'Imagining' for a community whose myths are so enmeshed with the irrational (emotion and sentiment, fantasy and the supernatural) may compromise the reading of any of the structuring narratives of the folk memory, reducing their application to mere psychic malady. But, equally, the imaginary has the potential to liberate and to allow the artist and critic to be creative in their engagement with the discourses of Scottishness. To use the fantastic infrastructure of the collective unconscious in a creative and abstract manner may also result in a version of culture where meanings are open for reinterpretation and narrative closure is a practical as well as a psychological impossibility. Thus one is faced with a drama characterised by emotional complexity, unsettled and extended narratives, a drama that analyses and celebrates sharing and social responsibility, that acknowledges and reflects a diverse and ever-changing society, played out by dynamic groups and potentially proactive in debates around community and identity.

Increasingly, writers of drama are responding to this idea of reassessing and re-creating in the context of existing cultural codes and conventions, thereby exposing the emotional uncertainties beneath totemic structures and, finally, taking knowing responsibility for the nature and the effects of our own culture. It is only with an awareness of the social and political importance of this shared responsibility to the meanings of Scottish culture that the drama can confront its cultural heritage and criticism can find fresh impetus to reassess its orthodoxies.

NOTES

1. Nina Auerbach *Communities of Women: An Idea in Fiction* (Cambridge, Mass. and London, Harvard University Press 1979) pp. 8–9.
2. Roddy McMillan *The Bevellers* (Edinburgh, Southside 1974); John Byrne *The Slab Boys Trilogy* (London, Penguin 1987); Sue Glover *Bondagers* in *Theatre Scotland* 6 (Summer 1993) pp. 32–44.
3. John Byrne *Tutti Frutti* (script unpublished: BBC Scotland 1987).
4. J. A. Ferguson *Campbell of Kilmohr* (London, Gowans and Gray 1915); Neil Gunn *The Ancient Fire* (unpublished: first performance 8 October 1929); Robins Millar *The Shawlie* (London and Glasgow, Gowans and Gray 1924); Paul Vincent Carroll *Green Cars Go East* (London, Samuel French 1948); Robert McLeish *The Gorbals Story* (Edinburgh, 7:84 Publications 1985); Ena Lamont Stewart *Men Should Weep* (1983. Edinburgh, 7:84 Publications 1986).
5. Alasdair Cameron *Study Guide to Twentieth-Century Scottish Drama* (Glasgow, University of Glasgow, Department of Scottish Literature 1990) p. 80.
6. Chris Hannan *Elizabeth Gordon Quinn* in Alasdair Cameron ed. *Scot-Free: New Scottish Plays* (London, Nick Hern 1990) pp. 105–46.
7. *The Plays of J. M. Barrie* ed. A. E. Wilson (Definitive Edition, London, Hodder and Stoughton 1942) p. 506.
8. *The Bevellers* p. 27.
9. Bill Bryden *The Ship* (unpublished: first performance 16 September 1990) and *Willie Rough* (Edinburgh, Southside 1972); Iain Heggie *Clyde Nouveau* (unpublished: first performance 29 August 1989); Chris Hannan *The Evil-Doers and The Baby* (London, Nick Hern 1991).
10. Iain Heggie *A Wholly Healthy Glasgow* (London, Methuen 1988).
11. John Byrne *Normal Service* in *Plays and Players* Vol. 26, nos 8 and 9 (May and June 1979).

12. *The Slab Boys Trilogy* p. 16.
13. Tony Roper *The Steamie*, in Alasdair Cameron, *Scot-Free* pp. 201–75; Donna Franceschild *And the Cow Jumped Over the Moon* (unpublished: first performance 2 November 1990); Sue Glover *Sacred Hearts* (unpublished: first performance 11 February 1994); Rona Munro *Bold Girls* (London, Samuel French 1991).
14. *The Steamie* p. 269.
15. *Bondagers* p. 33.
16. *The Steamie* p. 272.
17. *The Slab Boys Trilogy* p. 116.
18. *Study Guide* p. 136.
19. *The Plays of J. M. Barrie* p. 745.
20. *The Slab Boys Trilogy* p. 58.
21. David McCrone *Understanding Scotland: the Sociology of a Stateless Nation* (London, Routledge 1992) p. 190.
22. Benedict Anderson *Imagined Communities: Reflections on the Origin and Rise of Nationalism* [1983] (London, Verso 1990) p. 15.
23. Ibid. p. 16.
24. Tom Nairn *The Break-Up of Britain: Crisis and Neo-Nationalism* [1977] (Second ed. London, Verso 1981); Colin McArthur ed. *Scotch Reels: Scotland in Cinema and Television* (London, B.F.I. 1982); Craig Beveridge and Ronald Turnbull *The Eclipse of Scottish Culture: Inferiorism and the Intellectuals* (Edinburgh, Polygon 1989).
25. *The Break-Up of Britain* p. 172.
26. In this connection see *The Break-Up of Britain*; *Scotch Reels*; Cairns Craig *The History of Scottish Literature* Vol. 4: *The Twentieth Century* (Aberdeen, Aberdeen University Press 1987); John Caughie 'De-Picting Scotland: Film, Myth and Scotland's Story' in Timothy Ambrose ed. *Presenting Scotland's Story* (Edinburgh, HMSO 1989) pp. 44–58; *Understanding Scotland*; and the cultural magazine, *Cencrastus* (1980–).

9

A Scottish Trawl

EDWIN MORGAN

His head was covered with a singular profusion of light brown hair, which he usually wore coiled up under his hat. When he used to attend church on Sunday (of which he was at all times a regular attendant), after lifting his hat, he used to raise his right hand to his hair to assist a shake of his head, when his long hair fell over his loins and every female eye at least was turned upon him as with a light step he ascended to the gallery, where he usually sat.[1]

That was a description of the young James Hogg, aged about twenty, as seen by the son of his employer. Hogg was not good-looking, but he was strong and athletic, and he obviously had some head of hair – if it came right down over his loins it could well be the envy of the girls in the church who gazed at him. Why did he do it? Narcissism? Vanity? Desire to call attention to himself? It seems a double gesture – a man announcing his individuality and at the same time suggesting that he would like to be more a part of the body of the kirk than he actually was, a man who all his life, as things turned out, was to feel himself an outsider, one who did not quite fit in, either with the sophisticated Edinburgh society he barged into or with the peasant shepherd community he left and tried to return to. And his fiction is full of outcast figures, not least both Robert and Gil-Martin in the *Confessions of a Justified Sinner*. Any time I read that account of Hogg and his hair I am reminded of another quotation.

In the meantime, young Wringhim was an object to all of the uttermost disgust. The blood flowing from his mouth and

nose he took no pains to stem, neither did he so much as wipe
it away; so that it spread over all his cheeks, and breast, even
off at his toes.[2]

Is there anything more than a visual similarity between the cascading
of the hair and the cascading of the blood? The passage just quoted
is from the early part of the *Confessions*, where the young Robert
Wringhim is doing his best to disrupt a tennis game his brother
George is engaged in. George, intensely irritated, has hit him on
the face with his racket, making blood gush from his nose and
mouth. The point of the episode seems to be this: Robert had tried
but failed to kick George in the crutch and – hopefully – damage
his virility, but he now finds that he does successfully bring the
game of tennis to an end by less aggressive behaviour, as he runs
among the players, streaming with blood and, as the book says,
'courting persecution'.

In her book *Between Men*[3] Kosofsky Sedgwick discusses Hogg's
Confessions within a very interesting conspectus of the Gothic novel
and its relation to homosexuality and homophobia, and describes
the falling blood in the tennis episode as a 'feminization' of Robert,
who nevertheless goes on to pursue and destroy his very masculine,
very heterosexual brother George. Whether or not one accepts the
term feminisation, there is clearly an intense bonding, based on
hatred, between the two brothers in the first half of the novel, as
there is a more powerful bonding, based at first on quasi-erotic
attraction and then on fear and panic, between Robert and Gil-
Martin in the second half. The fact that Robert, the hero of the
novel, is driven to distraction, is defeated, is killed, as the outcome
of these bondings, does not mean that there is no positive homosexual undercurrent in the book, whether you think with Kosofsky
Sedgwick that the emphasis on power and control and domination is
essentially homophobic, or whether (as I would tend to take it) the
obvious and special attraction the story has for gay readers may indicate a painful homophilia rather than a drastic homophobia.

I would, however, like to move onto a different tack, taking
again the idea of the outcast. Douglas Gifford in his book on
Hogg remarks in passing that the novel might have been set off by
a reading of Marlowe's *Doctor Faustus*, but he does not pursue the
thought.[4] I believe there are instructive parallels. The theme of
damnation, the invoking of transhuman powers which you cannot
in the end control, the isolation of the central character, the theo-

logical discussions, the shape-changing disguises, the marginalisation of women, the slave–master bonding, and perhaps above all the panic and despair as the story hurries towards its final hellish outcome – these are all features that draw the two works close together.

> In particular, I brought myself to despise, if not to abhor, the beauty of women, looking on it as the greatest snare to which mankind are subjected, and though young men and maidens, and even old women, (my mother among the rest), taxed me with being an unnatural wretch, I gloried in my acquisition; and to this day, am thankful for having escaped the most dangerous of all snares.[5]

The unnatural wretch in that quotation is Robert, the Justified Sinner. It is as if he were following an earlier command.

> Thou canst not marry; thou canst not serve two masters, God, and my Prince: for wedlock is a chiefe institution ordained of God, and that thou hast promised to defie, as we doe all, and that hast thou also done: and moreover thou hast confirmed it with thy blood: perswade thy selfe, that what thou doost in contempt of wedlock, it is all to thine owne delight.[6]

That is the voice of Mephostophiles, addressing Faustus in *The Historie of the damnable life, and deserved death of Doctor John Faustus* which Marlowe used as a source for his play. But there is more to it than the many parallels. The real-life original of Dr Faustus, Georg Faust, a German wandering scholar of the early sixteenth century, was among other things homosexual, and had sometimes to move around fairly smartly to escape scandal. This is surely one of the reasons why Marlowe, himself homosexual, was attracted to the story, and to its suggestion that unauthorised behaviour, whether spiritual or carnal, carried fascinating but dreadful risks. As a final rider to that, and to the Marlowe–Hogg parallel, remember that it was the homosexual André Gide who as a novelist and critic rediscovered and recommended Hogg's *Confessions* after its long neglect and wrote the famous preface to it where he said: 'It is long since I can remember being so taken hold of, so voluptuously tormented by any book.'[7] That voluptuous torment appears as a link in a long chain.

> Frae joyous tavern, reeling drunk,
> Wi' fiery phizz, and ein half sunk,

Behald the bruiser, fae to a'
That in the reek o' gardies fa':
Close by his side, a feckless race
O' macaronies shew their face,
And think they're free frae skaith or harm,
While pith befriends their leader's arm:
Yet fearfu' aften o' their maught,
They quatt the glory o' the faught
To this same warrior wha led
Thae heroes to bright honour's bed;
And aft the hack o' honour shines
In bruiser's face wi' broken lines:
Of them sad tales he tells anon,
Whan ramble and whan fighting's done;
And, like Hectorian, ne'er impairs
The brag and glory o' his sairs.
    Whan feet in dirty gutters plash,
And fock to wale their fitstaps fash;
At night the macaroni drunk,
In pools or gutters aftimes sunk:
Hegh! what a fright he now appears,
Whan he his corpse dejected rears!
Look at that head, and think if there
The pomet slaister'd up his hair!
The cheeks observe, where now cou'd shine
The scancing glories o' carmine?
Ah, legs! in vain the silk-worm there
Display'd to view her eidant care;
For stink, instead of perfumes, grow,
And clarty odours fragrant flow.[8]

That is from Robert Fergusson's vivid poem of Edinburgh life, *Auld Reikie*, published in 1773. It is a splendid passage, but what is it all about? Is it possible to deny that there is a marked homoerotic feel to it? Boxing as a modern sport takes its rise in the eighteenth century, and there are many literary references to it, and to attempts at its regulation. Boxers in Fergusson's time, like boxers today, evidently had their male groupies. Fergusson's bruiser is drunk, he's big, he's swinging his arms, he's dangerous, but he's also past his best, he reminisces a lot, and Fergusson attaches a remarkable pathos to him after initially presenting him as a brute: 'And aft the hack o' honour shines / In bruiser's face wi' broken lines.' He reminds you of some of Peter Howson's early portraits of 'heroic dossers'. But if the boxer is a focus for pathos and respect, his followers are satirised as a 'feckless race / O' macaronies'. 'Macaroni' was a recent, fashionable word (the Oxford English Dictionary's first quotation is from 1764), and Fergusson enjoys using it, in other poems as well as this one. A macaroni was a fop, a dandy, with an underlying suggestion of effeminacy and homosexuality. 'There is indeed,' said the *Oxford Magazine* in 1770, 'a kind of animal, neither male nor female, a thing of the neuter gender, lately started up amongst us. It is called a Macaroni.' Notice the contemptuous 'it'.[9] In Fergusson's poem these macaronies are drawn, like moths to a flame, to the very macho character of a boxer, and they flit by his side from tavern to tavern, enjoying his propinquity even while they are afraid of it, finally getting drunk and collapsing in the gutter. Their rouged cheeks, their perfume, their pomaded hair, their silk stockings – everything is ruined. And Fergusson really lays it on. Why is he so hard on them? Does he perhaps protest too much? One of his closest friends was an Italian *castrato* singer, after all, and that cannot be too far from the macaroni class. Or does he genuinely despise them because he was, as we know, a very slovenly man, who seldom changed his clothes or combed his hair? And speaking of clothes: what are we to make of his poem 'To My Auld Breeks', where he laments the fact that his trousers are falling to bits, and are so much patched and holed that he will have to get rid of them – what will happen to them? – oh, they will end up under some woman's petticoats, 'mould and motty' as they are, receiving a new lease of life as a pair of whatever knickers were called in eighteenth-century Edinburgh, and this will help her secretly to 'wear the breeks'. Is that a piece of schoolboy humour, or should we call in a psychologist? I am full of questions about Fergusson!

And here is another one. We know that the poet was a great clubman, and Edinburgh was full of convivial clubs, mostly all-male clubs, at that time. Fergusson was a member of the Cape Club and greatly enjoyed it. But did he ever go to a club called The Beggar's Benison? This took its title from a proverbial phrase: if a man gave money to a beggar, the beggar thanked him by saying, 'May prick and purse never fail ye.' This club, like many others, had a lot of ritual, but its rituals were rather special. It was a Scottish example of the various homoerotic clubs which existed in England and France. When a new member was being inducted, he had to take out his genitals and place them on a pewter plate on top of an altar in the middle of the room. Then the full array of members, who were called Knights (as they were also called in the Cape Club), paraded up two by two and touched the novice's penis with their own penises (which were by this time presumably erect). There would then be toasts, speeches, erotic readings, obscene jokes and songs, and general masturbation.

> 24 met, 3 tested and enrolled. All frigged. The Dr. expatiated. Two nymphs, 18 and 19, exhibited as heretofore. Rules were submitted by Mr Lumsdaine for future adoption. Fanny Hill was read. Tempest. Broke up at 3 o'clock a.m.[10]

That extract from the society's records (which were kept in Anstruther – the society began in Anstruther and spread to Edinburgh) makes it clear that the 'frigging' or masturbation was quite open and ritualistic, and it also has the interesting reference to the two young women being 'exhibited', not to be touched apparently, but rather to provide a good stimulus to the wankers. What are we to call the goings-on at the Beggar's Benison clubs: homosexual, homoerotic, or merely homosocial? Were they no more than lurid forerunners of our rugby clubs and college fraternities? Most of the members probably regarded themselves as heterosexuals having a good night out by re-living their adolescence. Respectability was not sacrificed by joining; at Anstruther one of the members was Hugh Cleghorn, Professor of Civil History at the University of St Andrews. There must have been gay men among them: did they try hard to conceal their joy in the proceedings? If Fergusson, a sensitive poet, did attend such meetings, could this have contributed to the sense of guilt and self-disgust which eventually overcame him and drove him mad? This is pure speculation, but I offer it to you.

> In the evening I presided at the Celtick Club which received me with their usual partiality. I like this Society and willingly give myself to be excited by the sight of handsome young men with plaids and claymores and all the alertness and spirit of highlanders in their native garb. There was the usual degree of excitation, excellent dancing, capital songs, a general inclination to please and be pleased . . . I got home fatigued and *vino ciboque gravatus* [laden with wine and food], about eleven o'clock. We had many guests some of whom, English officers,

seemed both amazed and surprized at our wild ways, especially at the dancing without ladies and the mode of drinking favourite toasts by springing up with one foot on the bench and one on the table, and the peculiar shriek of applause so unlike English Cheering.[11]

That extract from Walter Scott's *Journal* (9 March 1829) shows that a lingering homoeroticism was still to be found in Edinburgh at that date, though the clubs were more conventionally respectable. Scott regarded such gatherings as purely social events, yet the English visitors were perhaps right in raising their eyebrows at the fact that these raucous, hard-drinking, thoroughly macho military men were dancing together, in skirts - to say nothing of another fact, that in the action of springing up for a toast in the way Scott describes they would reveal to anyone sitting on the opposite bench the answer to the ancient question about the Scotsman and his kilt.

> W[ill] C[lerk] mentioned to me last night a horrid circumstance about a very particularly dear friend who lately retired suddenly and seemingly causelessly from parliament. He ascribed [it] to his having been detected in unnatural practices – I hope there may be doubts though he spoke very positively and the sudden and silent retreat from a long wishd for seat look[s] too like truth. God, God whom shall we trust!! Here is learning, wit, gaiety of temper, high station in society and compleat reception every where all at once debased and lost by such a degrading bestiality. Our passions are wild beasts. God grant us power to muzzle them.[12]

That is another extract from Walter Scott's *Journal* (25 June 1826), in a very different mood. When you contrast it with the last quotation, and Scott's innocent delight in an all-male social event, it brings out very clearly the truth of what Bruce Smith wrote in *Homosexual Desire in Shakespeare's England*, about 'the schematic opposition that finally emerged as social dogma in the late eighteenth century and has remained in effect until today: a supposition that male bonding and male homosexuality are opposites, not different aspects of the same psychological and social phenomenon'.[13] The outrage Scott expressed in that last passage came from the fact that the homosexual scandal involved a personal friend. Richard Heber, a book-collector, had been a close friend of Scott and his family for over twenty years. He was caught with a young man; the newspaper *John Bull* published the story; Heber got a tip-off from a friend that he was about to be prosecuted, and fled the country to avoid execution, since homosexual acts were still a capital offence.

Scott not only did not lift a finger to help his old friend, but kept expressing his horror and revulsion in letters as well as in his *Journal*. Here was this man of the world, as he often boasted he was, a man who had a huge range of acquaintances, from peasants to royalty, from all social classes, a man who in the nature of things must have met many homosexuals – and yet his mind could not get to grips with this scandal, he regarded it as a personal betrayal, and he cut off Heber as if he had never existed. We, looking back, and perhaps deploring his reaction, may feel nevertheless that his trauma was good for him. At least something had been brought out into the open which had been secret too long, and it is interesting that when he talks about the bestiality of Heber's acts he goes on to say '*Our* passions are wild beasts. God grant *us* power to muzzle them.' His subconscious mind seems to want to bring Heber back into the human fold, even if he cannot do it consciously. It is also worth mentioning that Scott's circumlocutions and figures of speech in talking about the subject were not shared by the popular press at the time. I wonder if Scott read a broadside ballad in 1824 which told the sad tale of another respected Edinburgh figure, a clergyman called Dr Greenfield whom Scott knew, and who was caught with some students:

> Those who the Holy Craft despise,
>   And hold as mere humbugging,
> What can they think when Priests practize,
>   That blasted crime – *Bumbugging*.
>
> There was a certain grave Divine,
>   Esteem'd as wise as Mentor;
> Each Sunday did in Pulpit shine,
>   But B[u]gg[e]r'd his Precentor.
>
> He was the Church's prop and stay,
>   Penn'd a' her sage addresses,
> But yet forsook God's holy way,
>   And f[ucke]d in barber's a[rse]s.[14]

The coarse matter-of-fact humour of the anonymous balladist makes a nice foil to the angst of Scott.

*

His coat, consisting of pink-coloured silk, lined with white, by the elegance of the cut retired backward, as it were, to discover a white sattin waistcoat embroidered with gold, unbuttoned at the upper part, to display a broch set with garnets, that glittered in the breast of his shirt, which was of the finest cambrick, edged with right mechlin. The knees of his crimson velvet breeches scarce descended so low as to meet his silk stockings, which rose without spot or wrinkle on his meagre legs, from shoes of blue Meroquin, studded with diamond buckles, that flamed forth rivals to the sun! A steel-hilted sword, inlaid with figures of gold, and decked with a knot of ribbon which fell down in a rich tossle, equipped his side; and an amber-headed cane hung dangling from his wrist: – But the most remarkable parts of his furniture were, a mask on his face, and white gloves on his hands, which did not seem to be put on with an intention to be pulled off occasionally, but were fixed with a ring set with a ruby on the little finger of one hand, and by one set with a topaz on that of the other. – In this garb, captain Whiffle, for that was his name, took possession of the ship, surrounded with a crowd of attendants, all of whom, in their different degrees, seemed to be of their patron's disposition; and the air was so impregnated with perfumes, that one may venture to affirm the clime of Arabia Foelix was not half so sweet-scented . . . He also prohibited any person whatever, except Simper [his surgeon] and his own servants, from coming into the great cabbin, without first sending in to obtain leave. – These singular regulations did not prepossess the ship's company in his favour; but on the contrary, gave scandal an opportunity to be very busy with his character, and accuse him of maintaining a correspondence with his surgeon, not fit to be named.[15]

That frank and deckle-edged portrait of a homosexual sea-captain in Tobias Smollett's *The Adventures of Roderick Random* (1748) is only one of several striking references to homosexuality in the writer's works, and its open and unworried eighteenth-century worldliness makes a startling contrast to the inhibitions and revulsions of Scott. Although continuously satirical, the presentation of the nicely named Whiffle and Simper extends itself through a delighted profusion of detail that suggests something keenly observed beneath all the exaggeration (and Smollett was in a position to do the observing, as a surgeon's mate in the Navy), and makes the final 'not to be named' a joke (in fiction, if not in life). Roderick, the hero, has an even closer homosexual encounter in a later chapter, when he discovers that asking a favour from Earl Strutwell demands favours in return, though the naïve and eager hero is still unaware that Strutwell is 'notorious for a passion for his own sex', and allows himself (somewhat taken aback, but then, aristocrats have their ways and whims) to be hugged and kissed and given hints that might have issued from the lips of Oscar Wilde himself. Recommending the reading of Petronius's *Satyricon*, with its casual acceptance of homosexuality, the Earl works up a steam of eloquent argument:

> 'I own (replied the Earl) that his taste in love is generally decried, and indeed condemned by our laws; but perhaps that may be more owing to prejudice and misapprehension, than to true reason and deliberation. – The best man among the ancients is said to have entertained that passion; one of the wisest of their legislators has permitted the indulgence of it in his commonwealth; the most celebrated poets have not scrupled to avow it at this day; it prevails not only over all the east, but in most parts of Europe; in our own country it gains ground apace, and in all probability will become in a short time a more fashionable vice than simple fornication. – Indeed there is something to be said in vindication of it, for notwithstanding the severity of the law against offenders in this way, it must be confessed that the practice of this passion is unattended with that curse and burthen upon society, which proceeds from a race of miserable deserted bastards, who are either murdered by their parents, deserted to the utmost want and wretchedness, or bred up to prey upon the commonwealth: And it likewise prevents the debauchery of many a young maiden, and the prostitution of honest men's wives, not to mention the consideration of health, which is much less liable to be impaired in the gratification of this appetite, than in the exercise of common venery, which by ruining the constitutions of our young men, has produced a puny progeny that degenerates from generation to generation: Nay, I have been told, that there is another motive perhaps more powerful than all these, that induces people to cultivate this inclination; namely, the exquisite pleasure attending its success.'[16]

Roderick, thinking perhaps that his own opinions are being tested, warmly rejects the Earl's defence of 'this spurious and sordid desire', and the Earl quickly slides off the subject, but the passage remains for the reader a remarkable and instructive insert which gives testimony to Smollett's interest in the homosexual culture emerging among the upper classes in London at that time. A few years later, in *The Adventures of Peregrine Pickle* (1751), he returned to the subject in a very curious scene.[17] An Italian marquis and a German baron, observed on a couch in amorous embrace, are chased down the stairs in their dishevelled state by a landlady with a cane. So far so farcical; the proprieties are restored. But it is the sequel that is of peculiar interest. Peregrine Pickle and his friend Pallet, who are slightly drunk, have been watching this operation with pleasure and moral approval, but it is clear that some sort of devious sexual excitement has rubbed off on them, and Peregrine immediately proposes they should join a local masquerade, with Pallet dressed as a woman. The decision leads to a series of hilarious scenes in Smollett's most rumbustious style, with La Pallet gatecrashing the gentlemen's toilet and finally being groped in chest and crotch by a randy Frenchman. This is all, as they say, picaresque; but it is notable that Smollett, unlike Scott, could place homosexuality in the midst of life, not marginalised, and whether disapproved of or not, a source of unexpected, half-acknowledged interaction between homosexuals and heterosexuals.

> And, well-belovèd, is this all, this all?
>   Gone, like a vapour which the potent morn
> Kills, and in killing glorifies! I call
>   Through the lone night for thee, my dear first-born
> Soul-fellow! but my heart vibrates in vain.
>   Ah! well I know, and often fancy forms
> The weather-blown churchyard where thou art lain -
>   The churchyard whistling to the frequent storms.
> But down the valley, by the river side,
>   Huge walnut-trees – bronze-foliaged, motionless
> As leaves of metal – in their shadows hide
>   Warm nests, low music, and true tenderness.
> But thou, betrothed! art far from me, from me.
> O heart! be merciful – I loved him utterly.[18]

Unmistakably a gay love poem, a gay love elegy. It is by David Gray, a poet from Kirkintilloch who died in 1861 at the age of twenty-three. He grew up with a very close friend, Robert Buchanan, who long outlived him and became a well-known Victorian literary figure, with many volumes of poetry and criticism – best known probably for his attack on Swinburne and 'The Fleshly School of Poetry'. They arranged to go to London together, but in a mix-up they left from different Glasgow stations, and Gray spent his first night sleeping rough in Hyde Park, not the best thing for his tuberculosis, to say nothing of other dangers. He sought help from Monckton Milnes (later Lord Houghton), a rather strange choice. Did he know that this outwardly respectable literary man had a private library of erotica, and was specially interested in flagellation, being himself the author of a poem called *The Rodiad*? Timothy d'Arch Smith, an authority on Victorian Decadent literature, has written: 'I believe there is evidence that Buchanan's protégé, the young Scottish poet David Gray, was not averse to masculine charms. It is a coincidence at any rate that he was friendly with Baron Houghton, the author of *The Rodiad*. It is certainly very delightful to think of the tubercular Scottish Rimbaud having gently to remove Buchanan's hand from his kilted knee while he applied himself to a few more lines of *The Luggie and Other Poems*.'[19]

> Be it noted, however, that there was in Gray's nature a strange and exquisite femininity, – a perfect feminine purity and sweetness. Indeed, till the mystery of sex be medically explained, I shall ever believe that nature originally meant David Gray for a female; for besides the strangely sensitive lips and eyes, he had a woman's shape, – narrow shoulders, lissome limbs, and extraordinary breadth across the hips.[20]

That is from a long memorial essay on Gray published by Robert Buchanan, who also expressed his loss in two elegiac poems, 'Poet Andrew', and 'To David in Heaven'. The first is in Scots, the second in English, and between them they show how haunted Buchanan was by his friend's early death.[21] Gray may be a minor poet, but he is a part of the gay literary history of Scotland and should not be forgotten.

> Dear brother poet, dearest in the land,
> Friend of mine inmost soul, approved sincere,
> Born of the gods, love comes not at command,
> Nor yet art thou beloved though thou art dear,
> Would it were possible to mate thy strength,
> And feel the rapture of repose at length.

But I am as a weed on ocean's shore,
Scorched by the sun and driven by the breeze,
Shrivelled and crushed and trampled evermore
With scarce a memory of the fresh, salt seas:
My fainting strength thou canst indeed revive,
But how can love ill-mated hope to thrive.

I crave a beauty which I cannot see,
While yet methinks the world is fair enow,
And some eternal flame there burns in me,
Whose inward torture doth uplift and bow,
'Tis thus Apollo moulds me to his will,
Beneath his hand I suffer and am still.[22]

These lines are from a speech by the Greek poet Sappho, rejecting the love of Alcaeus, in a play called *The Lesbians*, by C. J. B. Birrell, published in a privately printed edition in Glasgow in 1914 (though it is undated). I have so far discovered nothing about Catherine J. Ballingall Birrell (*fl.*1889–1917) beyond the fact that she wrote and published plays and poems around the turn of the century. Is *The Lesbians* a lesbian play? Yes and no seems to be the only answer. At the time when the play was published, our modern meaning of 'lesbian' did exist, but would be found mostly in medical and psychological contexts; in common parlance a Lesbian would normally be an inhabitant of the island of Lesbos, though inevitably with some of the floating and accreted associations that have come down through the legendary history of Sappho and her loves. The title therefore gives nothing away, though the fact of private publication, coupled with the sexless initials of the author, would certainly suggest the circumspection of an undeclared interest.

The play deals with the last days of Sappho, leading up to her suicide after the disastrous *coup de foudre* of her falling in love with the young sailor Phaon, who cannot love her. Sappho is shown as unhappy, searching for a love and security that elude her, perhaps fearing the waning of her poetic power but still strong in many ways, and indeed the play has a political dimension which shows her as something other than a passive, suffering, or tragic figure. Lesbos is ruled by the quasi-fascist Pittacus who regards Sappho's house of girls, supposedly studying music, dance, and poetry, as a nest of dissidents against the order of the state, 'a hotbed of revolt and crime'. In an angry scene between the two, Sappho fiercely

defends the freedom of art and discourse ('Better out spoken word
than slavish thought') against the regimentation-for-the-public-good
arguments of Pittacus ('I and the state are one'). The very macho
Pittacus is, in fact, trying to rule an unruly island where it is the
women who are famous for making their presence felt, and the men
who are effeminate. When the sailor Phaon comes on the scene,
rough, impatient, very masculine, and so strikingly handsome that
he turns the heads of all sexes, he is disgusted by what he sees as a
reversal of the natural order:

> When I pick seamen 'tis my only care
> That they have thews to row and to exchange
> A sturdy blow if folk don't understand,
> As often happens in a foreign land.
>
> But what are looks? These Lesbians make a man
> Grow sick with their soft ways, now just to-day
> I caught a rascal at a polished pan
> Combing his elf-locks, well he got it quick
> And serve him right, he'll not forget that kick.
>
> Mirrors are for the girls.[23]

These Lesbians make a man grow sick – and that's only the men! I
know it's wrong to put a contemporary gloss on an eighty-year-old
play, but the sexual swirls and eddies which really are there are
sufficient in themselves to give us a considerable curiosity about the
nature and intentions of the author.

There would seem to be some lesbian interest in her play, *Two
Queens: A Drama*, published in Glasgow in 1889. The two central
characters are Lady Jane Grey and Queen Mary, clashing as they
seek to control the state after the death of Edward VI. Mary is (in
the main) the villain, 'a stubborn Papist', arrogant, good at burning
heretics, yet never able to be really happy ('I know I was not
throned for my own good . . . But to be champion of the Holy
Church'). Lady Jane, supporting the Protestant cause, is the tragic
heroine, strong but nice, and a bit of a feminist, as she shows when
she rejects her husband Guildford's claim to be King if she becomes
Queen:

> LADY JANE: If power be equal, I am set aside
> To whom the crown was due: what sense in that?
> Why should the King leave me an empty honour?

GUILDFORD: Who argues with a woman? They've no wit
    To know when they are beaten. I shall go.
    So great a Queen can never own a husband;
    Go, boast yourself in solitary state
    That you are Queen of England, I am King.[24]

Beyond the centrality of the two female characters, and their keen interest in one another as protagonists in a power struggle, there is nothing lesbian in the action of the play; at the same time, and thinking of it in connection with the Sappho play, there would appear to be an appeal to a lesbian readership or audience. More overtly lesbian themes do seem to surface in some of her poems, which were published as *Things Old and New*. 'Gulduc and Guldelaun' is a tragic ballad set in France and Devon. The two women of the title are both in love with Sir Iseldore, who loves them both, but the women are also in love with one another, an unresolvable tangle which results in all three retreating eventually to convent or monastery. The last two stanzas give little comfort to men:

> Then he became a holy monk,
>   And she [Gulduc] became a nun,
> And Gulduc loved fair Guldelaun
>   Until her life was done.
>
> But, take ye heed, fair maidens all,
>   How with mankind ye do,
> For the more love ye give to them,
>   The less they give to you.[25]

Maybe some day Catherine Birrell will emerge from the shadows and tell us whether these speculations are out of order.

You stand still. Again disdain in your eyes, disgust on your lips.

'But you don't want to claim that the abominable vice you have started to talk about has anything at all to do with love?'

Yes, I claim that, just as I claim that no love has anything to do with vice, if it is truly love. And I shall seek to prove my claim to you from the existence of this love.

But one thing I must ask of you: that you first banish from your imagination that dirty picture, which up to now has been the only way you could think of this love.

Think of your own love and you will understand me, you must understand me!

For since you are human, love cannot have remained a stranger to you: you love someone, you have loved someone.

Perhaps you are fortunate in love. Then you know the heavenly bliss of the heart, the agonizing pleasure of desire, the blessed feeling of understanding in two beings who belong to one another, the deep feeling of peaceful security on the beloved's breast.

Perhaps you are unfortunate in love. Then no torment of hell has remained a stranger to you: neither the infinite bitterness of not being heard, not being understood, the hopeless grief of futility, nor the passionate torment of never fulfilled longing, the raging pain of jealousy, the dull giving in to resignation and despair.

Now, *exactly so*, fortunate or unfortunate, do we feel our love. Thus it rejoices, thus it suffers, and it is distinguished in no way from yours, except in the one thing: that its object is not of the other, but of the same sex!

That is from a pamphlet of 1908 entitled *Listen! Only a moment! A cry*.[26] It is by John Henry Mackay, born in Greenock in 1864 of a Scottish father and a German mother, dying in Berlin in 1933 just at the time when Hitler came to power. His father died before he was two, and his mother took him to Germany, so he was brought up speaking and writing German, though he never gave up his Scottish name and was given to saying 'Ich bin kein Deutscher, ich bin Schotte!' Since he himself said that, we can claim him as the first thoroughly politicised gay Scottish writer, who despite endless harassment from censors and police managed to produce a series of important, pioneering books: fiction, poetry, socio-political and sexual polemics. As the quotation I have given you suggests, he rejected the late nineteenth-century medical and psychological theories of homosexuality either as a sickness or as the sign of a 'third sex'. He was upfront about its being natural and normal for a percentage of society, and his whole work was a plea for knowledge, understanding, open discussion, tolerance. He wanted a sexual revolution as part of a political revolution, as the titles of two of his main prose works might suggest: *The Freedomseeker* (*Der Freiheitsucher*) and *The Anarchists* (*Die Anarchisten*). His philosophy belongs very much to that intense period of argument at the turn of the century between anarchism, socialism, and communism, he himself inclining towards anarchism because of his strong feelings about personal freedom. But it is as a creative writer that he ought to be remembered and reclaimed, for his many poems, some of them set to music by Richard Strauss and Schoenberg, for his gay novels, *The Hustler* (*Der Puppenjunge* [1926]) and *Fenny Skaller* [1913], and for his non-gay or partly gay novel *The Swimmer* (*Der Schwimmer* [1901]), one of the earliest novels based on sport. Hugh MacDiarmid knew about his work and said he admired it, regarding him as belonging to the great Scottish diaspora which we should be willing to acknowledge as our own.[27] And that seems reasonable. His work is gradually being translated, in America, but I hope he will also be a focus of discussion in his native place, Scotland.

NOTES

This chapter proceeds as a mosaic rather than an integrated argument. Some discoveries and some reminders are juxtaposed with various questions and speculations, in keeping with what one must regard as the initiatory and exploratory nature of gay literary studies in Scotland. I am grateful to Paddy Lyons, Christopher Whyte and Hamish Whyte for suggestions and help.

1. *Memorials of James Hogg, the Ettrick Shepherd* ed. Mrs Garden (London, Alexander Gardner 1885) p. 37.
2. James Hogg *The Private Memoirs and Confessions of a Justified Sinner* ed. J. Carey (London, Oxford University Press 1969) pp. 23–4.
3. Eve Kosofsky Sedgwick *Between Men: English Literature and Male Homosocial Desire* (New York, Columbia University Press 1985) pp. 97–117.
4. Douglas Gifford *James Hogg* (Edinburgh, Ramsay Head 1976) p. 142.
5. *The Private Memoirs* p. 113.
6. Christopher Marlowe *Doctor Faustus* ed. J. D. Jump (London, Methuen 1962) p. 127.
7. James Hogg *The Private Memoirs* with an introduction by André Gide (London, The Cresset Press 1947) p. x.
8. *The Poems of Robert Fergusson* ed. M. P. McDiarmid (Edinburgh, Scottish Text Society 1956) Vol. 2 pp. 112–13.
9. *Oxford English Dictionary* Second Edition s.v. 'macaroni'.
10. L. Hutchison 'The Beggar's Benison' *Scottish Book Collector* 4 (Edinburgh 1988) p. 26.
11. *The Journal of Sir Walter Scott* ed. W. E. K. Anderson (Oxford, Clarendon Press 1972) p. 532.
12. Ibid. p. 162.
13. Bruce Smith *Homosexual Desire in Shakespeare's England: A Cultural Poetics* (London and Chicago, Chicago University Press 1991) p. 270.

14. R. Norton *Mother Clap's Molly House: The Gay Subculture in England 1700–1830* (London, Gay Men's Press 1992) pp. 215–16.
15. *The Adventures of Roderick Random* chapters. 34–5. Quoted from Paul-Gabriel Boucé's edition (Oxford, Oxford University Press 1979).
16. Ibid. chapter 51.
17. *The Adventures of Peregrine Pickle* chapter 49. Quoted from James L. Clifford's edition (London, Oxford University Press 1969).
18. *The Poetical Works of David Gray* ed. H. G. Bell (Glasgow, James Maclehose and London, Macmillan 1874) p. 78.
19. Timothy D'Arch Smith 'At Eton's door' *Gay News* 168 (31 May–3 June 1979) p. 25.
20. Robert Buchanan *David Gray and Other Essays, Chiefly on Poetry* (London, Sampson Low, Son, and Marston 1868) pp. 78–9.
21. Robert Buchanan *Poetical Works* (London, Henry S. King 1874) Vol. II pp. 53ff.; Vol. I, pp. 234ff.
22. Act 1, p. 15.
23. Act 2, pp. 26–7.
24. *Two Queens: A Drama* (Glasgow, James Maclehose and Sons 1889) Act 3, Scene 1, p. 56.
25. *Things Old and New* (no author, publisher or date: Brighton c.1917).
26. John Henry Mackay *Fenny Skaller and Other Prose Writings* translated by Hubert Kennedy (Amsterdam, Southernwood Press 1988) pp. 120–1.
27. Hugh MacDiarmid *Contemporary Scottish Studies* (Edinburgh, Scottish Educational Journal [1976]) p. 10.

Notes on Contributors

Jenni Calder was born in Chicago and has lived in Scotland since 1971. A graduate of the Universities of Cambridge and London, she has worked since 1978 at the National Museums of Scotland where she is currently Head of Publications. She has taught and lectured throughout the United Kingdom and in Europe, the USA and Africa as well as publishing numerous articles and reviews. Her books include *Chronicles of Conscience*, a study of George Orwell and Arthur Koestler, *There Must Be a Lone Ranger* on Westerns, *Heroes: from Byron to Guevara*, *Women and Marriage in Victorian Fiction*, *The Victorian Home*, *RLS: A Life Study* and editions of Stevenson's works. She is also the author of a study of the nineteenth-century Scottish novelist *Margaret Oliphant* and is currently working on a biography of Naomi Mitchison.

Margaret Elphinstone was born in London in 1948. She comes from a mixed Scottish, English and Jewish background and moved to Scotland in 1970. She lived in Shetland from 1971 to 1979 before settling in Edinburgh, where she is a member of the Pomegranate writers' group. She lectures in the Department of English Studies of the University of Strathclyde and has published a range of poetry and shorter fiction as well as three novels: *The Incomer*, *A Sparrow's Flight* and *Islanders*. *An Apple from a Tree* is a book of short stories. She is an enthusiastic gardener and the mother of two daughters.

Caroline Gonda was born in Kent in 1961 and educated at Blackheath High School and the University of Cambridge. She moved to

Scotland in 1989 to lecture in the Department of English Literature of the University of Dundee. Coming out as a lesbian in 1990 not only improved her social life (Dundee has a strong lesbian network) but also sparked off research interests in the relations between reading, writing and sexuality. She edited *Tea and Leg-Irons: New Feminist Readings from Scotland*, the first collection of its kind north of the border, and is currently completing a book based on her doctoral thesis, entitled *Reading Daughters' Fictions*. She is a member of Outright Scotland and of Dundee Lesbian, Gay and Bisexual Switchboard.

R. D. S. Jack proceeded from Ayr Academy to the University of Glasgow and subsequently the University of Edinburgh, where he now holds the Chair of Scottish and Medieval Literature. His earlier writings are principally concerned with opening up the neglected Renaissance period in Scottish literature. They include anthologies of verse and prose and a book on Alexander Montgomerie. He has also studied Scotland's links with Italy in *The Scottish Influence on Italian Literature* and *Scottish Literature's Debt to Italy*. More recently he has published *Patterns of Divine Comedy* on English medieval drama and a study of J. M. Barrie entitled *The Road to the Never Land*. He also edited the second of the four volumes of the Aberdeen *History of Scottish Literature* covering the period from 1660 to 1800.

Edwin Morgan was born in Glasgow in 1920 and educated at Rutherglen Academy and the High School. After serving in the Royal Army Medical Corps from 1940 to 1946 he returned to his native city to complete his degree and become a lecturer at its oldest university, where he was Professor in the Department of English Literature from 1975 until taking early retirement in 1980. His *Collected Poems* appeared in 1990 along with his collected essays *Crossing the Border*. This was also the year of his official coming out with the publication of a book of articles and interviews *Nothing Not Giving Messages*. His two most recent volumes of poetry are *Hold Hands Among the Atoms* and *Sweeping Out the Dark*.

Berthold Schoene graduated in English and Scandinavian Studies from the University of Freiburg in Breisgau in Germany. He gained a doctorate from the University of Glasgow with a thesis on the prose writings of George Mackay Brown which has the construction of narrative identity as its principal concern. He is the author of a volume of poetry in German *Die Reise zum Kern:*

Gedichte 1981–1990 (Editions Orionis). Current research interests are fictional historiography and the literary construction of identity amongst marginalised communities (regional, ethnic and sexual). He has a longstanding concern with the field of men's studies and is also working on the fiction of Salman Rushdie and Vikram Seth.

Adrienne Scullion is British Academy Postdoctoral Fellow at the University of Glasgow. Although she has a particular interest in Scottish theatre, her research activities cover the broader canvas of cultural studies. She has published on historiography, cinema history and radio drama; is preparing anthologies of works by British and American women playwrights of the nineteenth century; is writing on narrative in new opera; and was working, alongside the late Alasdair Cameron, on the development of arts policy and cultural politics in twentieth-century Britain.

Alison Smith was born in Inverness in 1962 and studied at the Universities of Aberdeen and Cambridge. She has published criticism, fiction and poetry in a wide range of magazines such as *Lines Review, Chapman, Gairfish*, and *Theatre Journal*. She is a contributor to *The Scotsman, The Sunday Times* and *The New Statesman* and critical essays have appeared in *Liz Lochhead's Voices* and *Tea and Leg-Irons*. Several of her plays have been produced at the Edinburgh Fringe and *The Dance* is to be published in 1995. Her work appeared in Harper Collins' *Scottish Short Stories* and she won the Macallan *Scotland on Sunday* short story award in 1994. A collection of short fiction entitled *Free Love* is due out from Virago in 1995. She is currently Visiting Lecturer in American Poetry at the University of Strathclyde.

Christopher Whyte was born in Glasgow and educated there, at Cambridge and in Italy, where he taught at the University of Rome from 1977 to 1985. He now lectures in the Department of Scottish Literature at the University of Glasgow. He has edited a bilingual anthology of recent Gaelic poetry *An Aghaidh na Sìorraidheachd/In the Face of Eternity: Eight Gaelic Poets* and his first volume of poems *Uirsgeul/Myth: Poems in Gaelic with English Translations* won a Saltire award. More recent projects are a volume of translations from contemporary Italian poets and a satirical portrayal of life in Catholic Glasgow. He teaches a module on gender and sexuality as an integral part of the degree course in Scottish Language and Literature.

Index